Europe and the Wolf

Europe and the Wolf

Political Variations on a Musical Figure

Sara Nadal-Melsió

ZONE BOOKS · NEW YORK

2025

ZONE BOOKS
633 Vanderbilt Street
Brooklyn, NY 11218

Printed in the United States of America.

Distributed by Princeton University Press,
Princeton, New Jersey, and Woodstock, United Kingdom

Library of Congress Cataloging-in-Publication Data

Names: Nadal-Melsió, Sara, author.
Title: Europe and the wolf : political variations on a musical figure / Sara Nadal-Melsió.
Description: New York : Zone Books, 2025. | Includes bibliographical references and index. | Summary: "This book explores how the work of several contemporary artists illuminates the current crisis of Europe, whose emancipatory values are mired in the brutal realities of exclusion and policing of borders" —Provided by publisher.
Identifiers: LCCN 2024031925 (print) | LCCN 2024031926 (ebook) | ISBN 9781890951856 (hardcover) | ISBN 9781942130970 (ebook)
Subjects: LCSH: Arts—Political aspects—Europe—History—21st century. | Arts and society—Europe—History—21st century. | Europe—Boundaries. | Harmony (Aesthetics)
Classification: LCC NX180.P64 N33 2025 (print) | LCCNX180.P64 (ebook) | DDC 306.4/842094—dc23/eng/20240826
LC record available at https://lccn.loc.gov/2024031925
LC ebook record available at https://lccn.loc.gov/2024031926

Contents

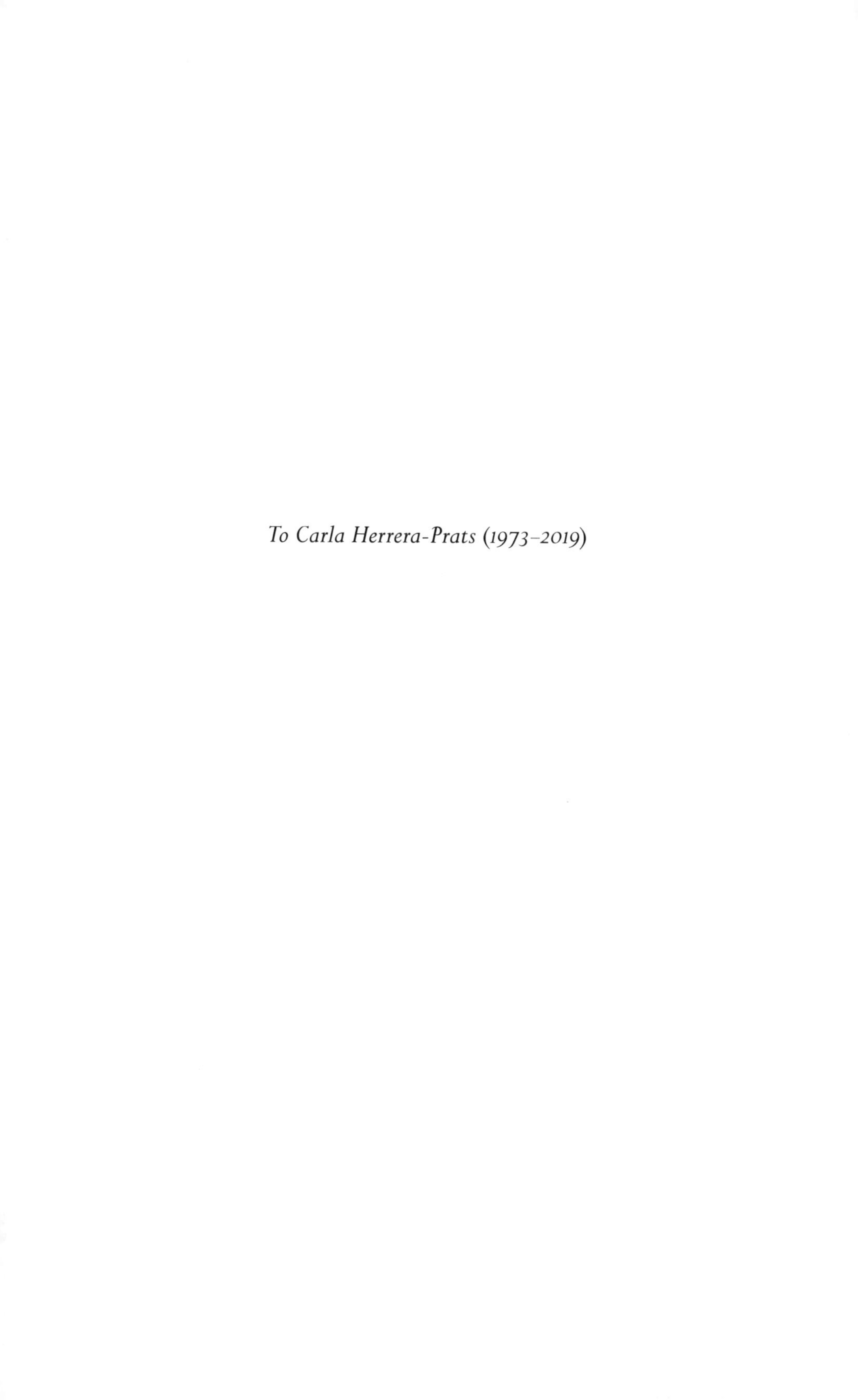

To Carla Herrera-Prats (1973–2019)

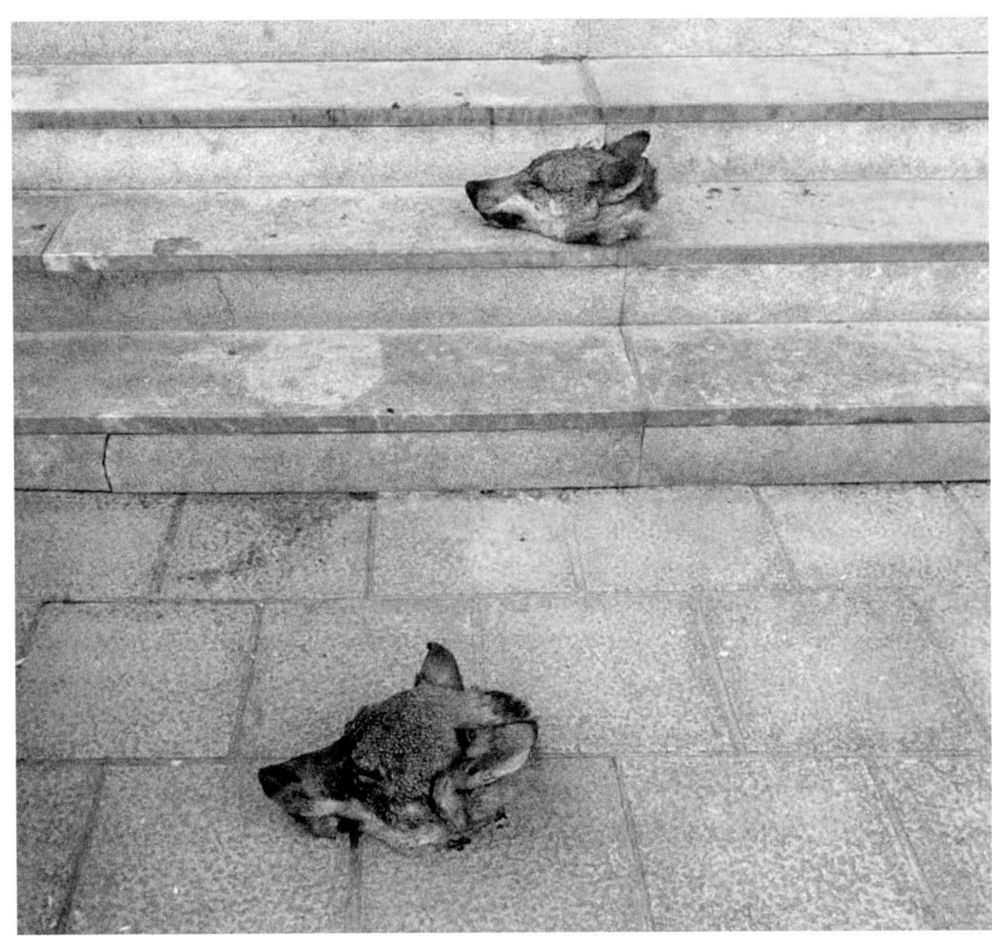

Protest action to demand the lifting of the Endangered and Protected Species Act for wolves in Asturias. Courtesy of *El Fielato*.

INTRODUCTION

The Wolf and Europe

> He said the wolf knew nothing of boundaries. The young don nodded as if in agreement but what he said was that whatever the wolf knew or did not know was irrelevant and that if the wolf had crossed the boundary it was perhaps so much worse for the wolf but the boundary stood without regard.
> —Cormac McCarthy, *The Crossing* (1994)

> The story of the last wolf was set in the Castillana de Vieja and began with the great wolf hunt to exterminate a whole pack with the help of a *lobero*, nine wolves to be precise, but the *lobero* only killed seven, so the remaining two, a young female and an even younger male, succeeded in staying alive, though the locals didn't really understand how.
> —László Krasznahorkai, *The Last Wolf* (2009)

On April 28, 2023, two wolf heads, one male, the other female, appeared on the steps of the town hall of Ponga, in Asturias, Spain. The composition of the scene was not only disturbingly violent, but also striking in its formal procedures. In the photograph that appeared in the local papers and eventually in *El País*, the head of a female wolf is resting on the marble steps. The stairs appear as lines of a musical staff or pentagram. Together with the governance and the laws the town hall building represents, they stand as a regime that integrates the decapitated head, one long, single monotone that resonates in the imagination like a hammer. Yet this wolf head and the space note that she becomes refuses to stand still. She is at once a displacement, a spacing, and an interval that reminds us that even the steps are themselves a liminal space. They are not yet the building, but a means of access to it—one across which one can either enter or exit the building and everything it represents. The second wolf's head, a larger, male head, sits outside the bounds of the rectilinear formation—not completely assimilated by the emblems of the rule of law, but not entirely beyond the violence that sustains it. And this because, to continue with my musical annotation of the image, it is incorporated as a ledger note, situated along a truncated horizontal line that is simply an extension of the staff. It signals a border that must not be crossed. The threat, macabre as it is, is eloquent. Performative violence goes hand in hand here with an agile and effective visual literacy. It not only kills the wolves, but also, by choosing a male and female, figuratively kills the possibility of more wolves or even the idea of what a wolf is by arresting the relentless movement that defines it.

It barely matters whether these formal procedures are intentional or not; the fact remains that the image's composition is a perfect articulation of the logic of the border, an articulation where wolves have played a crucial role from the very beginning. This image thinks and makes us think with it, alongside it; it immerses us in the logic that makes it possible. It tells us what a border is by becoming a border itself and by perching us at the threshold of that border and the violence it summons. A border is a violent cut. This image thinks like an artwork, disclosing as much as it hides, presenting itself with the force of an enigma. Like any artwork, it far surpasses the intent of its maker. It is a force field that sets each of its components in tension with one another. It contemplates and demands us to contemplate its unpredictable and violent emergence.

The photograph ostensibly documents a protest and an act of civil disobedience. An action designed to become an image, to be disseminated and multiplied, it challenges the rule of law and its boundaries by becoming a wolf itself, by materializing what the protesters say a wolf is and acts like. The protest calls for the lifting of the Endangered and Protected Species Act for wolves in the Iberian Peninsula. Wolves are now returning to their habitats after becoming almost extinct because of excessive and indiscriminate hunting. The story, both of the extermination and of the recent returns, repeats itself across Europe, in all of Eurasia, and the American continent. The reactions these wolves invariably trigger are also variations of the same — fear, hatred, fascination, and an intense need for fabulation and symbolization. Their capaciousness as emblems and enigmas matches the force of the sentiments they inspire.

Even as emblems of the wild and the unknown, wolves remain unbounded by discourses or boundaries. Wolves exhibit their unruliness through semantic excess as a form of fugitivity. They appear as musical figures and musical puzzles, as essential actors in certain political philosophies, as encoded figures for immigrants and strangers, as nurturing animals, as predators, as victims of human cruelty, as sacred animals, as commodities in colonial trade, as fellow travelers in America and Europe's Indigenous genocides, as guides and guardians of the mysterious wisdom of nature and her unwritten laws. The list goes on and on.

Figures are dematerializations that demand a relentless labor of interpretation, a contextual mobilization that will bring them back to life as essential participants in the composite ecology of the living. When they manage to come back, they come, no longer as figures, but as shards of life, as remembered experiences of becoming. At once beings and symbols, nexuses for borders and struggles over sovereignty and meaning, wolves become a conceptual problem, as well, because they are never just one just thing. Nothing is, but wolves are particularly splintered figures, depositories of an imagination that cordons them off, but cannot do without them. I begin with this image as an emblem of what this book wants to explore and, above all, think with, and this because my reflections here, if they are to be true to the questions they pose, must acknowledge the violence this image crystallizes. Not just the brute force that these two wolf heads inscribe, but also that of the ones that came before them and will surely come after and the things they are made to represent.

* * *

Europe and the Wolf: Political Variations on a Musical Figure begins by recuperating a baroque musical concept that acquires a renewed meaning amid contemporary aesthetic practices that seek to respond to the histories, violence, and promises contained in Europe, understood as the name for an ongoing conceptual and political problem. The "wolf" is the name baroque tuners gave to the dissonant and resilient sound produced in any attempt to temper and harmonize an instrument, the greatest challenge to the dream of complete harmonization.[1] By returning us to Pythagoras, and not just to his dream of absolute harmony but to his understanding of *logos* as music, interval, and number, the wolf becomes a solution, rather than a problem. The relational nature of this musical *logos*, a *metaxis*, transforms the task of tuning and harmonizing frequencies, pitch, scale, or temperament and deploys, rather than eliminates, the wolf by acknowledging that harmony is a carefully constructed acoustic fiction. This intervallic wolf, always present, but not always heard, is a form in flight, a border-crossing figure whose movement cannot be arrested and that always escapes capture.

The first mention of the wolf as a Western emblem of disharmony, however, predates tuning efforts against dissonant notes and comes from the Latin proverb "Homo homine lupus est," or "Man is a wolf to man," an endlessly appropriated and translated phrase that traces the pervasive fear and even hate for what is foreign and unknown, for what marks the borders of a community. Already in Plato's *Republic*, the tyrant is transformed from man to wolf, initiating the lasting bond between sovereignty and lycanthropy—a bond always traversed by mimesis and metamorphosis. Plautus's variation on the original proverb, "A man is a wolf rather than a man to another man, when he hasn't yet found out what he's like," extends and interprets it through a mirroring effect: we are the wolves, and we become wolves precisely because of our fear of the unknown.[2] For Plautus, violence stems from the misidentification of the self and from its dissociation from the other, from its refusal to acknowledge that the other is already inside, already constitutive of the self. Thomas Hobbes also turns to the phrase in the dedication of *De Cive* in what is possibly its better-known version, "man to man is an arrant wolf," as well as the one most often instrumentalized by reactionary thought. Passing through Niccolò Machiavelli, Hobbes's sovereign and his brute, prosthetic, and artificial force mark him as a political animal that imposes the law by first breaking it.[3] As Jacques Derrida puts it in *The Beast and the Sovereign*, unravelling the paradox that Hobbesian political philosophy so fully inhabits, "sovereigns and beasts seem to have in common their being-outside the law."[4] Picking up and weaving the threads of the always proliferating European political wolves, he describes "political man as superior to animality and political man as animality."[5] Hobbes's war of all against all, a world of men-wolves, still resonates in *Civilization and Its Discontents*, written between two world wars and during the rise of European fascism. There, Sigmund Freud famously echoes the original Latin proverb to explain the many forms of aggression and exploitation that plague group formations that deny their entanglement with others. As he puts it, "their neighbor is for them not only a potential helper or sexual object, but also someone who tempts them to satisfy their aggressiveness on him, to exploit his capacity for work without compensation, to use him sexually without his consent, to seize his possessions, to humiliate him, to cause him pain, to torture and to kill him. *Homo homini lupus*."[6] The wolf and its political genealogy is not exhaustive; it names a problem within the logic of community when that community is understood as the product of a social harmony predicated on the violence of exclusion and the expropriation of rights.

My mobilization of the wolf as an emblem that resists efforts to harmonize sound and to homogenize political communities activates all these resonances and adds a few more. The fact that not all notes can be reconciled in harmony or that musical codes or political community formations are not all-encompassing is materialized in the wolf as a conceptual emblem for various forms of disagreement and refusal. In the same way as the condensation of dissonance into a single note or interval—the exception that tempers the rule of harmony as a universalizing system and model—doubles as a mechanism of transference that allows dissent to persevere, the wolf as a fugitive figure carries within it the ability to transmit a dissent that can be politically resituated every time it is performed. As Derrida notes, "Without asking permission, real wolves cross humankind's national and institutional frontiers, and his sovereign nation-states; wolves out in nature [*dans la nature*], as we say, real wolves, are the same on this side or the other side of the Pyrenees or the Alps; but the figures of the wolf belong to cultures, nations, languages, myths, fables, fantasies, histories."[7] In the artworks I explore, a logic of encryption is at play: the figure of the wolf intensifies and retains an exceptional but necessary dissonance that allows for it to travel nested in the apparent harmony of cultural legacy, political consensus, and community formations. It smuggles a figure of dissent into the uses of organized sound and organized political communities alike, enabling it to inhabit—sometimes legibly but more often surreptitiously—the claims to universalization of the European *nomos*.

The sovereign, says Carl Schmitt, is the one who has the right to suspend rights through force, and to suspend rights is fundamentally to erect a border, to be able to expel.[8] To become identifiable as a sovereign—yet another baroque figure—to become the infrastructure that sustains both nation and state, means inevitably to enter the logic of enmity and exclusion. A projected but never actualized political formation, Europe is entirely articulated through the border, the most Eurocentric of concepts. The imaginary connotations of the wolf and its materialization in the person of the immigrant and the refugee are central to an understanding of how a political concept founded on the transnational and universalizing appropriation of the 1789 revolutionary Declaration of the Rights of Man and the Citizen proves to be the condition of possibility of border formation and a politics of exclusion and coloniality. Europe is at present an uneven economic coalition with no political content or democratic legitimacy that finds its center in the oscillation between the reductive operations involved in the opening and closing of borders—under the euphemisms of free trade on the one hand and of safety and preservation on the other. The free circulation of currency and "European nationals" (a nomenclature that points to a contradiction) conceals the very real border that Europe is. An aggregation of national sovereignties is, in practice, a multiplication of borders—proof of Europe's unwillingness or inability to supersede the nation-state.

While the Mediterranean has become Europe's most deadly border, it is literally an invisible one. A tomb for migrants and refugees, it is a maritime space where the continent's colonial violence continues to reverberate, entangling the old with the new and the dead with the living. The negativity structuring the slogan "no one is illegal" or the struggle of the *sans-papiers* is crucial to understanding its critical and political force. Like Derrida's insistence on the acoustic polysemy of *à pas de loup*, at once a description of the stealthiness of the wolf and a marker of its absence, these enunciations of the political are a negation and critique of the universalism of the European *nomos*, unveiling sovereignty and the law as instruments of violence. What they propose is a reconfiguration and metamorphosis of Europe from an identity or legacy that must be violently protected because it is always "in danger" into an accumulation of exclusions that, gathered as a force of dissent, constitute an alternative and always growing community that truly transcends the nation as an organizing political principle. As the intervals that would structure this collectivity, transit and absence are the vehicle of its becoming, the rhythms of a *pas de loup*.

Throughout, I will think *with* a select number of artworks that specifically experiment with Europe's musical legacy rather than give an art-historical or critical account of any of the artists, more accurately "producers," with whom I engage. I will treat these artworks as sites of intensity, of historical and layered density, that think, experiment, and compose through a complete immersion in the resonances of their specific contexts.

The book is structured in three movements, each of which includes interludes and variations that echo and multiply the main themes of the book—inheritance, collaboration, improvisation, violence—and the figures and tropes that repeat them with a difference—pianos, animals, bones, shipwrecks, demolitions. My subtitle, *Political Variations on a Musical Figure*, describes the configuration and structure of the project, a series of variations and relays between the musical and the political that in their complexity match the polysemic heterogeneity of the histories they mobilize. Like the artworks I think with, the argument of the book proceeds through layering, accumulation, and combination—procedures that allow resonances and echoes to proliferate and multiply as its pages and movements unfold. In the process, additional variations and associations are called into being—they take the form of interludes—and in this way match the underlying logic of complex, composite artworks that are produced as always expanding sites of encounter. My claim is that these transmedia artworks provide us with new relational compositional models that allow us to think through the aporetic logic of political communities that are wary of heterogeneity and to embrace instead endless metamorphoses that are both symbolic and material.

In Part 1, "The Labor of Sound: Pere Portabella and Carles Santos," I examine the work of the late musician and artist Carles Santos and of filmmaker Pere Portabella, particularly their collaboration on the film *Die Stille vor Bach*, and in Santos's musical theater piece

La pantera imperial. Going back to their early anti-Francoist conceptual practices — which are fully mediated by their participation in the collective Grup de Treball — there is an emphasis on labor and value production that extends into all of their subsequent productions. For them, culture is never innocent, and it is one of art's tasks to uncover the violence that inevitably fuels cultural capital. Against the backdrop of several political benchmarks, including the fraught political context of European fascism, the Spanish transition to democracy, and the fall of the Berlin Wall, they turn to music as a historical archive of the failures of a European collective, a collective that has too readily forgotten the violence that structures it. For them, music is a fully socialized labor force that cannot be instrumentalized because it remains immanent and historical, even if contentless; it is this absence of content that allows for historical resonances to multiply and gather in the contingency of their work. In their works, the acoustic functions as a speculative form that sustains the political undertones of a musicalized labor. In their hands, for example, Johann Sebastian Bach becomes a threshold from which to question the logic of cultural patrimony and patronymics by refusing to cover up the violence it demands. Santos's lifelong engagement with Bach in his performances, his love-hate relationship with the composer's music, is above all an attempt to listen more carefully to the fractures that inhabit it by making the wolf tones that Bach's achievements in harmony and temperance were intent on making less audible howl again.

In Part 2, "Acoustic Relations: Allora & Calzadilla," I focus on the artists' exploration of the relations between music, violence, and the question of the animal. Their work is presented as a compositional arrangement of different forms of acoustic existence, of multiple ways of being in the world — forms of existence that range from the human to the animal, from the organic to the mineral. My reading untangles the historico-political potential of Puerto Rico's ambivalent status in the United States as "foreign in a domestic sense" as the archipelagic anchor of their practice. Following María

Zambrano's call for a nonsacrificial history — which demands thinking without the inherited thoughts of the Western sovereign subject that articulate sacrifice as a requisite of imperial politics and its logic of enmity and domination — and juxtaposing it to the archipelago as an alternative form of political organization, I read Allora & Calzadilla's production of acoustic encounters through the violence encoded in the musical archive they mobilize. This violence becomes legible not only in their engagement in different forms of colonial extraction but also with the destruction of nature that is the signature of colonialism. Their works seek to resurrect the force of this destroyed nature — to hear its traces, but also its survival, in demolition sites, in prehistoric caves, and in animals that strike back by exposing the long history of accumulated annihilations, making themselves heard through bones, fossils, and different kinds of remains and debris. Indeed, their works feature a veritable bestiary — vultures, dogs, bats, elephants — that signals the limitations of humanism's approach to the compositive environments the artists construct and sometimes simply occupy. They explore the role of music as an organism that functions like a multitemporal and polyphonic ecology that permeates our surroundings, even when we cannot hear it.

In Part 3, "*Inter Canem et Lupum*: Anri Sala's Fictions," I attend to the complex role of fiction in Sala's acoustic and cinematic assemblages, which also feature a bestiary that is simultaneously literal and symbolic. As in Allora & Calzadilla or Santos and Portabella, Sala's acoustic and filmic reconfigurations of a European musical legacy cannot be insulated from the political violence, national and colonial, it encrypts and deploys — Tirana, Sarajevo, and the Germania pavilion at the Venice Biennale form a nexus of that violence. Sala's treatment of different media (acoustic, cinematic, spatial) and of different discourses (aesthetic, political, historical) produces a series of relays that intensify their relational dependence on one another. It is cinema, however, that allows him to elaborate an internal version of time through the musicalization of the image. Music, in his works, becomes an unfolding anamorphosis of historical time that intensifies and multiplies its complexity through a cinematic mediation that allows him to move backward and forward in looping motions that contract and densify the musical experience of time, making it more opaque and less legible, but also phenomenologically richer and more textured. His collaboration with saxophonist Jemeel Moondoc, for instance, brings these all to bear in relation to Black sorrow songs and the disturbances that inevitably plague collective historical memory.

Finally, in a brief coda, I turn to Tarek Atoui's collaborations with Deaf communities in his expansion of hearing beyond the aural and in the direction of a collective swerve expressing an endless connectivity to our environment.[9] Like all the artists I think with in the main three parts of the book and in the interludes that connect them, Atoui's speculations on a community briefly bound by the experience of listening are not *explicitly* political—they have no political content—but rather they are formally and *implicitly* political because they propose a composite and compositional organization that extends the logic of community beyond the logic of sovereignty, sacrifice, and identitarian exclusion.

The artworks with which I engage incorporate the wolves that Europe has willingly excluded through a series of historical and political choices. This is because they find in music the form of a promise that no longer thinks in terms of oppositions or of difference understood as inequality. Such promise emerges as a gathering force of historical relations that become manifest in collaborative and multimedia artistic practices. The speculative nature of these artistic approaches, with their layered acoustic and visual assemblages, enact a metamorphosis of Europe's musical legacies. In so doing they propose an imagined European community capable of surviving its foundational violence, a community that has too often been conceived either as a simple aggregation of wounded sovereignties or as an endless partitioning of these same sovereignties.

The collaborative relationship between music and cinema in many of the artworks I examine is also an exploration of their differences, each of them underscoring the singularity of the other, a singularity that remains intimately connected to their technological mediation. I underline the exceptional and paradoxical nature of the cinematic as a visual environment for the political and experimental potential of this disjunction by following the figure of the wolf, an acoustic condensation that bears witness to the discontinuous and dissonant ensemble, the fragile organization of differences, that we call "Europe."

The gesture is akin to understanding that Socrates learning to play the flute before his death is the mise-en-scène of a wordless and exceptional philosophical situation because it is conveyed in a medium other than the purely philosophical. In his reading of this scene in Plato's *Crito*, Derrida transforms Socrates into a musical instrument and philosophy into music through the mediation of a dream and the delay the dream demands. Although Derrida does not make it explicit, this is, indeed, *logos* as interval. Socrates dreams that with the flute he has learned to play, he must compose a melody to the god that, delaying the arrival of the ship from Sounion, has temporally stayed the philosopher's execution. "Socrates must thus transform himself into a musical instrument" to continue to do philosophy, but also to show, through this final metamorphosis, that philosophy is a kind of music, an interval, a delay, and a dwelling in place.[10] Similarly, the collaboration between image and sound asks us to rethink cinema and music altogether: if cinema and music can be thought only in relation to other media, even anachronistic and obsolete ones, it is because their unfolding calls other media and singularities into being. Or to put it another way, these media bear their own wolf within them, a wolf that, fissuring them from within, opens up their historico-political potential through the figure's latent mobility, metamorphosis, and heteronomy.

In the context of the acoustic turn taken by contemporary art practices, it is necessary to think about the specificity of sound as a mode of production, reproduction, and organization. Indeed, what Jean-Luc Nancy calls the "musical-becoming" of our times has changed the way in which we understand composition as a relational model.[11] Can we treat acoustic organization, its discontinuities and its complexity, as a blueprint onto which to project larger geopolitical forms? Is it possible to address Europe's failed political project through a musical understanding? The privileged relationship of music to number — think of scores, partitions, and algorithms — provides a unique representation of the contemporary economic realities that shape Europe's violent social and cultural legacy. The fact that European sovereignty is exclusively economic and that it functions fundamentally by tempering and harmonizing transnational fiscal dissonances underlines the centrality of musical models in our thinking of political communities.

The hour of the wolf is here the hour of the artwork, unsafe, because it belongs to the realm of the uncertain, the displaced, and the dissonant. Coming with the poetic presence of ghosts or artworks, wolves are ontological refugees. The urgency of rethinking European citizenship as open-ended is at the core of these artworks and takes the enigmatic shape of a wolf resisting harmonization, categorization, enclosure, and indeed any kind of limit or border. As Étienne Balibar puts it, "the relationship between politics and violence" is "illustrated by the operation of the 'border'."[12] Europe is fundamentally a series of operations of the border. However "harmonious" it may be in its conception, it consists primarily of an inscription of political violence, most often meant to domesticate the immigrant wolves at its borders or already within them. If these artworks incorporate the wolves that Europe has excluded, it is because they find in music a form that does not think in terms of opposition or exclusion, but rather emerges as a gathering of resonances that, woven together, become manifest in the imminent present of these collaborative practices.

FIRST INTERLUDE

EUROPA 2005, October 27

> This is not Europe gone mad; this is not aberration nor insanity; this *is* Europe.
> —W. E. B. Du Bois, *Darkwater: Voices from Within the Veil* (1920)

> We need to reinvent borders, destroy the Europe of Dr. Goebbels.
> —Jean-Marie Straub and Danièle Huillet, "Questionnaire on Globalization" (2001)

On October 27, 2005, in the Parisian suburb of Clichy-sous-Bois, two Parisian teenage boys of Mauritanian and Tunisian origin, Bouna Traoré and Zyed Benna, were electrocuted as they fled the police. Their friend Muhittin Altun survived, but was severely injured. As they were trying to elude their pursuers, they had hidden in a power substation, where they were burned alive. Their deaths were the result of a legally sanctioned police hunt and sparked nearly three weeks of uprisings and violent protest across France's *banlieues*. Vehicles and buses were torched, consumer goods destroyed—the highly visible violence was a television spectacle. There were thousands of arrests, a state of emergency was declared, and a curfew was imposed, based on laws passed during the Algerian war in 1955. Ten years later, the court in Rennes cleared Sébastien Gaillemin and Stéphanie Klein, the two police officers from whom the teenagers were fleeing, of the charge of failing to assist someone in danger.

The 2006 short film begins and ends five times. Same place, same pan, repeated but not identical—proceeding like musical variations. Each time, a date—*EUROPA 2005, October 27*—which is also the title of the film, appears on the screen, marking the singularity of a single and unrepeatable moment in time that still somehow keeps starting over again. Each of the five iterations is a variation of an invariant cycle of violence. First, in a static shot, we face a graffitied sign, "STOP. Ne risque pas ta vie." Then the camera begins to pan slowly to the right. It's spring—we hear birds, see a line of blooming trees next to the cars parked by the sidewalk. The light is slightly different every time. It is almost peaceful—the violence here cannot be represented, but it colors everything we witness. In succession, we see another series of variations of the same scene: a metal fence, a locked gate, another metal fence, barriers everywhere. There is another graffitied sign on a large metal door, a large building behind it: "STOP. L'électricité est plus fort que toi." There are electric towers in the background. The camera pans to the left. We are back at the first gate. The street is a cul-de-sac; it leads nowhere. A dog we cannot see barks every time we see the first sign again. It is either alerting us or guarding a gate, impossible to tell. These words, with the typographical disposition of poetic verses, appear on the screen: "chambre à gaz," "chaise électrique." It all starts again, one, two, three, four, five times—a cinematic accumulation. A little over ten minutes long, the film bears reference to a history of racialized violence, exclusion, and displacement.

Commissioned for Italian television on the centenary of Roberto Rossellini's birth, *EUROPA 2005* is Jean-Marie Straub and Danièle Huillet's final collaboration. It is their response to the neorealist filmmaker's *Europa '51*. Rossellini's film, part of his war trilogy, is a parable and female version of his earlier *The Flowers of St. Francis* and is set in postwar Rome. The likely suicide of a boy who has survived bombings and the deprivations of war, echoing the suicide of another child at the end of his *Germany Year Zero*, is the event that unravels the film, triggering the transformation of the film's protagonist. In her mourning, Irene, the child's mother, played by Ingrid Bergman, a wealthy immigrant living with her diplomat husband, is now able to see another Rome, a city still at war. By 1951, after the irreversible shattering of a world war, the struggle has taken the form of a brutal class war amid Europe's postwar reconstruction. In this merciless city, lodged within the city she thought she knew, and with a Communist journalist as mediator, she meets parents who cannot afford the cost of medical care for their son, a single and poor factory worker with a large brood of adopted children, a dying prostitute, and a petty thief fleeing the police. Once she assumes a place in the factory assembly line, there is no turning back. Irene chooses—her privilege is that she still can choose—to identify with Rome's underclass, and the results are jarring in her milieu, intolerable. Her husband decides to lock her up in an asylum for the insane, where she will meet other women also vanished and forgotten. There she is visited by her working-class friends, who think of her as a saint, as otherworldly. In the last shot of the film, we see Irene behind the bars of the asylum's window.

Straub and Huillet remain faithful to Rossellini. They, too, are talking about Europe, not just Rome or Paris. This Europe has internal borders within its metropoles, frontiers that are heavily guarded by the police.[1] Their version, however, replaces Rossellini's Christian humanism and its redemptive undertones with political militancy. That they decide not to compromise in their last film together should surprise no one. These are not accidents, they tell us, but executions. Their film is also part of a series on the violence of the state, which, in their hands, is a war—organized, targeted, efficient, and under cover of the law.

EUROPA 2005, October 27 is often screened with Straub's 2009 *Joachim Gatti, variation de lumière*, which, less than two minutes long, acts like a coda to the first and insists on what is invariant in relentless variations of the same. The film is a static shot of a photograph of filmmaker Joachim Gatti on the phone, positioned to the left of the screen and framed inside a red screen—it is film as an urgent political poster, a protest. Gatti was blinded by the police by a flash-ball gun during a peaceful protest in Montreuil, Paris. Straub's distinctive voice reads from Jean-Jacques Rousseau's preface to his 1755 *Discourse on the Origin and Foundations of Inequality among Men*. Evoking the European Enlightenment and implicitly its failure, he recites this passage on violence and inequality:

> Only the dangers of society as a whole trouble the philosopher's tranquil sleep and tear him from his bed. Someone can slit his counterpart's throat with impunity under his window. He only has to put his hands over his ears and argue with himself a little to prevent nature, which revolts within him, from identifying him with the one who is being assassinated. Savage man does not have this admirable talent, and for want of wisdom and reason he is always seen heedlessly yielding to the first sentiment of humanity. In uprisings and street fights the populace assembles and the prudent man distances himself: the dregs of the people, the women of the markets, separate the combatants and prevent honest people from slitting each other's throats.[2]

Rousseau's text is mobile and speculative in its arguments. It relies on rhetoric, irony, and understatement and incorporates the ambivalence that the writer associates with philosophical statements in general. While it is a philosophical and literary text, however, it is not a militant one. It reinforces Straub's emphasis on violence and inequality as invariants that permeate the European Enlightenment, but in Straub's filmic jab, covering one's ears is not an option, and the idea of a self-regulating mass has become almost utopian. The "*reduction of politics to the police*"[3] both simplifies and intensifies Rousseau's scenario. There are now only two possible identifications: either with the police or with the victims of the police in the permanent segregation of the *banlieue* and in the criminalization of its uprisings. Straub seems to be wary of any ambiguity in this context, a luxury he can no longer afford. After a brief pause, he indicts the violence of the police, sanctioned as it is not only by the state, but by the "Europe" of 2005, of 2009, and beyond: "And I Straub, I say to you that it is the police, the police armed by Capital, who kill."

PART ONE

The Labor of Sound: Pere Portabella and Carles Santos

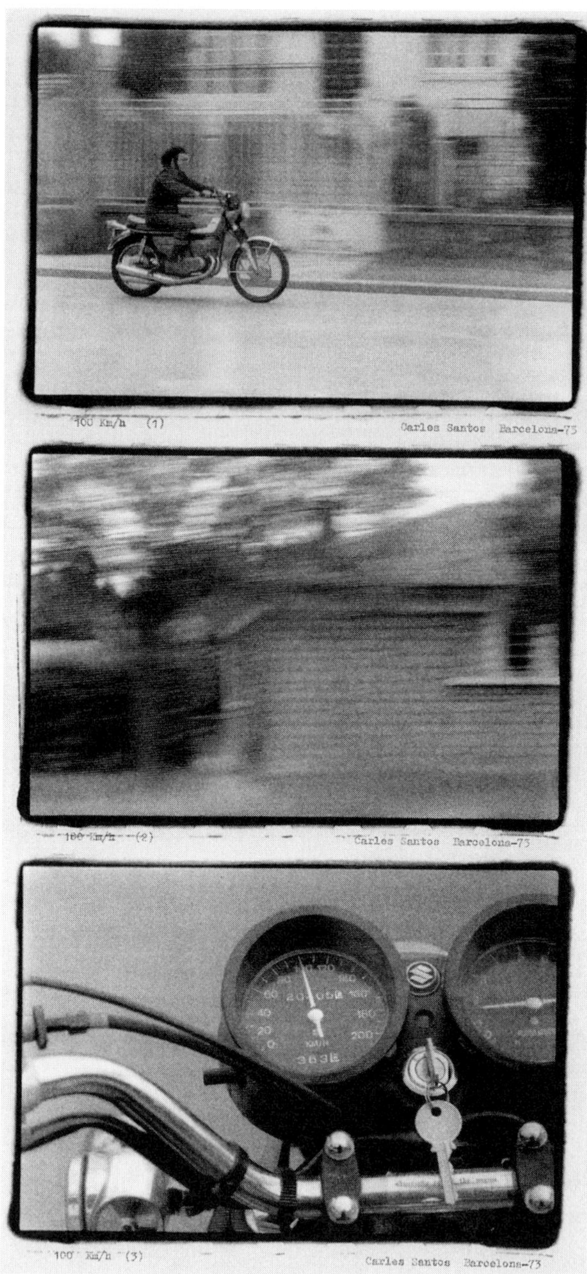

Carles Santos, *100 km/h, 1, 2, 3*, 1973. Performance documentation. Fons Carles Santos, Caixa de Vinarós.

Bach at the Modelo

> We do not understand music — it understands us.
>
> — Theodor W. Adorno, *Beethoven: The Philosophy of Music* (1998)

I begin with a story the Catalan filmmaker Pere Portabella loves to recount, a story regarding avant-garde composer, artist, and musician Carles Santos's return to piano playing after a self-imposed hiatus that lasts three years.[1] In 1971, before Portabella's narrative begins, Santos decides to intensify his refusal to play and sells his piano, buys a motorcycle with the money he receives, and in 1973, records the performance *100 km/h, 1, 2, 3*. The piece consists of a series of photographed intervals of the pianist speeding on his new motorcycle, a view of his surroundings, now blurred and transformed by the rush of motion, and a close-up of the motorbike's speedometer. The metronomic focus of the piece suggests the transposition of musical technology and its temporal movements onto a motorized movement materialized in space, as well as in time — an allusion to early chronophotography. The speed indicator brings to mind the urgency of the piece's political and historical context — the last violent and agonizing years of Francoist rule in Spain — and suggests a revolutionary acceleration of history as an antidote to the ideological ossification of the regime.[2] It is also an artistic reflection on the question of what can and cannot be measured, on the hesitation between the calculable and the incalculable as the interval of the possible.

That same year, Santos devotes himself to clandestine political activities in order to put an end to Francoist rule. In October, he is arrested together with 113 members of the Assemblea de Catalunya, an anti-Francoist platform founded in 1971 and active until 1977,[3] and incarcerated in the Modelo prison in Barcelona. Upon arrival, Santos cannot be fingerprinted by the police, because his daily piano practice, and this despite his motorcycle interlude, has worn out his fingerprints. As we will see later, this failure of biometrics resonates loudly in the context of the musician's investment in the impersonality and anonymity of artistic and political practices.

In the prison, his cellmate is none other than Portabella. It is here that the raconteur's story begins: on learning that somewhere in the building there is an abandoned piano, Santos decides it is time to play again. He proceeds to play an entire Bach sonata on a hopelessly out-of-tune piano, and in doing so, joins risk and violence to the act of playing, using virtuosity in defiance of itself. His playing is now of a different order, and it will remain so. He no longer plays the piano, but plays *with* the piano and even against it—as an incongruous piece of furniture in the prison, as a conceptual object, and as the symbolic carrier of a fraught cultural tradition and political order. He finds a way to connect his virtuoso skill as a renowned pianist to the political dissonances of the Spain of his time, transforming the concert form into a performative "action." He deploys the disharmony of the wolf to intervene militantly in the biopolitical regime of a Francoist prison—forcing a listening that falls far outside the signifying references of the space where it resonates and, in doing so, emphasizes music's disidentificatory potential. His performance is at once an interpretation and a labor of composition that defamiliarizes both music and location. It is the expression of a musical inheritance that is set to work by unveiling the disharmony any legacy carries within it—by wrestling out into the open the strangeness in every patrimony.

In this instance, the unstable anachronism that exists between the production of sound, its resonance, its transit through space, and finally its reception by the ear calls into presence the dissident political community in the prison through the notion of an interval—through what is at once belated and new, too late and too early. This gap or hesitation, this unavoidable delay, is an important element that underscores the temporal intensity of music and its unfolding—its capacity to make us feel time in the body through intervallic modulation. One could even say that music is a direct effect of these delays, intervals, and spacings. Or that in music, time itself becomes polysemic—rhythm and tempo, extension and contraction, regularity and variation, memory and anticipation. Additionally, the fact that in the Western musical tradition in which Santos is embedded, intervals can be viewed as either consonant or dissonant—can be perceived as antagonistic—is precisely what allows for the emergence of "wolves." Wolves are another name for the encounter of these opposing beats as they clash together in disharmony and dissent, for the unstable border between music and nonmusic. Their howling is simultaneously the negation, the denial of a metric and its rules of containment, and the expansion of a structure that can no longer hold them inside it. It is also a multiplication of the uncountable—after all, when three wolves howl together, they sound like several more; their number remains forever uncertain. The impossible reconciliation between the one and the many structures the movement of the political and of the artwork itself.

In the prison, those who listen may well hear their dissent temporally echoed and amplified in every out-of-key sound Santos plays. They may even experience it as an acoustic and transient reenactment of their physical displacement, as an inscription of their multiplicity, alone, yet together, singular in their anonymity. The acoustic semblance of harmony is revealed here as an auratic mirage that echoes Spain's vexed sociohistorical context, resonating with all its contradictions. Through Santos's action, the listener, albeit briefly and in an intermittent refraction, recognizes himself (the Modelo was a male-only prison and a panopticon designed to increase a sense of isolation) through the critical distancing effect of having his own dislocation resonate in the dissonant sounds of the out-of-tune piano and in the newly found strangeness and splintered uncertainty of Bach's music. If the political prisoner exists outside the bounds of the prison as a political actor, that is, he has an active life that has been displaced elsewhere, Santos's militant mobilization of the emancipatory potential of an artwork, a deviation of Bach's music, in this case, functions like a heterotopia, or better still, as a practice and rehearsal of freedom. It transports the prisoners forward and elsewhere to a differential space-time that, until now invisible or inaudible, cannot be accounted for within the logic of a Francoist prison and does so through the free play of an unpredictable artistic action. It materializes the musical fugue as a flight, as an experiment and a speculative encryption of both freedom and its impossibility within material, formal, and ideological constrictions.[4]

Santos's piano performance embodies what Adorno calls "a desire for dissonances," an "expression of the suffering, simultaneously autonomous and unfree subject" for whom music "is Utopia as well as the lie that Utopia is here now."[5] Political and aesthetic freedom are understood here as ephemeral and performative sites of production, aftereffects of a singular labor that cannot be predicted, counted, or extracted. It is this performative aspect of artistic practice, its engagement with its present context together with the demand that we somehow play along, but also move forward, that opens the door to political possibilities. It bears no relation to content or expression but rather hinges, in the words of Trinh T. Minh-ha, "on the complex task of generating, arranging, altering, arresting, modulating, inflecting, distorting, adjusting, tempering, perfecting, purifying, setting, and standardizing intervals."[6] In other words, music always operates negatively and through silence—the source of its proliferating contentless content—and produces, above all, a condensation, intensification, and shattering of different temporalities.

Santos's expansion of physical and political spaces through acoustic temporalities implies a negative understanding of the artwork, and its unchosen legacies, that, as we will see, he shares with Portabella. Sound's ability to traverse walls and enclosures speaks to an emancipatory potential that calls for a redistribution of a cultural capital no longer understood as a closed archive and no longer embedded in the logic of property and inheritance. Bach's music and the physical resistance to it performed by Santos's playing, in collaboration with the materiality of the piano's out-of-tuneness, transport listeners beyond the boundaries of the ideological and aesthetic harmonization of cultural patrimony, a form of unfreedom that both prison and concert hall eerily share. The duration of Santos's performance—he played the *entire* sonata, uninterrupted—takes the form of an attack,[7] and his mobilization of the wolf underscores the violence of his musical charge on Bach's temperance and harmonization as carriers of a larger social and political normativity they often have been instrumentalized to represent, preserve, and transmit. Violence and rupture play a prominent and often playful and comical role in Santos's relationship to Europe's musical heritage, and his choice of Bach is key.

The Panther

> Love, hatred, attraction, repulsion, suspension: all are music. The more the displacements one has gone through, the more music one can listen to.
> —Trinh T. Minh-ha, *elsewhere, within here: immigration, refugeeism, and the boundary event* (2010)

> This little book is *a great declaration of war*, and as for sounding out idols, this time they are not just idols of the age, but *eternal* idols that are touched here with the hammer as with a tuning fork.
> —Friedrich Nietzsche, *The Twilight of the Idols: Or, How to Philosophize with a Hammer* (1899)

According to art historian Fèlix Fanés, when Joan Brossa—a visual artist, early cinema fanatic, magician, playwright, mainstay of the Dau al Set, principal instigator of a conceptual Catalan avant-garde, and one of Santos's future collaborators[8]—met Carles Santos in the Barcelona of the 1960s, he demanded a piano recital. In such encounters, Brossa often called for a performance as a "carta de presentació" (formal introduction). The young avant-garde pianist and composer, who had studied with John Cage and was successfully introducing Fluxus noise music and Minimalism to the hungry and stifled Spanish audience of the *tardofranquismo*, responded by playing Bach.[9] The notoriously demanding Brossa retorted to the virtuoso display by simply declaring that Santos clearly knew how to play the piano and then provocatively asked, "*I ara qué?*" (And now what?). Santos's lifelong engagement with Bach's music, his love-hate relationship with it, can be understood as a protracted attempt to answer this question.

Bach himself advocated on behalf of the new technology that resulted in a tuning that compromised the Renaissance pursuit of pure fifths in favor of a system that eliminated wolf tones and facilitated the development of modern tonality. Bach is the crucial figure in baroque aesthetics because he employs traditional forms—the fugue, most of all—in the service of a new technology, an intensified formal speculation, and a modern harmonic system. His music resounds simultaneously forward and backward in progressions and inversions, augmentation and diminution—musical figurations that recur constantly as variations and contrasts in his compositions. Santos's relationship with Bach is crucial in understanding what one might call, with Adorno, his "musical conduct" and, with Baruch Spinoza, his *affectus*, that is to say, his being at once affected and affecting. While the loops that adorn the first page of Bach's "The Well-Tempered Clavier" visualize a circular temperament where all keys sound in tune and produce a loop of call and response that harmonizes them, Santos reminds us that despite Bach, and maybe because of him, not all sounds—and the cultural capital they are made to carry—can be reconciled in harmony.

Santos's rendition recalls Bach's towering figure in the dream of harmony and the fragility of such a dream in the context of Europe's cultural legacy. With Bach's developments in harmony, which call musical modernity into being, dissonance is neutralized, integrated, and subsumed into a larger system. Harmony becomes an ideological mystification that in turn echoes a fabular idea of Europe. In addition, the connection of Bach to imperial ideology and its logic of domination, on the one hand, and to subservient artistic labor, on the other, holds the key to Santos's 1997 musical theater piece *La pantera imperial (Dedicat, com el 1802, als "admiradors patriòtics del vertader art musical")* (The imperial panther [Dedicated, as in 1802, to "patriotic admirers of the true musical art"])[10]—one of his first collaborations with Mariaelena Roqué, responsible here for the costume design and art direction and a turning point in Santos's increasing dramatization of the musical. The title of the piece refers as much to Bach as it does to the piano, the instrument that entirely mediates Santos's relationship to Bach. In fact,

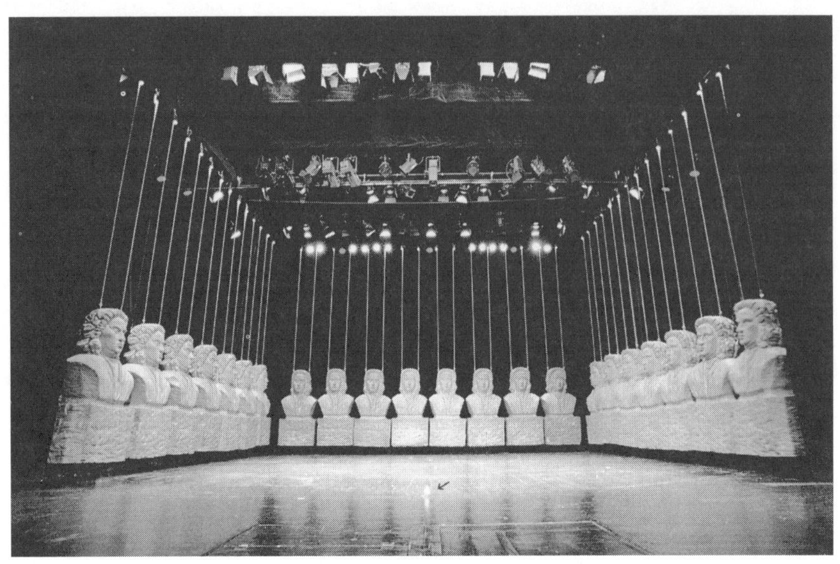

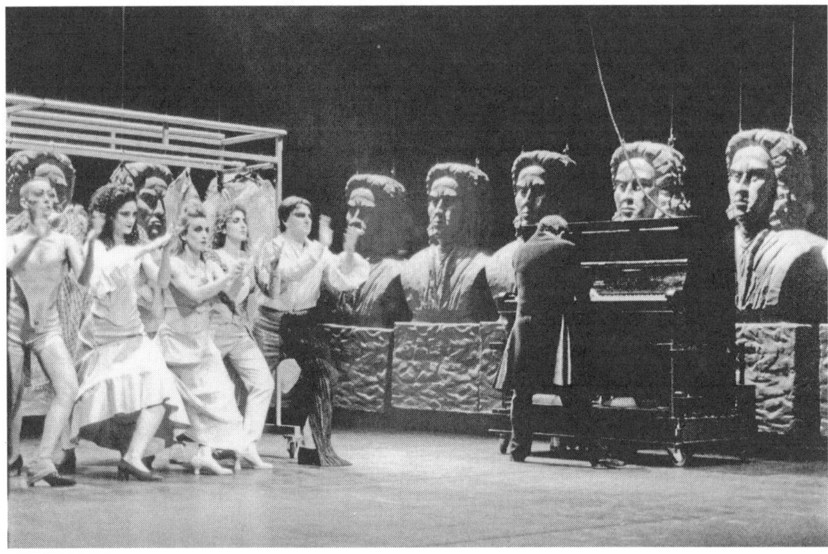

Carles Santos, *La pantera imperial (Dedicat, com el 1802, als "admiradors patriòtics del vertader art musical)*, 1997. Performance documentation. Fons Carles Santos, Caixa de Vinarós.

Santos often referred to his Imperial Bösendofer grand piano as a "panther," a small, but revealing detail that tells us much about the feral nature of an instrument that is no longer understood as a tool but as a mechanical yet living organism, part of a larger assemblage of associated producers that freely play with and against each other in the intensified libidinal economy of his music. With Santos, the piano itself can no longer be fully detached as a value form, as an object that represents cultural capital; it must be seen as a relational ensemble of dependent parts, human and nonhuman, that often play in opposition to one another.[11]

If in Santos's hands (and head, arms, and indeed his entire body, all of which are used during his performances) the piano must be fully untamed and undomesticated, it is not surprising that the same fate must befall Bach's music and his monumentality — which relies on the arrested movement of a representation it fiercely protects. Bach was well known for being an astonishing improviser on the organ, as well as adopter of new musical technologies, such as the pianoforte and, later, Silbermann pianos. There was little that was archaic in his experimentation and speculation with musical form. Even his anachronism must be put in relation to the innovations that, on occasion, could hardly be fully realized with the instruments and orchestration available at the time. It is also worth recalling that Bach's monumentality and iconicity is mostly a posthumous construction; for most of his life, Bach was an overworked and underpaid church composer in the decentralized Lutheran denomination.[12] His numerous letters to his employers are a testimony to the difficulties of his musical labor and consist above all in complaints about his lack of time — after all, labor, like music, is measured in time.

Bach's monumental figure in *La pantera imperial* is embodied and materialized in a neo-Dadaist theatrical landscape that recalls a boxing ring, an avant-garde trope Santos had used before (notably for concert announcements that echo Arthur Cravan's boxing matches).[13] Bach's overwhelming musical stature is broken down into a series of moving and threatening busts that fill a stage defined by an excess of bodies, voices, and sounds, all fighting for harmonic ascendancy. The busts arrange and rearrange themselves into several variations, as does the music. Bach's legacy is transformed into a wildly anachronistic performance. Santos's violent splintering stems from loving Bach as a transgressor, as a conflicted musical worker who at times resists the emergence and commodification of specialized labor in the time texture of his music. By literally decomposing Bach as a subject, he also brings forth the possibility, already present in Bach's music, of turning polyphony and multiplication into technologies that, in Adorno's words, "resist the inexorable growth of the commodity-character of music, a process . . . linked to its subjectivization."[14] With Santos, Bach disappears as a subject in order to metamorphose into an anonymous and nonharmonic collectivity caught in a continued process, or fugal loop, of being made and unmade. Santos materializes this conflict, or rather antithesis, between subject and object in Bach's music through the motorized movements of a mechanical pianola that haunts the stage playing the *Goldberg Variations*. Tradition is presented here as an infinitely mediated mode of relation, one where transmission and inheritance travel under the cover of rejection: Santos needs Bach, Bach needs Santos. Their complicity is not a choice. By means of a radical exercise in the labor of advanced composition, Santos literally makes the heterogeneous and dynamic unfolding of Bach's music both visible and audible, rescuing what still remains hidden in his work from cultural stagnation, transporting arrested identity toward dynamic becoming. Adorno describes the task in the following way: "The entire richness of the musical texture, the integration of which was the source of Bach's power, must be placed in prominence by the performance instead of being sacrificed to a rigid, immobile monotony, the spurious semblance of unity that ignores the multiplicity it should embody and surmount."[15]

Santos's compositional realization of Bach's music—his interpretation *and* performance—resists the commodity character of music

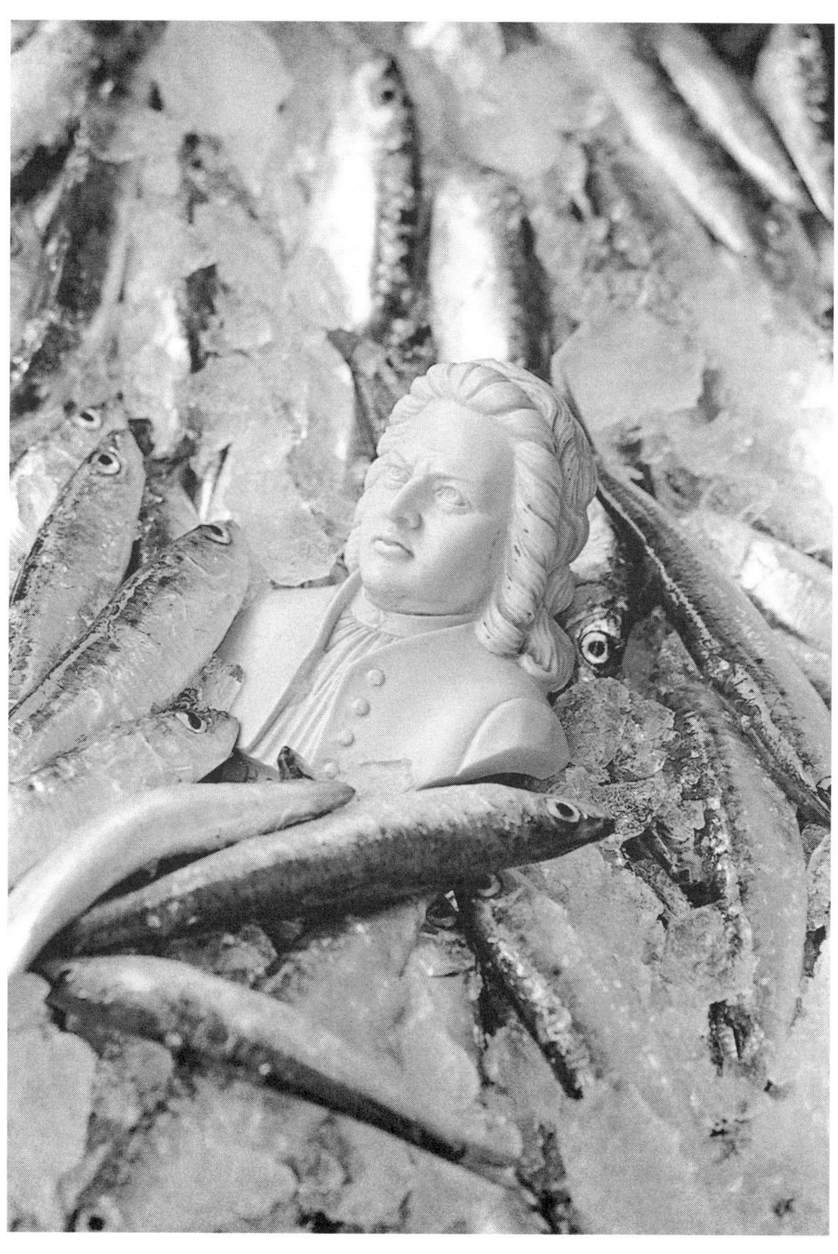

Carles Santos, *Sèrie B-A-C-H. Tema amb variations*, 1997–98. Courtesy of Actar.

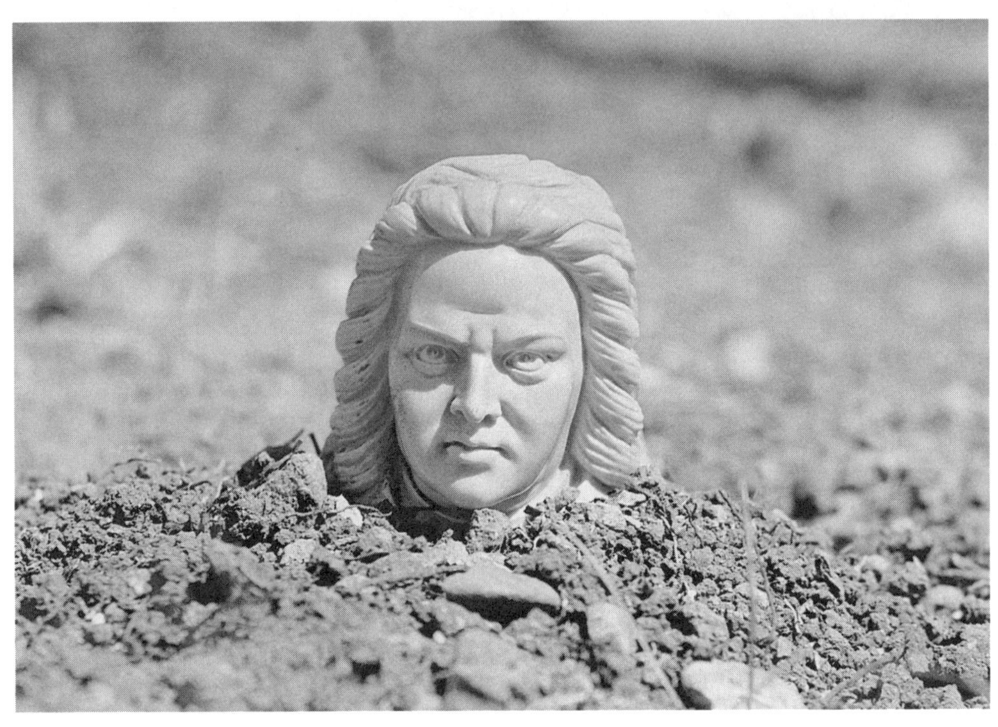

Carles Santos, *Sèrie B-A-C-H. Tema amb variations*, 1997-98. Courtesy of Actar.

and of musical labor through the intensification and multiplication of arrangements. Turning Bach's music into a theatrical situation where listening to music and the composition, interpretation, performance, and recording of it cannot be compressed or separated, he transforms it into an event and a mode of production opposed to productivism that challenge cultural commodification by denying its self-identity, pluralizing it to become, in Adorno's words, "a force field that tears all moments of the artwork into itself."[16] Music is never a conflict-free zone, either for Adorno or for Santos or even for Bach. Framing his homage in the form of sacrilege—literally kneeling like a penitent to play Bach, with each arm extended to play separate pianos—Santos actualizes and desacralizes Bach's legacy by returning it to its formlessness and heterogeneity, to the uncertainty of an internal violence that is its true legacy, a veritable force field. His performative emphasis on physical endurance thematizes corporeal limitations and markers of finitude that traverse musical experience through an embodiment that belies any transcendent understanding of the medium.

Furthermore, and in contrast to Adorno's elitism, Santos insists that this legacy must be seen in relation to popular traditions rather than in opposition to them. In his performances, Bach can also be played with feet stomping on the stage through the percussive rhythms of a *zapateado*. The novelty of Santos's approach, like that of Bach, is often the result of the recombination and remediation of already existing forms, a reminder that variations contain endless possibilities. His approach is also an at times slapstick acknowledgment that music can be described or discussed only through the nonmusical. One of the numerous versions of *Pantera imperial* (the piece never ceased to be a work in progress) begins with a female actor forcefully declaiming a description of the musical notations on the score, becoming out of breath during her recitation as she tries to catch up with the rhythmic and anticipatory unfolding of the fugue. When the actor articulates her words with a minute and fastidious precision—reading every single note, bar, return and repetition—her breathlessness underscores the impossibility of ever fully representing or giving an account of the enigma of Bach's music through notation, further emphasizing the conundrum it is for Santos but also for anyone truly listening to it. One is also reminded of Deleuze and Guattari's description of Glenn Gould playing Bach: when he "speeds up the performance of a piece, he is not just displaying virtuosity, he is transforming the musical points into lines, he is making the whole piece proliferate."[17] Put another way, the virtuosic speed of the actor and pianist allows us to feel the infinite in the finite, the limitless numerical possibility lurking behind the carefully measured tempos of Bach's music and its textural dissonances. The limits of representation and analogy, their ties to notions of measurement and countability, are on full display. The actor's breathlessness and Gould's humming, strange singing, and even howling express the finitude that traverses Bach's infinite play, a reminder that music is indeed a form of breathing, a way of being alive in the world—and for Santos, a matter of life and death.[18] This may seem like an exaggeration, but Santos literalizes this point when he reenacts one of the fictionalized torture scenes in Portabella's *Informe General* by having a singer's head repeatedly and forcefully submerged in water so that his intermittent singing is as much music as it is an index of breath and survival.

Throughout Santos's work, the relationship between music and survival—at once existential, artistic, and political—hinges on a potential for multiplication and intensification that, springing forward spontaneously, anticipates the emergence of the new. The question of the possibility of the new, or more explicitly of the emergence and possibility of a future, is closely connected to an understanding of composition itself as a mode of production and reproduction and indeed variation of older forms—one that employs dissonance and the multiplication of intervals and differentials to derail a mode of production that would rely on divisions of labor, on the fetishization of authorship, or on the immediacy of agency. Because composition has a relational value, it constantly produces something new by interrupting modes of productivism that present themselves as resolutions, as the completed and detachable objects of dead labor. In the act of composition, acoustic dissonance cuts across and reorganizes formal economies and temporalities while acting as a challenge to harmonic modes of representation, offering alternative forms of association and alliance that privilege the risks of becoming over the certainties of being. Association and differentiation are no longer opposites but stages in a process of unfolding. The enactment of antagonism and difference, dissonance plays a role in the activation of a multiple political agency through resonance and multiplication and in a performative actualization and unfolding of Europe's musical patrimony that takes the form of a scattering and a decomposition of the *Homo europaeus* it has come to represent.

Indeed, every listener becomes implicated in Santos's performative labor of decomposition and composition, a labor that articulates the piece's musical and dramaturgical collage with its acoustic montage. As Adorno puts it, Bach's "heritage has passed on to composition, which is loyal to him in being disloyal; it calls his music by name by producing it anew."[19] The stakes of this legacy could not be higher for Adorno, who comes to see the movement of music as the best expression of the movement and duration of thought, the latter having become obscured by the disciplinary certainties of philosophy and its resolutions in a manner that in turn echoes musical commodification. Let us not forget, Adorno was as much a musician as he was a philosopher: as he notes in "On the Contemporary Relationship between Philosophy and Music," the "analysis of the current status of music should give itself up to philosophical insight as, conversely, the philosophical reflection [is] not to be separated from the contemporary situation of music."[20] For Adorno, philosophy cannot move without music. Santos's performative conceptualism needs to be equally understood as a musical expression of the survival of bodies and minds. He, too, knows that *music thinks.*

Metronomics

> "Poème Symphonique" (for 100 metronomes) requires,
> as its primary condition for performance, 100 metronomes.
> —György Ligeti, *Poème symphonique*, score (1962)

The social and political imaginaries of Francoist Spain created a singular instance of dislocation in the Catalan avant-garde of the 1960s and 1970s. The commitment to avant-garde practices emerging from an established tradition in the Catalan context pushed the envelope of political possibility by establishing an elective affinity and an affective and social transfer between the political and the aesthetic. Grup de Treball (Work Group), initially called Equip Conceptual, a heterogeneous Catalan art collective with a short lifespan (1972–1976), affiliated predominantly with Marxist politics and conceptualist aesthetics, is an excellent example of this double bind. Both Portabella and Santos were members of the collective.[21] Their collaboration in Grup de Treball provided both artists with an experimental platform on which to work through the successes and failures of an ideological conceptualism. One of the interventions of the group stands out as a mouthpiece for the main political concerns and conceptual protocols of the group, namely, the use of the record or the chronicle, together with the precise segmentation and impersonal measuring of subjective experiences that are then gathered and collectivized. The 1973 piece *Recorreguts: Treball col·lectiu* (Routes: Collective work) clearly echoes Santos's *100 km/h, 1,2,3*, produced earlier the same year. The collective project recorded three possible measurements of the route taken in Barcelona by 113 people from October 28 to October 31, 1973, after their detention and arrest during a meeting of the Assemblea de Catalunya. When the police raided their meeting, participants were first taken to the infamous Via Laietana police station and from there divided and taken to two different prisons: men went to the Modelo and women to the Trinitat. These itineraries were presented on a map of Barcelona at different scales, kilometers, centimeters, and fingerprints (maybe an allusion to police biometrics), and through a variety of measuring devices, a motorcycle odometer, a finger on a map, and traditional topographical maps.

The *Recorreguts* project was conceived as a book publication to raise money for political prisoners through the activist platform Solidaritat amb el Moviment Obrer and had a companion piece, *Treball col·lectiu que consisteix a verificar la distribució de 44 professions entre 113 persones segons una nota apareguda últimament a la premsa* (Collective work that consists of verifying the distribution of 44 professions among 113 people according to a note recently published in the press), which omitted the names of the 113 detainees and replaced them with a list of their professions. The group's central preoccupation with different forms and assemblages of formally collectivized and anonymized experiences and labor functions as a critique of capitalism under Franco and finds echoes in all their subsequent output. In 1975, a year before its dissolution, in its *Autodefinició del Grup de Treball*, a manifesto mostly written by Santos, the group described its practice as follows:

> Heterogeneous grouping of individuals whose degree of union is established on the basis of a double articulation consisting in 1) ideological positions—implicit and explicit in the artistic practice, individual and collective, of the group, and in other types of articulated practice realized by the group—and 2) of the style of work in terms of the dialectical articulation of three types of practice: artistic practice, theoretical practice and the practice of influence on and intervention in artistic and intellectual sectors.[22]

The manifesto presents the group as a coalition of singularities and differentials created through the collective labor of associated producers, a labor that, emerging from an interactive assemblage of the artistic and the political, manages to preserve their difference. This bridge between art and politics extends to the protocols that constitute their collective amalgamation: temporal encounters, restricted movements, and associations that intervene in the ideological and artistic stagnation of late Francoism by setting themselves to work that recalls an idiomatic rendition of the Heideggerian *Werksein* (literally: an artwork that works). The group relies on a configuration of practical, theoretical, and artistic means, a triad that spells out their definition of the labor of conceptualism and of the artwork's own conceptual thinking. Their artworks come into the world as labor. Joining their conceptual work with that of the artwork itself, they hope to produce a multiplicity of forces of production with no predetermined outcome. These forces encapsulate but also exceed the artistic contributions of the members of the group, and they do so by refusing to be measured through elaborate artistic procedures that, in turn, parody and deconstruct capitalism's estimation, computation, and extraction of labor power.

The group's organizing principle understands the artwork as a composite or arrangement of disparate forces that the artist can never fully predict or control but that nevertheless creates and activates a force field of political energy. It insists on the irretrievable ephemerality that structures any aesthetic experience and that will become an essential component of Santos's lifelong iconoclasm. Because of this, his work retains the multiple traces of the collective, even when it appears under his individual signature. In one of his performances, the 1979 *La Re Mi La*, Santos metamorphoses into seventy-four different characters, materializing the plurality and multiplicity his practice seeks to intensify. The same could be said of Portabella and, perhaps to a lesser extent, even Brossa. While the dissolution of Grup de Treball after the end of Francoist rule speaks to the centrality of its sociopolitical location and its strategic use of the mutual interference of aesthetic and political militancy, its ethos remains alive in the production of each of its former members. Once Franco died, so did Grup de Treball. The group's self-declared obsolescence is proof of the dependence and incompleteness of art and politics in their militant practice, which is a historicized process of mutual mobilization, in contrast to the stasis and indifference to one another displayed in the Francoist milieu, themselves forms of complicity and instrumentalization.

In the case of Santos, the group's artistic protocols point to a mode of listening otherwise, in languages that, not only musically, expand what music may be or may become. In 1974, once Santos is out of prison and has returned to public piano performances, he conceives and produces, under the collective signature of Grup de Treball, *1 Preludi de Chopin, opus 28, núm, 18*, employing and extending the group's conceptual conventions.[23] The piece consists of 264 photographs documenting and fragmenting the gestures and bodily positions of the pianist at play, translating musical movement and intervals into a visual splintering and silent recomposition. This mediation between music and the visual becomes the crux of Santos's performative actions and is at the heart of his collaboration as a writer and composer in Portabella's films. Transforming the score into a storyboard, into an impersonal and yet embodied abstraction of an ephemeral musical experience we do not get to hear, Santos produces a model for his subsequent conceptual practice: he demonstrates that listening is always listening back and listening otherwise, beyond the musical.[24] It is hard not to read one of the few "screenplays" we have by Santos and Portabella (who famously did not use any), consisting of a sketch of the movements in the 1972 film *Umbracle* (Greenhouse), as a musical notation of the compositional unfolding and the fugal relation between images in their films. By taking up the idea of musical or even choreographic notation in order to move beyond it, the two collaborators engage in an endless negotiation between different languages, each one of them insufficient by itself, but carried forward through its relationship to another, spiraling into a movement that is entirely unpredictable.

Before continuing, let us pause for a moment and consider the space of the Fundació Joan Miró in Barcelona, where Santos's 2006

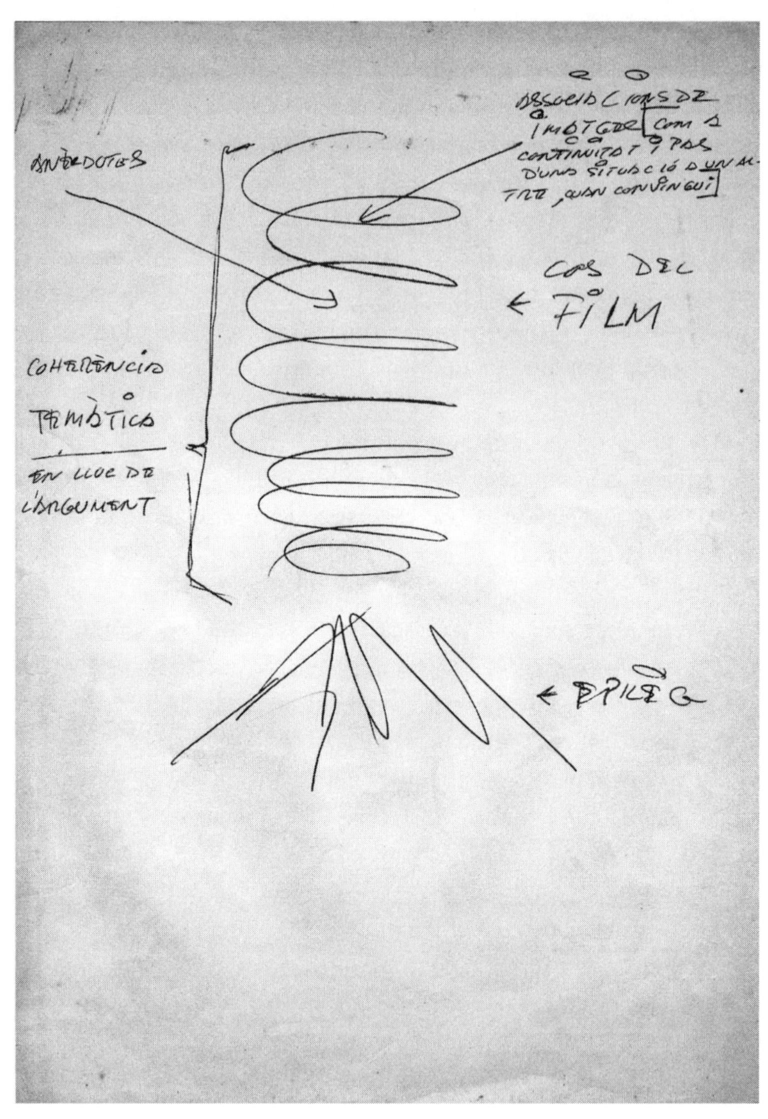

Umbracle, 1972. Screenplay.

retrospective *¡Visca el piano!* (Long live the piano!) takes place. The collection on view is a testimony of Santos's lifelong commitment to an aesthetic and political avant-garde. Two details, however, stand out in a way that is relevant to our discussion. A mechanical pianola (the same one Santos used in his *Pantera imperial* and that reproduces a recording of him playing Bach) moves through the space, which is filled with artifacts, forcing the audience to negotiate its transit through the exhibition carefully. In another room, Santos is working. He arrives every day to sit at his piano and practice for a few hours and to devote, as is his custom, some of his time to playing Bach. He also plays one of his new compositions, using a white ball as a prosthetic extension of his left arm, so that the performance becomes an assemblage of human and nonhuman agents. Pere Portabella joins him there to record the rehearsals of Santos's composition, *No al no* (No to no), to document Santos working in the museum, and to begin shooting the prelude that opens their 2007 film *Die Stille vor Bach* (The silence before Bach).[25] The long-time collaborators engage once more in the visualization of labor through the durational complicities of the performative and the cinematic, reminding us that the artwork comes into the world as living labor. Together, they insist that every one of their forceful negations, their collaborative "no to no," must be understood as enigmatic and militant affirmations of the possible, that is, as an emphatic "yes."

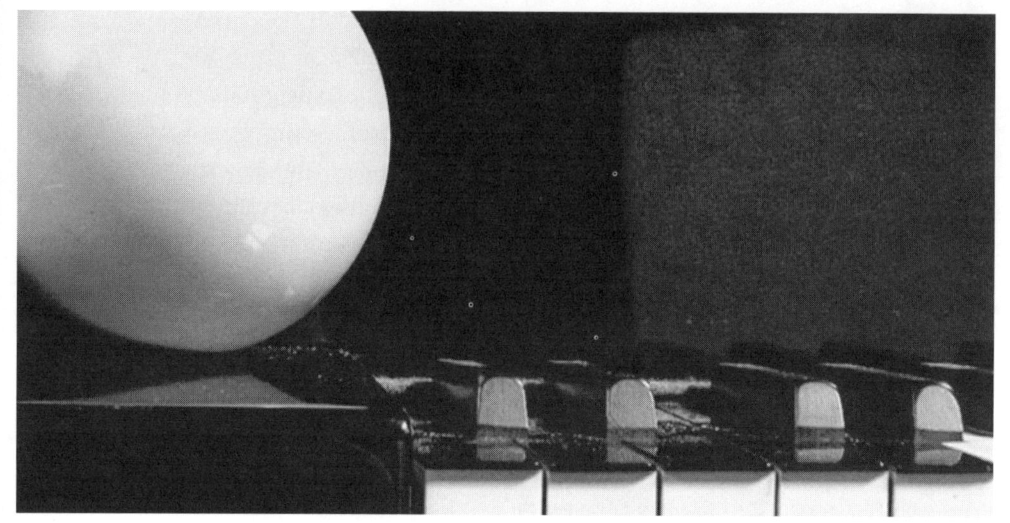

Pere Portabella, *Visca el Piano (No al No)*, 2006, film still. © Pere Portabella-Films 59

Music Is a Nomad

> Instead of having at his disposal just two or three sea noises, for example, all roughly in the same tone, the composer will be able to play on a keyboard of twelve or twenty-four or thirty-six or forty-eight different tonalities (with transpositions at fractions of an octave), whose combination at the premixing stage will also allow him to diversify the resource infinitely. It thus becomes possible to create chords and dissonances, melodies and symphonies of noises, which are the new, specifically cinematographic music.
> —Jean Epstein, "The Close-up of Sound" (1955)

As far as geopolitical contexts are concerned, the role of the peripheral is also relevant here: a Catalan filmmaker and a Catalan musician take a sideways glance at Bach as a musical landmark that has been used to universalize European identity and its modes of cultural production. Santos and Portabella mobilize the peripheral and precarious sovereignty of Catalonia as a vantage point from which to make the wolf audible again, to listen to the incomplete harmonization that lies at the dead center of Europe. Because we are concerned with music and cinema as forms in movement, the political agency that Portabella and Santos's collaboration reenergizes is intimately tied to the transit of sound and image across the specific temporalities and physical locations on which they fleetingly anchor themselves historically. These times and places are not simply settings or contexts, but rather histories that are called into being by the music itself, creating a loop or a transfer by which they activate one another in the fragmented and layered continuum that constitutes historical experience. Europe is not just the "location" for these aesthetic interventions, but the very thing they construct and then destabilize. European sovereignty and its discontinuity are at the core of these musical and musicalized artworks and take the shape of a nomadic wolf that crosses its borders and resists harmonization.

In addition, the centrality of cinema as yet another site of encounters, collaborations, and compositions is key to understanding the counterpoint between sound and image in the Portabella-Santos tandem—a counterpoint that depends on the memory of previous sounds and images. If, following Deleuze, Alain Badiou argues that cinema names a "philosophical situation," because it allows for "an encounter between terms that are foreign to each other," the concrete relationship of music and cinema is an exploration of their difference in which each of the terms of the encounter highlights the exceptionality of the other.[26] I wish to underline the exceptional and paradoxical nature of the cinematic as a visual environment for the political and experimental potential of this disjunction by following a wolf that is an acoustic condensation of this same disjunction. The dissonance of Santos's wolf resonates only insofar as it relates to the nonmusical, to the silence of Portabella's image, to a linguistic organization, to a dramaturgy, or to a sculptural configuration. Santos and Portabella's collaboration asks us to rethink cinema altogether: if cinema can be thought only in relation to other media, it is perhaps never itself. Or to put it another way, cinema—but cinema as the name of the encounter of different media—bears its own wolf. As we will see, through Portabella's cinematic images, these acoustic wolves, like the ghosts and the buried that hound his films, are ontological refugees, inhabitants of the border, culprits of the violence of the partition that articulates Europe as a political problem. They are also the acknowledgement of those who are missing. As Deleuze puts it, "This acknowledgement of a people who are missing is not a renunciation of political cinema, but on the contrary a new basis on which it is founded.... Art, and especially cinematographic art, must take part in this task: not that of addressing a people, which is presupposed already there, but of contributing to the invention of a people."[27]

Portabella's 2007 *Die Stille vor Bach* presents us with an extended reflection on these questions and locates them in a Europe with an uncertain future. The film recovers the lessons of Catalan experimental production in the 1970s and transposes them onto a larger geopolitical scale. It is also the last collaboration between Santos and Portabella and an archive of the visual and acoustic tropes that accumulated in their previous works and that are now recirculated and multiplied in a new series of variations. Like Santos's *¡Visca el piano!*, the film functions like a retrospective, one that likewise insists on expanding and transforming earlier work, always moving it forward. It also marks Portabella's return to filmmaking after more than a decade devoted primarily to political and institutional engagement — notably, as a senator in the Spanish Parliament involved in the writing of the country's vexed post-Francoist Constitution and later as a member of the Catalan Parliament. Written in collaboration with Santos and musicologist and theater director Xavier Albertí, the film confronts the absences at the core of Europe and speculates how to imagine a different organization that would acknowledge and multiply these absences and then to put them to work otherwise. Its political center is articulated through a reflection on Europe's cultural legacy and acts as a counterpoint to the European Union's championing of a free market, one that allows for the free movement of financial capital, rather than people, that has triggered the current free and unregulated circulation of debt, and that has facilitated the multiplication of refugees, both economic and political. The film instead advocates for a legacy capable of containing the traces of Europe's shattered history of violence and displacement, together with the mourning and the dead labor it continues to demand and also fears.

Die Stille vor Bach begins, silently and almost programmatically, with a white wall and ends with a blank screen. In this prelude to the film and its procedures, Portabella engages Bach's music as an early cinema of attractions. The naked presentation of the material conditions of film production destabilizes the mechanism of

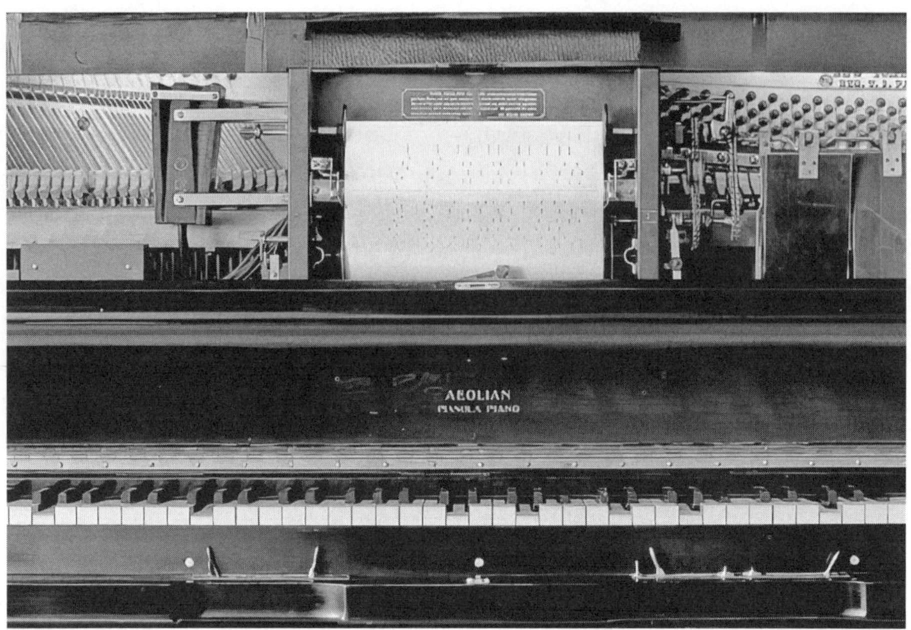

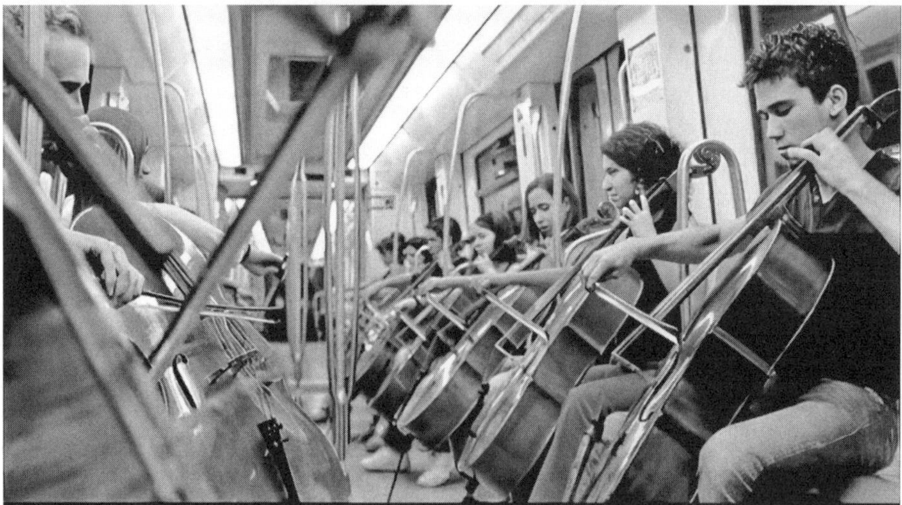

Pere Portabella, *Die Stille vor Bach*, 2007.
Film stills. © Pere Portabella-Films 59

representation and conceptualizes the process of production in yet another echo of the Grup de Treball's manifesto. In the opening scene of the film, the camera pans over the silent white walls of a gallery space. By filming the scene in Josep Lluís Sert's Fundació Joan Miró, emptied of all its paintings, Portabella opens the film by putting his Catalan avant-garde heritage to work through an absence that defies cultural identification because it operates through negation.[28] The scene speaks a sort of silent Catalan, evoking a collective and a legacy that are nowhere to be seen or heard. The slow camera movements and the film's silence are suddenly interrupted by the sound of the *Goldberg Variations*. The notes strike a disturbingly inhuman tone and double as an invocation of dead labor. The camera searches for a diegetic source of sound and finds it in the form of a wheeled mechanical pianola. The camera follows the pianola and its twirling motions through the gallery space. When both camera and pianola stop, we see a close-up of the musical scroll. The metronomic inscription of the music on the white scroll, itself a remediation of the musical score, recalls a mathematical algorithm and the pervasive fantasy of complete harmonization. It strikes a menacing chord by eliminating the human from this final equation, abstracting violence through an anachronistic technology.

By going back in order to move forward, anachronism functions here as a dislocation of cultural legacy that allows for a different and more enigmatic mode of transmission. The strategic use of anachronism is a constant in the film and in his work more generally and functions like the truth of time because it reveals time's layered opacity and history as an enigma. The sequence of effacements the opening scene portrays — silence, absence, anachronism — serves as a playful model for the dislocation of Europe's cultural capital, as a negative and nonidentitarian enactment of its legacy.

Die Stille vor Bach consists of a nonnarrative musical transport across Europe that structures itself across three centuries (eighteenth, nineteenth, and twenty-first); among three locations (a

Barcelona museum, Leipzig, and Dresden); via three modes of sound production (silence, "found" noises, and formal music-making); incorporating a variety of individual presences: a piano tuner and his dog, a bookseller, a shop owner, two truck drivers, Bach, Bach's impersonator, Felix Mendelssohn, Mendelssohn's butler, Mendelssohn's butcher, the present cantor of St. Thomas, a female cellist, and most noticeably, the music itself, performed by soloists, collectively, but not always in ensembles, and at times mechanically, and featuring the compositions primarily of Bach but also of Mendelssohn and Ligeti. The scenes or, better still, the intervals of the film are not sutured. The intervals between spaces in the film, the sudden cuts it contains, reflect on the production and transport of cultural and ideological meaning. Although the film moves from one century to another and one medium to another, from human bodies to machines and animals, from trains to rivers and roads, from computer screen to film screen and cell phone, it is movement as such that links and structures a sense of an aggregated collective and foregrounds its absence, and this movement is enacted acoustically and musically.

Music and cinema move, unfold, and come together as they navigate the force field of European history and the vexed heritage it incorporates and at times encrypts. The film is an extended political and aesthetic effort to put the legacies of European cultural capital compositionally to work and to set them in motion. It is also a reminder that ideas and violence are transmitted together, one often traveling under the cover of the other. The disenchanted realities of contemporary Europe after the fall of the Berlin Wall—which have since only been doubled by economic crises, refugee emergencies, and genocidal wars—provide the context for a film that is as much a critique of Europe as it is a call for the reactivation of aesthetic and political legacies that will no longer neglect the violence Europe contains and exports. Portabella establishes aesthetics and politics as practices of interruption that propose a different kind of violence, that mutually interrupt each other, and that together disrupt the ideologies that have transformed them into products of cultural capital, property, identity, and consumption. Geographical markers, cultural capitals, and musical landmarks (the river Elbe, Dresden, Leipzig, and Bach's music) have become culturally reified, yet their immanent history contains discontinuities that the film makes audible and visible in an attempt to bring life to a legacy that may still yield some political momentum if it is mobilized differently.

Die Stille vor Bach presents us with a Europe that is made out of cuts and interruptions and whose dissonance is the preferred mode of transmission for cultural capital represented by Bach's music and echoed in absences located in the very heart of this uncertain European identity. That such a large of part of the film takes place in Leipzig, though still shot in three different centuries, is not just a matter of Bach's biography. It is in Leipzig that the revolutions of 1989 started under the banner "We Are the People," which was a statement of the absence of one German collective and an echo of the '68 graffiti "We are all German Jews." Bach's impersonator in Leipzig's Thomaskirche — a former academic in East Germany, whose daily routine we follow in the film — is a marker of the economic inequalities that followed Germany's reunification in 1990. The different temporalities the film inhabits establish a nonsynchronic continuum that in turn allows for the incorporation of the past into the present, weaving a historical texture that is layered and durational and fundamentally unequal.

European collectivity is thus enacted as a transit among identities, temporalities, institutions, different modes of transport, and languages. Instead of presenting Europe solely as an unsolvable aporia, a broken promise, a cultural legacy tainted with violence — and Europe is all these things — we are presented with an acoustic performance of a collective as the transient relation that binds together a disjointed, fragmented, and splintered political entity that exists only as a fiction that the very act of binding together briefly materializes. The aesthetic and political role of transit as a structural analogy linking the various elements of the film underscores

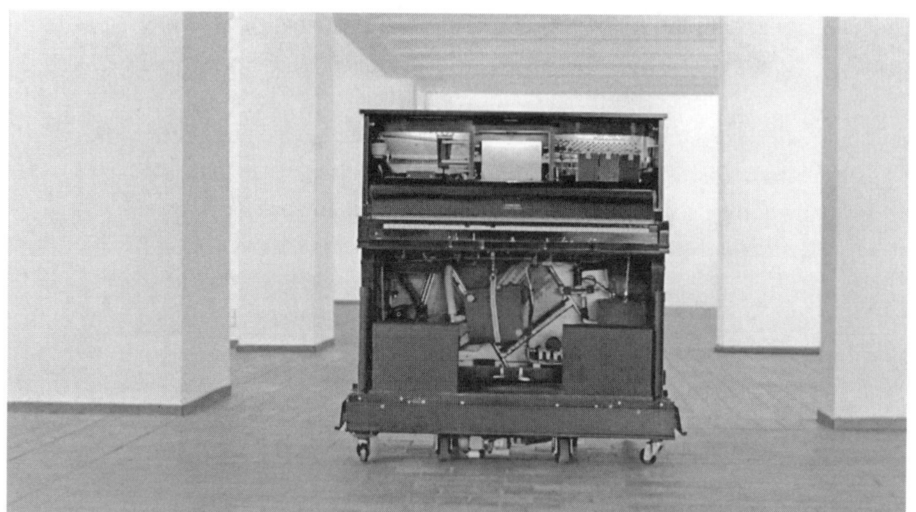

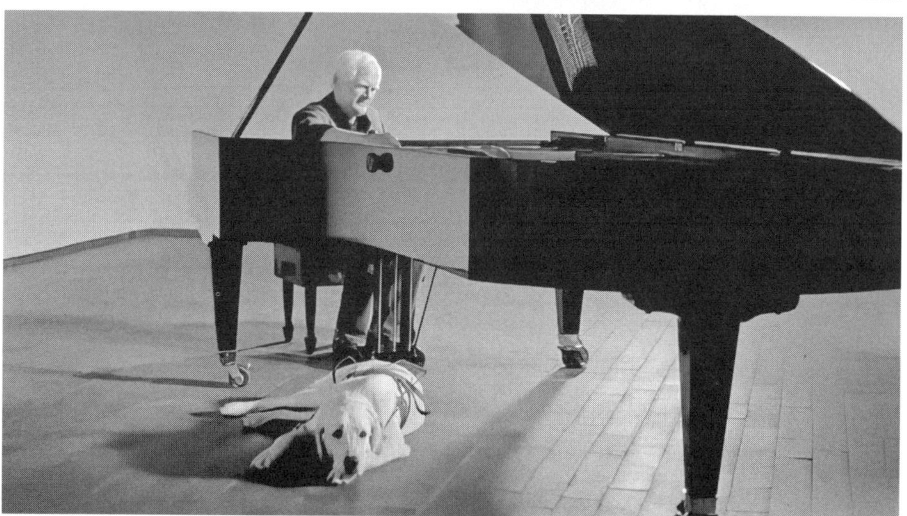

Pere Portabella, *Die Stille vor Bach*, 2007.
Film stills. © Pere Portabella-Films 59

Portabella's larger governing assumption that historical conditions must always be understood as material conditions, which in turn can be experienced only in the shared contingency of work as a practice and of art as the speculative playground for nonalienated labor. The film asks the following questions: How much does a work of art cost? How many people work, and for how long, to transport art or simply to make it happen? Labor, transit, and cost are the material conditions and the intensified contingency that Portabella insists we not forget.

Thinking Ears

> I had greeted the revolt like a musical ear recognizes a right note.
> —Jean Genet, *Prisoner of Love* (1986)

> But indefatigably at issue is the ear, the distinct, differentiated, articulated organ that produces the effect of proximity, of absolute properness, the idealizing erasure of organic difference. It is an organ whose structure (and the suture that holds it to the throat) produces the pacifying lure of organic indifference. To forget it—and in doing so take shelter in the most familial of dwellings—is to cry out for the end of organs, of others.
> —Jacques Derrida, "Tympan" (1972)

That the prelude to the film and its emphasis on dead labor is followed by a slow and meditative scene that addresses both the film's hidden conditions of production and the tuning and maintenance Santos's piano requires further highlights Portabella's sustained affinity to the conceptual tenets of Grup de Treball.[29] We see again the same rooms of the Fundació Miró where the mechanical pianola twirled around in the prelude. This time, however, the lighting props and cables are fully visible, revealing the skilled manual labor hiding behind the pristine beginning of the film, with its uniformly lit white walls. The camera now follows the purposeful and slow itinerary of a blind piano tuner and his guide dog, whom he repeatedly instructs in French, *doucement* ("go slowly"), a command that could double as a direction to the film crew, who will now slow down to accommodate a new cadence, the hesitant sounds of a piano being carefully and patiently tuned. Once the tuner has reached the rehearsal room, the camera will be focused on the dog. The animal becomes central to the compositional scene, an essential part of the working assemblage we now witness: a human, an instrument, and an animal; sets of tools, hands, and ears; all engaged in a labor of tuning that is above all an exercise in attentive listening and an encounter between different sources of life and movement. In fact, the slight movements of the ears of the dog recall Santos's eyebrows in the 1973 *Acció Santos*, where we observe the pianist with his headphones, listening to a Chopin prelude he has first played, recorded, and then plays again as a recording. While the audience can no longer hear the piece Santos now privately hears through his headphones, we still remember it and are able to trace its musical movement in the musician's face, and in the rolling of the camera reflected on his glasses; he is now transformed into a defiant Chaplinesque figure. Music is here transmitted through gesture, as the movement of an embodied thinking. The guide dog's moving ears must be similarly understood as thinking ears, acute mediating instruments for apprehending a world to which we are not privy, that we may be able to acknowledge but never fully understand.[30] As the notes get longer, louder, with longer intervals between them and increasingly dissonant, the scene changes to moving images of a road from a truck. The acoustic "close-up" of the soundtrack, these serializations of "sound objects," a trademark of Portabella's earlier clandestine experimental low-budget films, fully saturate the image and transform the ocular into an extension and resonance of the aural.[31] On two occasions, both in *Nocturn 29* and *Vampir-Cuadecuc*, Portabella even shoots by using the sound band to create poor, overexposed, and high-contrast images, materializing the conceptual tenets of his use of sound more generally. Movement in the film is always initiated acoustically through diegetic sources. It calls for a different organization of the syntactical relation between sound and image, which is no longer subservient but contrapuntal and entirely associative and musical in its logic.

Additionally, the use of direct sound emphasizes the finite duration of an action, its temporal materiality, as much as the expenditure of the different kinds of labor it requires. A heightened sense

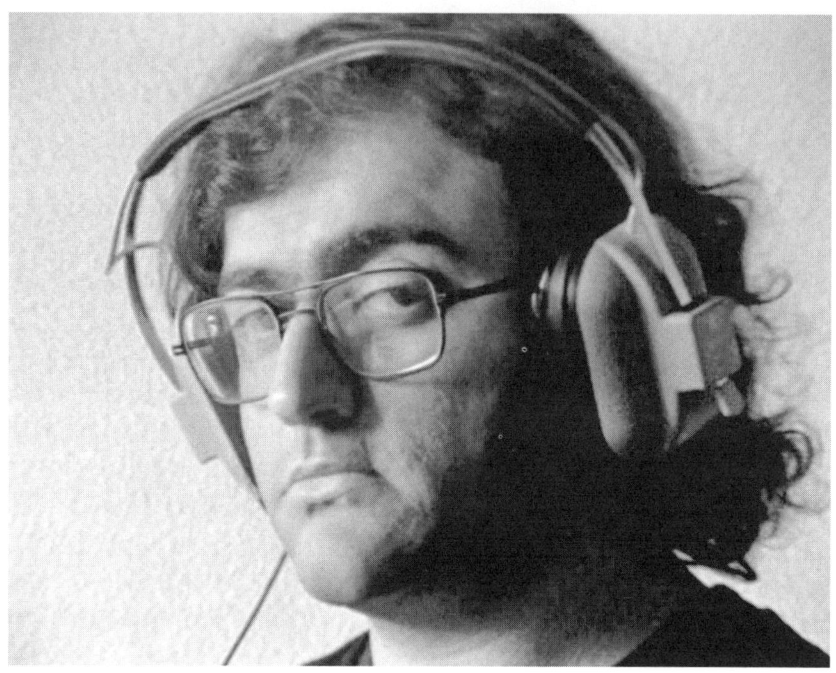

Pere Portabella, *Acció Santos*, 1973.
Film still. © Pere Portabella–Films 59

of finitude and an often-eroticized embodiment of music feature prominently in Santos's musical performances, belying any notion of transcendence or historical detachment. Through the film's frequent reliance on direct sound, which clearly references Jean-Marie Straub and Danièle Huillet's 1968 film, *The Chronicle of Anna Magdalena Bach*, music is surrounded by the everyday sounds of gendered domestic labor, by its cadences and interruptions. Straub and Huillet are not only procedural references for Portabella, but above all, political ones. Their understanding of the image as a political work force is already in full display in their first feature, dedicated to Bach and more than ten years in the making.

When *The Chronicle of Anna Magdalena Bach* finally opens, Straub and Huillet, in exile in Munich for refusing to participate in the repression of the Algerian people by the French government, dedicate the film to the expropriated peasants in the Bavarian forests and to the Vietcong. On this occasion, despite it being a full collaboration with Huillet, Straub signs the film alone.[32] It is the first installment of a long career of political dissent that parallels Portabella's and whose traces are legible in his collaborative practice of cinematic representation. The film is a technological tour de force of sound recording nestled inside an anachronistic series of "authentic" renditions of a wide range of Bach's compositions, performed with historical instruments in mostly original locations, all of which work to intensify the experience of distance. This is exactly the kind of "historicist" performance Adorno decries. Yet despite the apparent search for "authenticity" in their choice of instruments and settings, Straub and Huillet find their multitemporal and dialectical force field elsewhere.

By isolating music in the claustrophobic interiority of a single take of a live performance, by restricting space and time and increasing the intensity and movement of a sound that violently agitates the stillness of the camera, Straub and Huillet allow music to break open. This restriction and isolation are extended to still shots of manuscripts, letters, scores, and open books, together with extremely fleeting shots of moving water and of clouds. History will also occasionally break open from the film's cloistered and restricted settings, for example, in the single scene shot in an exterior location depicting Bach, played by Dutch harpsichordist and musicologist Gustav Leonhardt, directing an orchestra over an angled film projection of a building, the Thomas School in Leipzig, that was completely destroyed by bombings during the Second World War. The violence of European history traverses the film—resonating throughout, making it inescapable. This is why it is important for the filmmakers that all the "actors" in the film are musicians and also that Bach be played by a non-German: this directorial decision prevents any national identification from aligning itself with Europe's nationalist aggressions.[33] In the *Chronicle*, itself a reflection on the opacity of this form, the fictionalized voice of Anna Magdalena, played by the musician Christiana Lang, reads Bach's letters as well as those of other family members, together with public proclamations and the obituaries of many of her children. None of the words we hear her speak are her own, and her voice is always heard off camera. Delivered in a fast, affectless, and heavily accented English, a match for Leonhardt's accented German, her speech becomes a paradoxical enactment of her silence. From then on, the transit across languages and inflections—among French, German, Italian, English—remains an essential component, even a linguistic enactment, of the transnational communist politics of Straub and Huillet's films.

Leonhardt, who plays Bach in the double sense of the word, though without ever ceasing to be himself, as well, remains unchanged and ageless as Bach's biography moves forward in time. After a series of takes of different manuscripts and scores, the last one that of an unfinished and blotted fugue, we see the last shot of the film: a motionless Leonhardt/Bach staring through an open window onto a beautiful landscape, passive and, for the first time in the film, not working or performing, but silently projecting an intimacy with nature. While Anna Magdalena reads a description of his loss of sight and fatal illness, a faint music can be heard in the background, the only nondiegetic instance in the entire film. In this final scene, we get a brief glimpse of the possible analogy between art and nature and of the capacity of film and music to render death beautiful by connecting the finite to the infinity of its variations, the personal to the impersonal, and to the free and opaque play of the imagination. (In the scene, Bach contemplates by listening to what he can no longer see.) All the elements in the film—image, speech, inscription, music—create a mediated force field that, disjunctive and offering no reconciliation, belie the apparent peacefulness of a scene that simply cuts to a black screen. The film becomes an inventory, an affidavit of the opacity of Bach's life, that explores primarily the enigma and the tension of, in Straub's words, the "patience and violence [that] is hidden in Bach's art itself."[34] Similarly, découpage is the patient and violent act that makes cinematic movement possible. It is also a reminder that "in reality, we don't know what a film is" because every film is singular and contingent, historical through and through, like music.[35]

The conviction that there is no whole, only a relationship between fragments, and that the gap between them demands that we believe in the possibility of a connection, is also essential to Portabella's politicization of the infrastructure of the cinematic image. In *Die Stille vor Bach*, the musical fragment is continually tampered with, and this tampering serves to create an alternative space that transforms the perception of what is given and puts it back in motion. The situations the film records in real time and with direct sound function like moving readymades or "sound sculptures," as Santos might put it. The constant reminder of duration, of the finite human temporality of work, of human effort and its costs, of culture as human expenditure, are the basis for the militant politics and conceptual aesthetics of *Die Stille*. Bach's toil as a worker is as central to the film as the cultural capital his legacy becomes. The redeployment of aesthetic autonomy as critique is a means for exploring the political in all of Portabella's cinematic interventions — Kant looms as large as Bach in the film. The emancipatory potential of the aesthetic is contained in its *sensus communis*, that is to say, in the communicability, attunement, and assembly of a community through the experience of taste, understood as the aesthetic organization of the sensorial and as an irreducible differential.

This community can potentially become political because taste, like music, is contentless, enigmatic, and free. This understanding of taste as singular and communal is articulated in *Die Stille vor Bach* by a butcher in a nineteenth-century market as he describes his culinary methods with irrepressible gusto, all the while wrapping his merchandise in musical scores. The butcher alludes to the Kantian *jedermann* ("each and every one," the formula for a differentiated multiplicity), extolling the freedom and inclusiveness of aesthetic judgment, or rather of the capacity to make a judgment, as a model for democratic disagreement while insisting that *De gustibus non disputandum est* is also "where we renounce ourselves in favor of others."[36] The question is, as Hannah Arendt puts it, "Why then should taste — not beginning with Kant but ever since Gracián — be elevated to and become the vehicle of the mental faculty of judgment?" Together with Kant, her answer is because it relies on the "imagination."[37]

Portabella makes the point, in both *Die Stille vor Bach* and the film that precedes it, *Pont de Varsòvia*, by having the most philosophical — and occasionally the most arcane and philological — arguments be debated by workers, waiters, butchers, cooks, or truckdrivers. The point is not to dismiss our Western philosophical and musical inheritance altogether, no matter how violent and conflicted this inheritance is, but rather to fight its tendencies toward elitism and exclusion and replace them with what Kant calls "a broad-minded way of thinking." This more inclusive mode of thinking would take "account of everyone else's way of representing in thought in order, as it were, to hold its judgment up to human reason as a whole and thereby avoid the illusion which sets [one] apart from the subjective private conditions of the judgment, within which so many others are as if bracketed, and reflects on [one's] own judgment from a universal standpoint."[38] This universal standpoint, which is contentless, is nothing else but the intuitive capacity of imagining and putting oneself into the standpoint of another; it is the aftereffect of a relationship based on the differences between one another that cannot be interiorized and can never be fully completed because there are always others we fail to take into account. It is another name for the transit and transport among bodies and minds that accumulates into a shared heritage that is carried within the infrastructure of our social and historical relations, with all its poignant contradictions, violence, and human costs. This transport, however, is also and above all the communication or transmission of the aesthetic as an enigma, together with the exposure to others this enigma activates in the imagination.

Composition: Bach with Kant

> Transcendence: a specifically European disease.
> —Gilles Deleuze and Félix Guattari, *A Thousand Plateaus* (1980)

> We must fully acknowledge the particularity of Europe's reconstruction of the world because only then will it be possible to transcend it.
> —Immanuel Wallerstein, "Eurocentrism and Capitalist Development" (1997)

Many of the concepts we use in relation to music—affinity, attunement, harmony, conduct—are also echoed in the philosophical language not just of Adorno, but also of Kant. And this despite Kant's ostensible devalorization of music because of its sensuality and impermanence, even when he connects it to mathematics and number. Nevertheless, his linguistic choices tell a different story because he emphasizes the possibilities of "Stimme" (voice), "Übereinstimmung" (correspondence, accord), and "Zusammenstimmen" (to tune together) to describe the faculty of aesthetic judgment in his *Third Critique*. Michel Chaouli reads this lexical network in relation to "what Kant calls free play, a sort of synchronized vibration in which harmony is neither imposed from above (by force of rules or reason) nor achieved from below (by virtue of a harmony woven into all facets of human existence), but rather by means of a fortuitous, improvised play that happens somewhere in between."[39] This improvised free play heralds a different kind of engagement with the world, one mediated by making as a modality of attunement and identified with *poesis* as a prerequisite for both aesthetic judgment and pleasure, binding reception and production into a symbiotic ensemble—one for which music might be the better model. This free play can be retroactively extended to the architecture of the first two critiques, allowing them, in a formulation by Michael Wayne, to be read "as a polyphonic structure whose tensions and contradictions give off many different notes, whose very discordance should be a matter of great interest."[40] That this description would be fitting for Bach's music is hardly a coincidence because it sheds light on an incipient and embryonic philosophical modernity that uses older forms to express an experience for which a new and generative language must be invented. The form of the *Third Critique*, which at times reads as a work in progress or a struggle, is further proof of what Deleuze calls Kant's "*free and indeterminate accord* between all the faculties," "a free harmony, a harmony without fixed proportions."[41] It is also the basis for Kojin Karatani's conception of "transcritique," a critical oscillation and a sustained vibration of the antinomes of Kantian thought, and of Lukács's statement that Kant "bluntly elaborated . . . contradiction[s] and presented [them] in an undiluted form."[42]

In the *Third Critique*, the bridge between the conceptual and the perceptual lies in the imagination and undoes the dichotomy between thought and experience by articulating a functional interval between the two through the aesthetic realm's infinite heterogeneity. The universality of the aesthetic as a bridge and compositional reorganization of the faculties is not found in "the pleasure, but [in] the *universal validity of this pleasure*."[43] We could say that the aesthetic is not only not self-identical, as Adorno insists, but also larger and more capacious than it appears, since in order to function, it must always contain the nonaesthetic, the external, and the foreign—hidden in its depths and unfolding topologically as the internal rhythm and breath of the artwork.

Furthermore, Chaouli notes that Kant's judgment, which is more a process than an end result, should also be understood as a medium, a form of transport and binding between faculties and minds: "Judgment is, then, a *Mittel*, a means and a medium: it is what is betwixt and between, what joins and binds."[44] While judgment is a means of transport between differentiated faculties, each of them unable to account for aesthetic experience, it is also a spontaneous assemblage and interplay between them. It is the relationship and brief coalescence brought about by the conceptual irregularity, displacement, and strangeness of an aesthetic experience that cannot be reduced to the beautiful because it far exceeds its normativity and recognizability. As Kant puts it, "the imagination's freedom consists precisely in its schematizing without a concept."[45]

Indeed, none of these descriptions of the aesthetic phenomenon have to do with intelligibility or understanding, but rather with the encounter of a code or enigma, one that hovers between sense and non-sense and for which new logics and rules must be invented and experimented with. The artwork appears as a new kind of organism, a new composition, an energetic and dynamic holding together of different forces that cannot be accounted for or predicted because the performance of its free play exceeds, alters, and expands the organization of the given and forges a new relationship with it. Herein lies the relational, emancipatory, and political potential of the artwork: a thinking otherwise that is fully performative and has no closure or resolution—an organism that, while fully exposing the viewer to others, is itself never disclosed. Music thinks through the expansive possibility contained in its sounding, which is always new, always experienced as a surprise, which, in turn, is at the source of the wonder and freedom it can instill in the listener.

Deleuze, who writes *Kant's Critical Philosophy* in 1963, also speaks of cinema's "Kantian revolution" in his foreword to Éric Alliez's *Capital Times: Tales from the Conquest of Time*. There he describes how "time ceases to be originary or derived, to become the pure form of interiority, which hollows us out, which splits us out, at the price of a vertigo."[46] Later in *The Time-Image*, Deleuze will make the motion of postwar cinema depend entirely on time, as it does in music, and rely on the immanence of its autotemporalization, forcing us to face and reflect on the intensity and awareness of our incessant production of time, of our embeddedness in the absolute contingency of history and its violence. Indeed, the violence of war is at the core of Kant's 1795 *Toward Eternal Peace: A Philosophical Sketch*, a late political text that might at first sight seem unconnected to his reflections on aesthetic phenomena.[47] That the text is written after the 1789 Declaration of the Rights of Man and the Citizen suggests that for Kant, the aporia of the relationship between politics and violence continues to pose a problem, particularly at the level of collective identities defined by exclusionary national models. (The imminent Napoleonic Wars would provide ample proof of this.) In response, Kant proposes a transnational principle of federation based on the contingency of choice and association, rather than on identitarian membership in a predetermined sovereignty. On closer inspection, this principle of federation follows from the same relational structure that undergirds the relation and transit between faculties in the aesthetic, one that allows a people to be more indeterminate, in a sense, freer and more equal, because of this association and interplay with others. Because this relationality is dynamic and always unfolding, this community can never be identical to itself at any given moment and is therefore able to move beyond the constrictions and borders of the nation-state and its universalization, beyond a simple aggregation of national sovereignties and its capitalist economies. As Kant puts it, "it must not be a nation consisting of [other] nations," which are themselves simply materializations of market borders.[48] Kant associates the rights of the nation with the violence of protecting borders and property and indicts the peace treaty as a mere postponement of a structural violence. Pointing to a contiguity between war and peace that can result only in a "grave that covers all the horrors of violence and its perpetrators," he proposes "a federalism of free states" that "guarantee the rights of each," arguing that "without a contract among nations peace can be neither inaugurated nor guaranteed."[49] This kind of transnational association or coalition "will be distinguished from a *treaty of peace* (*pactum pacis*) because the latter seeks to stop *one* war, while the former seeks to end *all* wars forever."[50] It would be "a league of peace" that would ensure the reciprocity and equality of rights based on the relations *between* rights.

The defining characteristic of the federation or world republic, which functions like a regulative idea and a means, is what Kant calls a "cosmopolitan" right, which he defines as the right "of an alien not to be treated as an enemy upon his arrival in another's country." The right to visit, which quietly undoes the tenets of nationalism, he continues, "belongs to all men by virtue of the common ownership of the earth's surface."[51] This is why, he adds, colonialism, which is nothing else than the export of national border violence, is the starkest example of the "terrifying" violation of this mutual right since it uses the "cruelest and most ingenious slavery" as a training ground for war and domination, a confirmation of the complicity between capitalism and war and between nationalism and imperialism.[52] It is here that his argument turns to the artistry of nature, a subjectless and relational force that echoes the artwork's creativity: "Perpetual peace is *insured* (guaranteed) by nothing less than that great artist *nature* (*natura daedala rerum*), whose mechanical process makes her purposiveness [*Zweckmassigkeit*] visibly manifest, permitting harmony to emerge among men through their discord, even against their wills."[53]

Like an amalgamation of faculties and sensations that vibrate and sound together in aesthetic experience, this free association, led by the subjectless mechanism of a nature that is simultaneously purposive and purposeless, recalls Karl Marx's association of free producers and the scene in *The Chronicle of Anna Magdalena Bach* of Bach's own dissolution of art into nature. Karatani's reading of the text *Toward Eternal Peace* further reinforces this resonance when he writes that "what Kant calls 'perpetual peace' is not simply the absence of war, but rather the abolition of all antagonism between states—meaning, that is, the abolition of the state itself."[54] What Kant proposes, then, is a deposition or abolition of the nation as a form based on antagonism, a form of relation that can end only in violence. Like Bach's conception of a modern harmonic system, where the foreign or dissonant is integrated into a larger system rather than eliminated, this is an abolition that increases the complexity and possibilities of the system.[55] Because of this, the impurity of acoustic resonance transforms dichotomies into a variety of differential intervals. When understood not as oppositions but as delays and spacings, the relationships between cause and effect, the contingent and the predictable, the actual and the possible, and the passive and the active become associative, rather than merely antagonistic.

Works of art think. But they do not think like us because they never fully disclose the enigma that articulates their knowledge; they never feel the need to determine their thinking. When they transmit their knowledge to us, they transmit precisely this enigma, a space of nonresolution that expands the world as we know it or as we assume to know it. Artworks think freely and in ways that defy the partition between being and knowing, thinking and doing. This absence of determination, this suspension of contradiction, is another name for freedom in Kant's work and for autonomy in Adorno's. But neither exists as an abstraction that can be separated from individual artworks. Instead, they remain materially grounded in the specificity of each singular instance—of each sounding.

If we return to Adorno's understanding of the role of inherited tradition in musical performance and in the playing of Bach in particular, if we recall his insistence on producing this music anew, his emphasis on music's dialectical movement and its disruption of harmonious appearances, the exemplary character of music now appears as autonomous because it creates its own rules and because these rules can never be predetermined. Music and artworks demand an indeterminate thinking, a thinking without concepts, which is the source of their mobility and freedom. It is what Kant calls "*force without enforcement*."[56] If there can be no musical thinking without improvisation, it is because it functions like an indeterminate force of deregulation, exercising its own modality of violence against the normativity and stasis of received ideas.

This musical force is also the incommensurable imagination contained in every mind and body. The bodies that fill the screen in *Die Stille vor Bach*—the Bach impersonator, the cellist, or the musician and truck driver—cannot be reduced to the product of their labor or to any determinate identity, national or social. That their "extended imagination" enables them to participate in the aesthetic as a supplement that resists stasis and identification is one of the critical points here. If the emancipatory potential of an aesthetic phenomenon is contained in its freedom to transport us elsewhere, in *Die Stille*, acoustic and filmic displacement contain the enigma of a political community still to come, one where one is always something *more* and something *else*. Any approach to the musical is necessarily traversed by the nonmusical and can have no claims to purity or self-containment. Europe is not absent because it has disappeared. It is absent because it has never yet existed—not just as the phantasm of a single, homogeneous, self-identical political formation, but above all, as a complex and difficult crossroads that would succeed in including those who are no longer and those who are not yet.

The aesthetic functions as this crossroads; it is both a relation and a movement, simultaneously a displacement of antagonism and a bond across distances. An extended imagination demands participation and composition, not only for the actors and musicians, but also for the audience that is given a chance to imagine new relational possibilities for a Europe that may be possible only because it has never existed before. A Europe that would acknowledge that "if today nothing is harmonious, this is because harmony was false from the beginning."[57]

Anamnesis

> The true eye of the earth is water. Within our eyes it is water that dreams.
> — Gaston Bachelard, *Water and Dreams: An Essay on the Imagination of Matter* (1942)

> Nothing is more beautiful than water. But since everything in life has a reflection in our unconscious, I wouldn't like my love for water to be seen from too narrow a viewpoint. Maybe it's an ancient memory, my ancestors energizing to life from water, who knows? In any case . . . I couldn't make a film without water.
> — Andrei Tarkovsky, *A Poet in the Cinema* (1983)

The film that precedes *Die Stille vor Bach*, the 1989 *Pont de Varsòvia*, is again written in collaboration not only with Santos, but with the translator and anti-Franco communist militant Octavi Pellissa. *Pont de Varsòvia* marks a reassessment and transformation of Portabella's experimental and clandestine anti-Francoist production in the context of an emergent neoliberal democracy, as well as a caesura that marks the beginning of his almost two decades of silence that will follow. It is also a dress rehearsal for *Die Stille vor Bach*. Some of the procedural avant-garde protocols of his earlier films used the experiential infrastructure of a country closed to the outside world and expressed it via acoustic out-of-frames, loops, and repetitions. In *Pont de Varsòvia*, these protocols are treated as processual and are mobilized instead to underscore the fluidity of a plastic cinematic medium capable of opening to a new sense of possibility, even against the violent and often hidden forces of enclosure and containment — whether these be political, national, or statist. The changed sociohistorical circumstances within which Portabella's

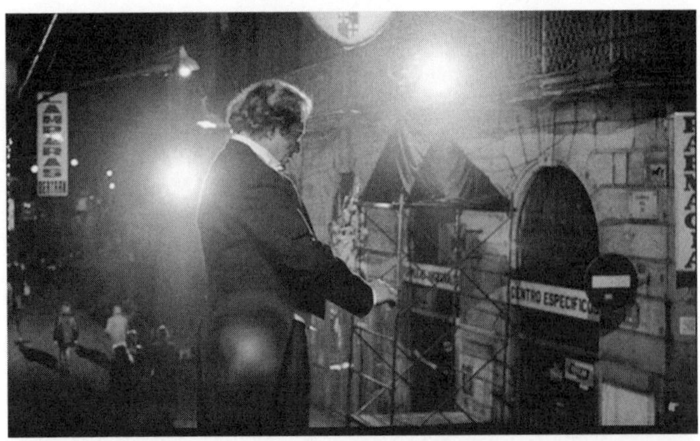

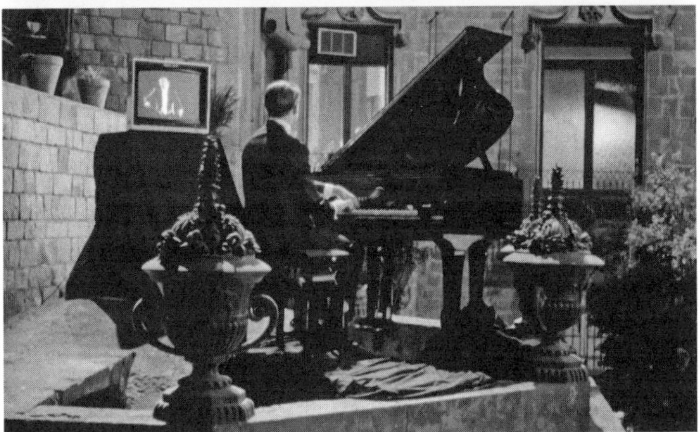

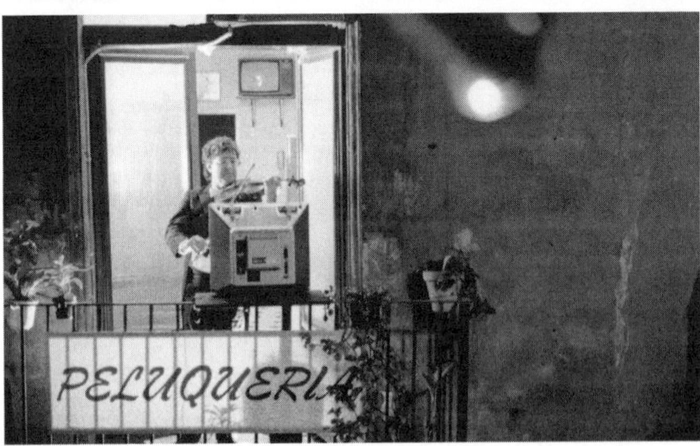

Pere Portabella, *Pont de Varsòvia*, 1989.
Film stills. © Pere Portabella-Films 59

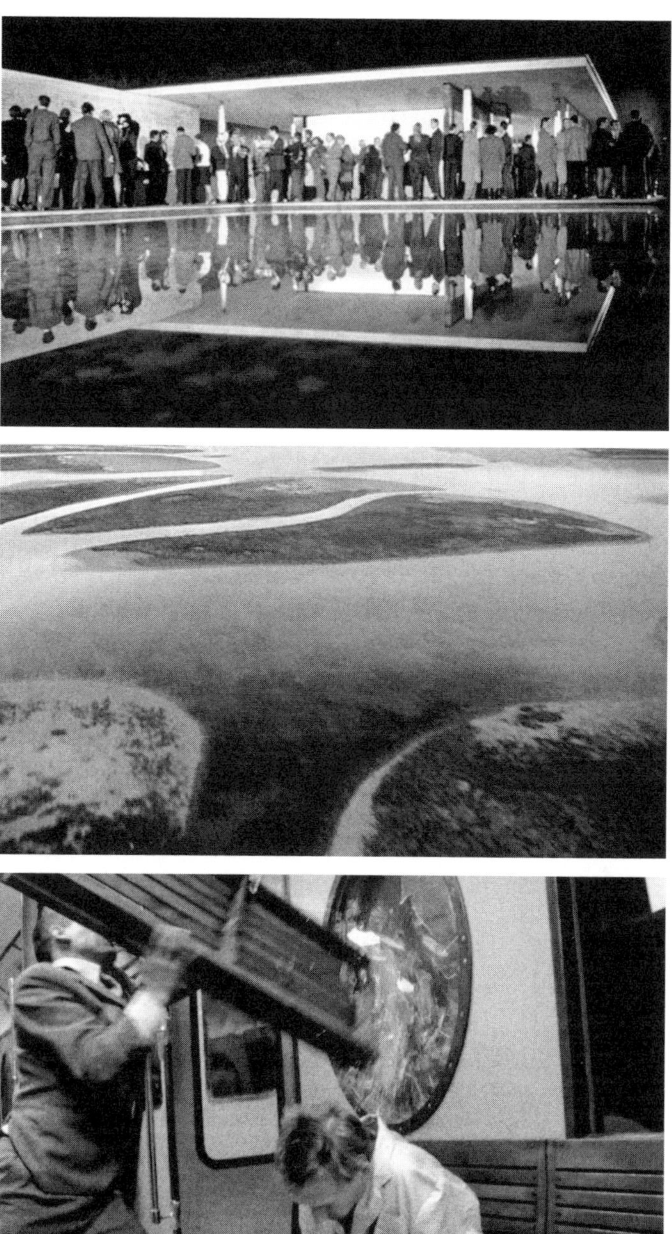

film is produced are, as before, never addressed directly. We are instead given glimpses of a fragmented reality that can be captured only through the arbitrariness of the banal, or through what the filmmaker likes to call a "realismo de resultados," a gaze that forces us to see the circumstantial determinations that undergird the most random of gestures.

These determinations are always to be understood cinematically: this is to say that in Portabella's work, there is a destruction of the distance between cinema and history, an interdependence of cinematic forms and historico-political contexts that must be read as a political and materialist gesture. Portabella's cinema is a symptomatic reading of the spectral materiality of every image, of the way in which images, whether still or moving, always carry forward the history that traverses them, as music does in Kant and Bach. Such a reading brings to mind the political activism legible in Jean-Luc Godard's making and unmaking of filmic language in his 2004 *Notre musique* or his 2019 *Film socialisme*, or even in Manoel de Oliveira's 2003 *A Talking Picture*. Like Godard, Portabella does not redeem physical reality through cinema but instead uses cinema to indict physical reality and to show us the violence it hides within its various manifestations. Cinema reveals the social and technical infrastructure that sustains each image, often in the most enigmatic ways. Insisting on the enigmatic character of not just the world, but the cinematic medium itself, *Pont de Varsòvia* and *Die Stille vor Bach* are above all a reminder that there are no innocent images. This is why we can say that Portabella's films contain a pedagogy on how to read cinema, and even history, materially and historically.

We could say that Portabella's cinema thinks spectrally because it thinks historically and self-consciously. Populated by the corpses of the undead and the half buried, it is always a conversation with the dead, an exercise in associative memory that knows it can only be incomplete and that demands to be constantly restarted. Besides the 1970 cult film *Vampir-Cuadecuc*, an experimental meditation on spectrality as a cinematic remainder, three of the films Portabella shoots after the death of Franco, the specter par excellence of his 1960s and 1970s production, continue to contain corpses, graves, and mausoleums, pointing to the analogies between the state, the nation, and capitalism and burial sites.[58] After all, the mausoleum that we see at the beginning of his *Informe General* is in fact a cover for the mass graves of political prisoners that were conscripted to build the Francoist monument.

A film that appears as a warning and a lament that nobody in Spain was ready or even willing to hear, the ominous *Pont de Varsòvia* portrays a series of encounters that devolve into violent collisions. Pellissa, who was responsible for the often very literary dialogues in the film, was tortured and imprisoned by the regime and had lived in exile both in France and in Germany, specifically, in Leipzig, then part of the German Democratic Republic. He introduces the idea of the bridge as a reminder of the persistence of borders and walls and of the difficulty of crossing them. In the film, we become witnesses to the inability to cross bridges, the failure to connect the fragments of a broken history, and the reluctance to undergo the full metamorphosis that the Spanish transition to democracy would have required.

These failures are already legible in Portabella's previous film, the 1976 *Informe General*, and find their echo in the larger context of Europe after the fall of the Berlin Wall. We witness the dismantling of the militant left and the virtual disappearance of the Communist Party, which had been key to anti-Francoist resistance, in favor of a spectacularization of culture as a consumerist distraction that culminates with the celebration of the 1992 Olympics in Barcelona. This dismantling and disappearance announce the failures of the German *Wende*, a last-ditch attempt to democratize the German Democratic Republic that only accelerated its demise, and the organization of the European Union as a museum of dead patrimony that must be administered, preserved, and cordoned off in order to sustain itself, even as an idea. In Portabella's hands, the still-peripheral status of Spain within Europe—caught in the aftermath of the prolonged and enforced anachronism that Francoism was—is a prolepsis of what Europe will become, or more accurately, of what it will fail to become.

While *Pont de Varsòvia* points to many of the themes and compositional approaches of *Die Stille vor Bach*, it remains committed to the portrayal of political failure and of institutionalized culture as an instrument of deception, betrayal, and forgetting. The title of the film refers simultaneously to a novel, a dream, a place, and a time. Perpetually displaced, it becomes a placeholder for the collective enunciation of a buried memory. Stories are buried within other stories that can barely contain them, and the film becomes a polyphonic chamber that not only brings them together, but also unravels them. When one of the film's characters asks, "How long have I been dead?" her question quietly resonates through all the empty buildings the film's opening evokes. In place of a structure or an organizing memory, there is simply a gap, a void, where multiple voices reverberate.

Portabella's commitment to a nonidentitarian understanding of collective agency remains rigorous throughout his long career and has its analogue in the film's embeddedness in a vast network of cultural references that, binding it to an ever-extending number of disciplines—architecture, opera, theater, painting, digital culture (then just emerging), sculpture, science, literature—function as an anchor and dead weight in the midst of a film committed to a discontinuous but relentless and disquieting movement. The circulation of these references and disciplines belongs to this movement and even enacts it, as it were, in a kind of cinematic liquidity, in an unpredictable and itinerant set of transits and transmissions.

Indeed, in asymmetrical counterpoint to the architectural voids of the film, the enigmatic role of water, windows, and apertures of all kinds, the proliferation of screens and reflective surfaces throughout, operate in a continuum with the musical composition of the film as an uncontained, uncontrollable, and unmeasurable flow. We are directly reminded by a marine biologist that water is a zoological source of life in a constant state of metamorphosis as she gives a lecture while feeling she is speaking through someone else's voice, herself becoming yet another device for transport and mediation in a film that, like *Die Stille vor Bach*, is entirely constructed around the possibility of multiplication, metamorphosis, and movement — between past and present, music and literature, bodies and images, architecture and dreams, the living and the dead. The length of an autopsy scene, the fragmentation of the bones and the twisting of the corpse, echoes Portabella's directorial approach, a dissection of traditional narrative in favor of scatterings, encounters, violent collisions, and a continued movement that again belies the distinction between the dead and the living. In the film, water itself, or more precisely what Deleuze calls the "thread of water,"[59] becomes the medium for a multiplicity of voices belonging to the living and the dead, a medium that itself already contains cinematic references that are in dialogue with Portabella's images. (Think of the history of water in early film and of the films of Tarkovsky or Jean Epstein.)

The German *Wende*, which begins the same year the film is produced, is also present in the film as an undertone and explodes in the brutal shattering of a subway car in Berlin. Performed by the theatrical group La Fura dels Baus, the highly choreographed scene does not present violence as an inevitable outcome, but as a permanent undercurrent that, triggered by a small gesture or a simple equivocation, or even without apparent cause can erupt with the condensed force of its latency. If the geographical center of Europe becomes undone underground, it is because its original violence has been willingly forgotten and buried there.

Like many other scenes in the film, the subway car as a choreographic spatial continuum recurs in *Die Stille vor Bach*. In the later film, however, Portabella and Santos propose a musical organization of this continuum, allowing the camera to move back and forth following the tempos and returns of Bach's prelude to his *Suite 1* for cello, filling the subway car with rows of cellists playing in unison. Emphasizing the multiplication and pluralization of the young musicians, foregrounding the sounds of the train tracks, and making Bach's music sound like a crowd, the subway car is no longer conceived as a space of confinement, but as a transport that can accommodate the fluidity of music's transient assemblages. Transport here becomes the condition of possibility of a new relationship, the brief coalescence of a community brought about through displacement and strangeness. This gesture is repeated in a piano store later in the film, the last appearance of Santos in a Portabella film, playing among the many, disappearing into a row of pianists playing together but not in unison, a musician among other musicians in a world of multilayered sound.

Entirely scored by Santos, *Pont de Varsòvia* also contains a musical performance that stands out in the film as an experiment in the constitution of a collective of associated producers, one of the film's two iterations of earlier performance pieces—the other being a direct reference to *Acció Santos*. The scene begins with Santos exiting a building in busy downtown Barcelona, dressed in a tailcoat, walking toward an elevated podium surrounded by cameras and a lighting apparatus to direct an orchestra we at first hear but do not see. As a surprised audience begins to gather around Santos (exercising a right of public assembly that did not exist during the filming of any of Portabella's previous films and also acting as placeholders of the numerical mass of an invisible orchestra), we start to see a montage of orchestra musicians playing alone on different balconies as they follow his direction through a televised transmission. What the cinema audience hears is a compositional record, an inner synchronization, both visual and acoustic, that adopts an Eisensteinian understanding of polyphonic montage—the result of the "collision of independent shots," where "each sequential element is perceived not *next* to the other, but on *top* of the other."[60] Encompassing both production and reception, it is no longer simply a procedural aftereffect but an assemblage that is also the performance's condition of possibility—and the film's, as well. As often happens in Santos's performances, the composition takes place in an act of mediated reception that cannot be distinguished from its production. This compression and intensification follow the rhythmic crescendos of Santos's score in the film and, through an apparatus of production that is fully mediated by technology, call for the multiplication of participants, and present music and cinema as means of aggregation, endless labor, and tactics of incorporation.

In this way, the simultaneous fragmentation and gathering of distinct compositional elements proposes a kind of organization that stands in contrast to the cultural consumption and institutional spectacle of the literary prize the film proceeds to depict. While this later scene emphasizes the passivity of culture as a site of consensus and a closing of class ranks—as an instrument in the displacement and pacification of political violence—the staged assembly around Santos's musical intervention in the streets offers another way of conceiving the potentially shattering force of cultural acts that, targeting the violent complicities of culture, exceed it with a different act of violence, with the force of an eruption.

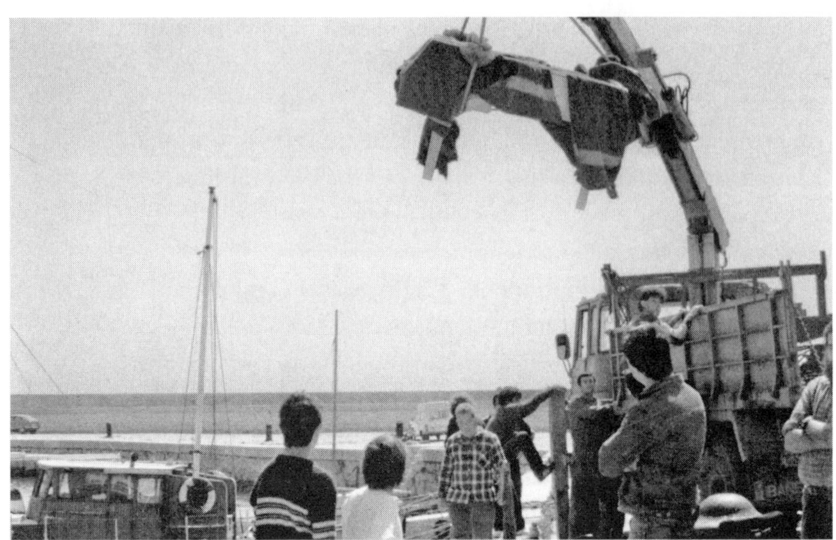

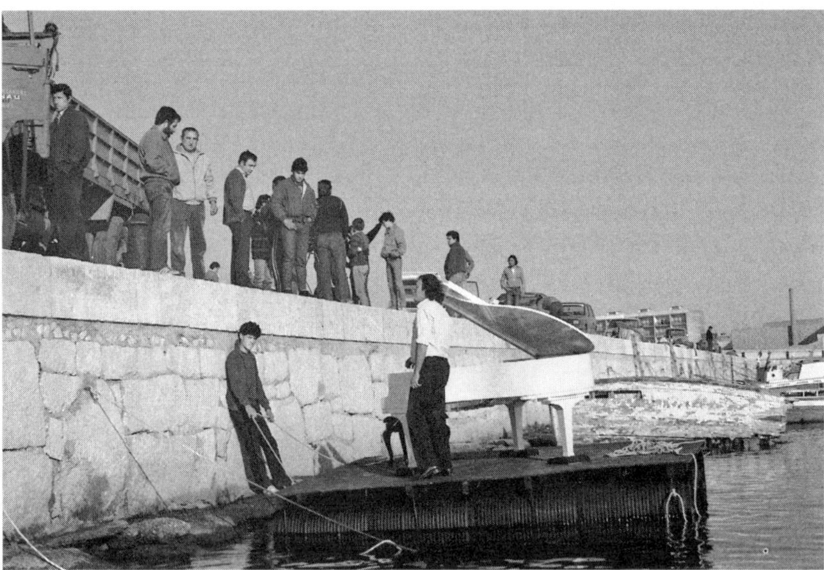

Carles Santos, *Minimalet-sur-Mer*, 1988. Performance documentation. Courtesy of Fons Carles Santos, Caixa de Vinarós.

Variation One: Music Floats

A pianist is alone with his instrument on a floating platform on the sea, the movement of the music encountering the undulating movement of the water. The movements of the camera that records this scene and the rapid montage further emphasize the motility and fluidity of the piece, a rhythmic composition on different modalities of transport and transmission. Santos's 1988 video recording of Minimalet-sur-Mer, *produced by the Catalan public television network TV3, is perhaps the most direct example of his associative relation between music and water, which is a recurrent leitmotif in all his music theater pieces.*[61]

Shot on location in his hometown of Vinarós, it also transforms the piano into a biographical anchor that refuses to sit still. A parenthetical intertitle in Catalan at the beginning of the video invites us to consider the singularity of what we are about see, its existence against all odds, as it states, "(did anyone ever think this would ever happen)." We then see the piano suspended in the air, wrapped up in fabric and with a piece of crinkling plastic casually attached to it, moving to the sound of seagulls, as it is lowered perilously close to the water, with no platform to be seen anywhere. In the next scene, Santos uncovers the instrument, which is white and reflects the sunlight to become an even more incongruent and bright object in its maritime surroundings. It is then that we hear music for the first time, through the voice of the soprano Carina Mora singing one of Santos's compositions, herself hoisted onto the top of Vinarós's cement harbor tower, hair and red dress billowing with the wind, notes lengthened and in a high pitch that seems to carry them further. Her singing resonates like a call directed to the sea. We then begin to hear the crescendo of Santos's percussive playing and see a very fast long shot of Santos drifting along in the middle of the water, becoming increasingly smaller as the music grows louder, stretching the visual and the aural in opposite

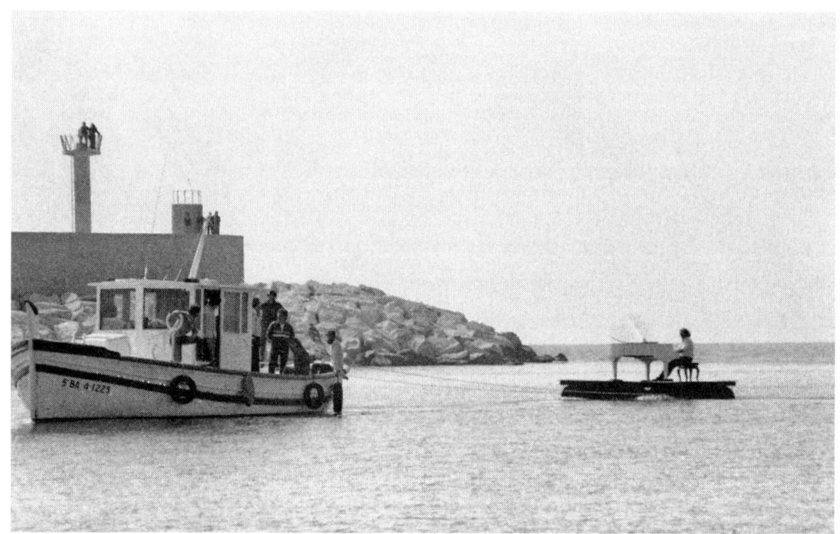

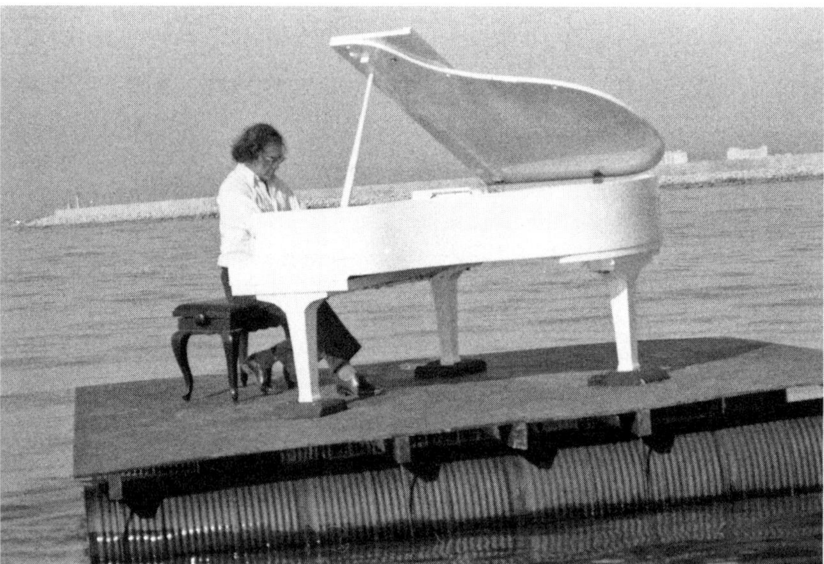

Carles Santos, *Minimalet-sur-Mer*, 1988.
Performance documentation. Courtesy
of Fons Carles Santos, Caixa de Vinarós.

directions. For the duration of the piece, the piano and the soprano will engage in a call and response that amplifies the distance between them and spatially materializes the composition of the piece. They will also alternate between sustaining their soundings and rapidly syncopating them, between prolonging and cutting. As the piano continues to drift across the water, we see intermittent shots of Santos's feet, hands, face; of the piano hammers, lid, keyboards, legs, and pedals; taken at long shots, close-ups, crane shots, and at different angles. The same is true of the soprano, but with her, the camera movements appear more circular and repeatedly use low-angle shots, as if to mimic the tower's architecture. The montage is structured musically, and the camera functions like a third, silent instrument that mediates the relationship between pianist and soprano, behaving with a liquidity of its own.

The last scene appears as the aftermath of a shipwreck. The piano has now disappeared, and we see the bodies of pianist and singer stranded on the beach, both softly singing. Santos begins to crawl toward the soprano. The montage now includes black screens separating each shot, breaking the continuity in the movements of the two bodies. We then see the two musicians together, crawling back into the sea and then beginning to swim. Throughout, we continue to hear their singing, a reminder that the sound in the film has been recorded in the studio and that synchronicity is an acoustic mirage. The final image freezes the musicians swimming against the waves, returning to the water.

With Santos, we might say, music always overflows to become a liquid passage into pure movement. It becomes, as Deleuze would have it, a "vibration with an infinity of harmonies or submultiples, such as an audible wave."[62]

Time has happened because music has conceptualized and materialized it.

Corpses and Fables

> From the point of view of death, life is a production of corpses.
> —Walter Benjamin, *Origin of the German Trauerspiel* (1928)

> Death makes its promise to us by way of the cinematograph.
> —Jean Epstein, "Le cinèmatographe dans l'archipel" (1929)

Something is new in *Die Stille vor Bach* that was not present in Portabella's extraordinary productions of the 1960s and 1970s: the use of myths or fables, another mode of transport by a filmmaker that has insistently announced his rejection of narrative. After *Pont de Varsòvia* and the political "*desencanto*" (the disenchantment with the Spanish transition to democracy), Europe's failed political spectacles and its historical amnesia may have taught Portabella that a collective myth or a fable are necessary tools not only for the construction of collectivity, but also for the practice of a shared sense of accountability. Both *Pont de Varsòvia* and *Die Stille vor Bach* recover fable as a linking mechanism because in the end, the commons always needs a story to transform contingency, which is opaque, into an experience that can be shared.

I am not referring here to historical narratives but to orally transmitted popular legends, songs, and myths as carriers of a condensed truth they merely point toward, without fully disclosing. *Pont de Varsòvia*'s tentative and bitterly ironic plot is structured around the incongruity of a newspaper notice, which appears on screen at the end of the film as a sort of postscript. It describes the corpse of a scuba diver, one of the two orchestra directors the film intermittently follows, this one fictional, found in a burned forest. The diver's body, having been sucked in by one of the amphibious aircraft collecting water to extinguish one of the many fires that typically burn forests in the Catalonian summer, appears on screen *before* we follow the same character in his transit across several of the film's locations. The suggestion here seems to be that the newspaper chronicle is a testament to the failure of narrative and an example of the false causalities that structure our relationship to contingency and violence.

Die Stille vor Bach takes up this question again and takes a much more complex approach to it. The legend of the discovery of Bach's *Saint Matthew's Passion*, wrapping a brain that Mendelssohn's butler has just purchased in the market, is another example of Portabella's rediscovery of fable as a mode of transport and condensation. This legend is sung in the movie by a woman doing laundry. In the song, with lyrics by Xavier Albertí and a melody by Mendelssohn, the ambiguity of the German phrasing "Mendelssohn's butcher," which is also the butcher of Mendelssohn (Mendelssohn did get butchered by Nazism) contains the trauma of Jewish extermination, which is explicitly addressed in the film. Together with all the violence that preceded and followed it, this trauma remains lodged in the Romantic construction of the nation-state, of fantasies of assimilation through high culture, and of capitalism's commodification and instrumentalization of music.

The Shoah, one of the greatest examples of the complicity between culture and violence, is openly addressed in a bookstore scene that also introduces the title of the film. The scene contains a recitation of quotes that foreground the ambivalence of music as a source of solace and underscore the brutality it is capable of hiding. Beginning with Lars Gustafsson's 1982 poem "The Stillness of the World Before Bach," from which Portabella takes the title of the film, it describes a Europe of everyday sounds that, seemingly unmusical, are music's precursors and counterparts:

> There must have been a world before
> the Trio Sonata in D, a world before the A minor Partita,
> but what kind of a world?

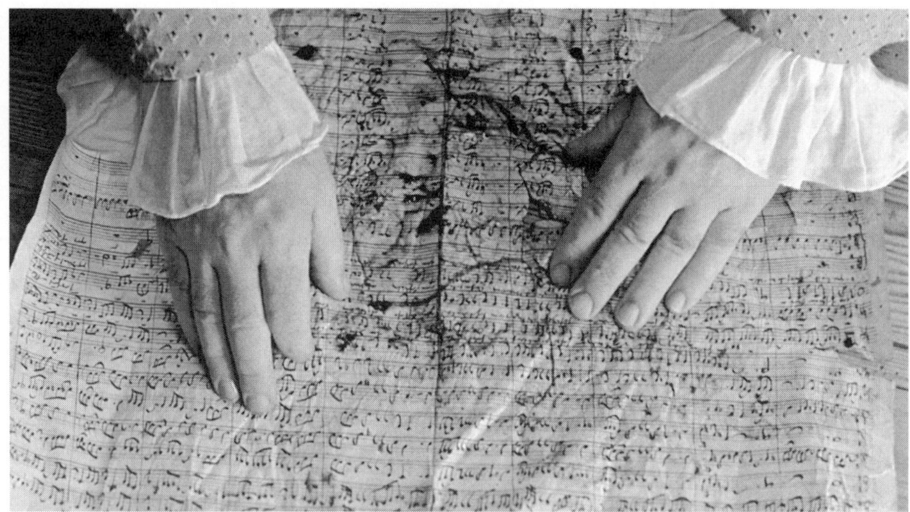

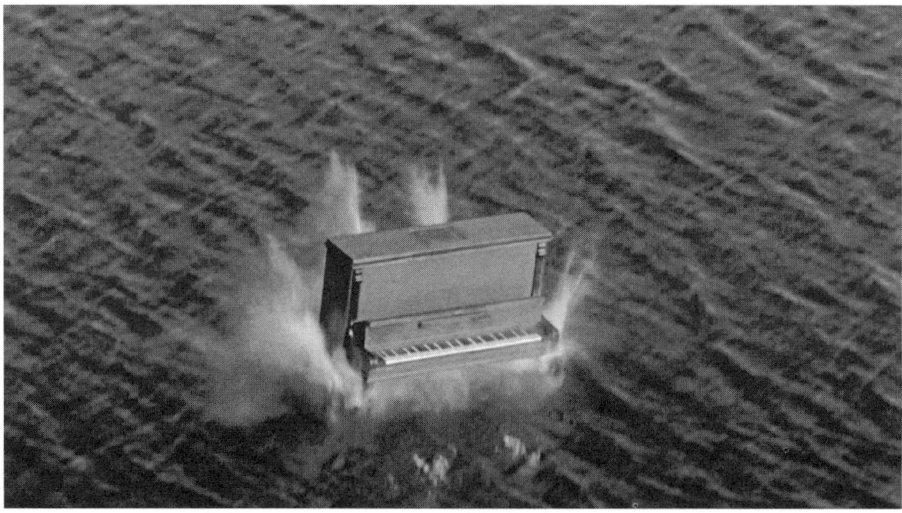

Pere Portabella, *Die Stille vor Bach*, 2007.
Film stills. © Pere Portabella-Films 59

A Europe of vast empty spaces, unresounding,
everywhere unawakened instruments
where the *Musical Offering*, the *Well-Tempered Clavier*
never passed across the keys.
Isolated churches
where the soprano line of the *Passion*
never in helpless love twined round
the gentler movements of the flute,
broad soft landscapes
where nothing breaks the stillness
but old woodcutters' axes,
the healthy barking of strong dogs in winter
and, like a bell, skates biting into fresh ice;
the swallows whirring through summer air,
the shell resounding at the child's ear
and nowhere Bach nowhere Bach
the world in a skater's stillness before Bach.[63]

The reading aloud of the poem by a rather sinister piano shop owner prompts the bookseller to reference Primo Levi, then Szymon Laks's phrase "music hurts" from his 1948 memoir of his time at Auschwitz-Birkenau, in which he describes his directing an orchestra of prisoners, *Musiques d'un autre monde*, and finally a lapidary quotation, this time by Emil Cioran, simply stating "music kills." The film then cuts to a piano crashing silently into the sea, a cinematic allegory of the barbarism of civilization that—contrasting the reversibility of the cinematic image with history's crushing irreversibility—also questions the possibility of silence, since after Bach, we have been taught to listen to the world differently and more attentively, to hear things in it we had never heard before. In Cage's words, "try as we may to make a silence, we cannot."[64] Silence is as singular, contingent, and durational as music. Although we do not hear the piano fall into the water, we do hear its loud, violent splash in our minds. What we hear in the midst of the silence is an aural memory that affects our experience of the image and prevents silence from remaining silent; we hear the aural inscription of history in the mind. After Bach, silence is no longer possible; we hear things because, even in his absence, our ears still can hear everything his music enabled us to hear—nothing less than all the sounds of the world. Indeed, the scene's sound montage engages our *anamnesis* at every level. If the disappearing piano visually suggests a world without Bach, a world that, having heard Bach, cannot but hear the world musically, then, after Bach, "a bell," "whirring," "barking," and any form of "resounding" is also a musical variation.

This newly figured silence is, according to Gustafsson's poem, a mirage, an idea that is more ideological than material because it assumes a separation between sounds that in Bach's world is not possible. Indeed, with the attention that Bach bequeaths to us, we are invited into a world of infinite resonances and vibrations that suggests an often invisible and silent continuity between the animate and the inanimate and all the sounds that, together, they produce in the world. The immanence of music is contained in its own subjectless act of listening, one we in turn reflect and reflect upon as we listen. Bach's music appears as a force of transformation that breaks the world's silence—it proves that silence, like autonomy or harmony, is a phantasm—because it can often be made to envelop, hide, and enclose the signs of violence. This happens especially when Bach and his music are instrumentalized in the name of creating a sense of harmony—be it musical, political, national, or "European." Such instrumentalization domesticates the radicality that Portabella and Santos wish to retrieve and move in other more plural and heterogeneous directions. In their work, Bach is a resource for another politics, another way of conceiving Europe—a Europe that would welcome its wolves, rather than kill them, because it knows it is nothing without them.

In the face of European history as an accumulation of violence, *Die Stille* asks the question: What, then, can be done after this dislocation, after this break in the historical continuum, has taken place?

What can we do after the pages of Bach's *Passion* have been used to wrap up dead flesh, as happens in a rather remarkable moment in the film? Minimally, we can bring to bear on the scene—and its strong visual suggestion of an entanglement between Bach's sacred oratorio and the violence of slaughter, between Bach's cultural significance and his instrumentalization in the direction of mass death, between Bach's legacy and the butchering of Mendelssohn—the moving meditation on community and violence, on the complicity between victims and perpetrators, between mourners and the effects of the violence they lament, that the *Passion* is. What we see here is the instrumentalization of a musical piece that, if listened to differently, can be a resource for acknowledging and then resisting the violence and slaughter so evident in the Shoah. As Kant reminds us, the artwork is a site for contemplation—not because of the kind of object it is, but because of the reflective space it opens up in us. "We *linger* in our contemplation," he adds, because "this contemplation reinforces and reproduces itself."[65] It is a form of attention that in turn makes us more attentive to the world and to others.

Portabella's cinema also asks us to connect what has become disjointed, giving us the space to contemplate Europe's fractured history. It tells us that the traces of history and all its violence can be read in even the most mundane and everyday activities and that music can play a role in these everyday activities and in the most horrific historical events. It urges us to understand that innocence no longer exists; that, like music, we, too, bear the weight of history, and we must learn from the love and wonder so evident in Bach's music. They are part of what we can inherit from him to counter what can always go in the direction of the worst. Bach enables us to imagine how we might gather a force of resistance from music's own capacity for transformation, for imagining the impossible, an exit from the endless cycles of violence and death that have for so long been Europe's signature and most significant export.

Deleuze makes a similar plea in a passage in which, referring to

Artaud's intolerable state of permanent banality and in the aftermath of the violence that traverses and anchors European postwar cinema, he writes: "Which, then, is the subtle way out? To believe, not in a different world, but in a link between man and the world, in love or life, to believe in this as in the impossible, the unthinkable, which nonetheless cannot but be thought: 'something possible, otherwise I will suffocate.'"[66] Deleuze's conviction is that cinema must create not the world but belief in this world. For him, belief is our only resource, however diminished and destroyed it so often has been. It must be understood as a means of relation, as a linking mechanism—one that finds its counterpart in what Portabella sees as the quotidian role of music in film, in turn supported by the cinematic image.

The passage by Deleuze, and Portabella's sentiment regarding the centrality of music, is echoed in the film in a cafeteria conversation between two truck drivers, one of them a likely offspring from the exodus of Spanish workers to Germany from 1960 to 1973, who are transporting musical instruments across the now open borders of the European Union. One of the drivers, who is also an oboe player, describes music as a vital breathing space that allows him to cope with the violence of the other's reductive preconceptions of him as a truck driver and the monotony of his job. This ostensibly banal breakfast conversation (which will comically result in a sustained equivocation regarding the perceived violence of others)[67] is a reminder that the link between people can be mediated only with a relationship to the world and that music is a mediating force. This is exactly what happens when one of the drivers opens up an alternative space, indeed a *breathing* space, by playing the fourth *Goldberg* variation on a harmonica, surrounded by the sound of other trucks passing by. This is cinema as the philosophy of everyday life at its very best, as a kind of secular faith in the finite and the fragile. Like music, it provides a link to the world by interrupting the repetitive nature of work as labor, by establishing a passage that, briefly and somewhat miraculously, connects what has become disjointed. The scene is also a good example of the compositional complexity of the use of diegetic sound in the film, which allows a more complete experience of the unfolding of time and grounds us in the here and now of the possible.

Portabella does not describe or depict situations in *Die Stille*; he creates them as acoustic events that are made possible and then recorded and made possible through this recording, locating himself between the before and after, which is the place of the blank screen and of silence in his film—a silence that can always overwhelm us, either before or after Bach. He relies on the interstices between these situations, which, never constituting a sequence, construct new relations through transit, interval, and resonance. We should not forget that Portabella belongs to a second avant-garde from the late 1960s and early 1970s that championed the "situation" over painting or the readymade. To this, one should add Cage's influence on conceptual art's "dematerialization," on a more expansive understanding of sound (one that exceeds the musical and its presumed emancipation of sound), and on Santos, in particular.

These musical experiments move both backward and forward in relation to musical history. When the present cantor of Saint Thomas, Georg-Cristoph Biller, plays Györgi Ligeti's Organ Study No. 2, "Coulée," on Bach's organ, we hear both Bach and Ligeti transformed by the relationship to one another, less certain and more speculative in their structural consistency.[68] It is an enactment of what Lauren Berlant and Lee Edelman describe as the irruption that such encounters produce: "Structural consistency is a fantasy; the noise of relation's impact, inducing incompletion where it emerges, is the overwhelming condition that enables the change that, within collaborative action, can shift lived worlds."[69] The collaborative and associative relation between sound and image and between music and cinema echoes the materiality of the creative process of the Santos/Portabella tandem by mobilizing an affinity that also preserves their difference. Composition and the redistribution of cultural capital is the key to the internal logic of the film. Nancy puts it this way: "What distinguishes music . . . is that composition, in itself, and the procedures of joining together never stop anticipating their own development and keep us waiting in some way for the result—or outcome—of their order, their calculations, their (musico)logic."[70]

This "joining together" also describes the encounter between music and cinema and between aesthetics and politics in the film. The film produces a situation that is shared by all its participants and collaborators without ever becoming a means to an end because it follows a singular compositional logic that cannot be anticipated and that exceeds any calculation. As Jacques Attali puts it, discussing the political economy of composition as a dynamic practice: "Composition—a labor on sounds, without a grammar, without a directing thought, a pretext for festival, in search of thoughts—is no longer a central network, an unavoidable monologue, becoming instead a real potential for relationship."[71] This is what *Die Stille* is made of: the record of a relationship as a disjunctive synthesis, the conjunction of two incomplete singularities in the making that manage to connect through a composition that interrupts the continuum of ideological narratives, namely, Bach's music, understood as patrimony and, given the role of Bach's sons in the commodification of his music as a "style," as a patronymic machine.[72] But the link between music and cinema needs to be constructed because the real is made out of cuts. This is what the specificity of the cinematic brings to the table: cinema is made by cutting, as music is made through the syncopation of silence. The collective labor of composition, its socialization, demands an aesthetic practice of collaboration and of sustained negation, a resistance to the stasis of identity that turns artistic practices into culture, patrimony, and patronymics.

The filmic actualization of a Marxian coalition of "associated producers" proposes a different kind of inheritance, one not entirely governed by ownership, subservience, and violence—one whose vast relationality resists all delimitations and forms of possession and instrumentalization and whose incommensurability of entanglements cannot be organized in a predictable way.[73] The film indexes not just our inscription within a network of shifting relations — within a growing association of producers — but also our duty to continue to examine critically our place and responsibility in it. It is the measure of the extent to which we have inherited the archives that, shaping our present, can be drawn upon and added to in order to facilitate a different future, one that is inseparable from the possibilities of dissent and production. What is at stake is reconceptualizing "culture" so that — no longer a token of class, nation, expertise, or what we have come to refer to as "cultural capital" that can be possessed but instead a formation to be disassembled and constantly recomposed — it is transformed through the multiple modes of its transmission, its plural forms of inheritance. It is when "culture" is thought of as one, when it is identified as a European bourgeois form, that it displays its barbaric underbelly, and this contradiction puts its conceptualization in crisis. Interrupting culture as an "object" that can be appropriated for national, ideological, or "cultural" purposes is one of the tasks of Portabella's film. If culture is a site of production that detaches itself as an object, partly by becoming a document of its own production, it is because it is culture from the perspective of producers, and not from the vantage point of consumers or guardians of cultural capital. This point of view breaks culture open in order to show its fissures, to expose its complicity with violence of all kinds. It pluralizes and multiplies culture from the "inside," as it were, but in forms that are not identifiable, countable, or calculable.

Associative Logics

> The materialism of the encounter is the materialism, not of a subject . . . but of a process, a process that has no subject.
> — Louis Althusser, "The Underground Current of the Materialism of the Encounter" (1982)

> Music innovates by opening gaps, by cracking; the composer's pen and the musician's fingers and lips are pliers, which wrench open or tear the existing fabric of music, enlisting countless forces in their service.
> — Aden Evens, *Sound Ideas: Music, Machines, and Experience* (2005)

Film, for Portabella, is above all a performative and collective practice of the possible, even when it appears as finished and is technologically reproduced. It is a participatory activity with unpredictable effects, one that refuses to be ideologically instrumentalized. This is because it demands a singular engagement, with Catalan as an idiomatic anchoring in the context of the here and now of an audience willing to play along and in this way make the performance a publicly political event. Indeed, the full title of his longest, most polyphonic and essayistic political docufiction, the 1976 *Informe General para un proyección de interés público* (General report for a screening of public interest), calls attention to this possibility. That during Francoism, Portabella, Santos, and Brossa were involved in underground networks of clandestine distribution and screenings that were, above all, occasions for political debate and conversation surely informs an understanding of cinema as an expansive event that is never exclusively cinephilic.[74] Such an event calls for a participatory audience and proposes an uncertain and agonistic democratic structure based on the possibility of plural disagreement. This historically grounded cinematic dispositif traverses Portabella's conception of the medium and is embraced as both a political and an aesthetic choice. The fact that his cinema was "rediscovered" in its transposition to the art gallery after a long period of critical neglect,[75] artificially extending the protocols of this expanded event, surely does not escape Portabella. It is explicitly thematized in a reconfigured relation to the museum as a site of production in his 2015 *Informe General II: El rapto de Europa* (General report II: The abduction of Europe). The exhibition value of his work in the museum normalizes the labor of defamiliarization and the experimentalism that undergirds Portabella's oeuvre and risks domesticating it.

With *Pont de Varsòvia* and *Die Stille vor Bach*, Portabella and Santos willingly occupy the commercial space of the movie theater to reach a wider and transformed audience—one already highly trained by professional cinema and now able to access a wide range of expressions. Rather than retreat into the prestige circles of an "artistic" film, they enter mainstream distribution to generate a different kind of conversation, one in which now many more can potentially participate. While *Pont de Varsòvia* fails to connect with this wider and more diverse audience because it rubs against everything that culture was instrumentalized to become in the consensual and amnesic milieu of the Spanish transition and the German *Wende*, two events that would completely restructure the political organization of political dissent in Europe, the success of *Die Stille vor Bach* took everyone by surprise. The accessibility of the film, which repeats several of the choices that had labeled *Pont de Varsòvia* opaque and elitist, are now hailed as reinventions of the relationship between music and image and between film and the constitution of a public.

We could say that Portabella and Santos go back to the extraordinary experience of the Modelo prison piano performance in order to amplify and multiply it. The question is why now? The answer is twofold: by the time *Die Stille* comes out, the reality of a system with no alternatives, the unraveling of Europe as a political promise, its failure to integrate Eastern Europeans fully, the ten-year Yugoslav Wars, the unbridled hostility toward immigrants and refugees and the exploitation of their labor, and the exponential restriction of asylum rights make the bleak warnings of *Pont de Varsòvia* almost unnecessary. While acknowledging all this present violence, together with the violence that preceded it and prepared for it, the film focuses instead on the form a different kind of political organization might take, without ever falling into the trap of giving it a fixed content. What the audience seems to have experienced is the creation of a void as a site of possibility and a breathing space: not the description of a world, but only the reminder of the plurality of worlds and their infinite encounters and combinations.

The Piano: Fabrica Mundi

> In his *Trapper's Guide*, [Sewell Newhouse] says the trap goes before the ax and the plow, forming "the prow with which iron-clad civilization is pushing back barbaric solitude" and causing the wolf to give way "to the wheatfield, the library, and the piano."
> —Barry Lopez, *Of Wolves and Men* (1978)

In the liner notes for his 1984 *Piano track*, Santos writes, "with or without piano, there is always a piano."[76] The statement synthesizes the musician's ambivalence toward a mechanical organism that overwhelms his entire production. In one of his most notorious performances, the 1972 film *Miró sculpteur*, a collaboration between Santos and Clovis Prévost around the figure of Joan Miró, Santos delegates the complete destruction of an upright piano in an empty swimming pool to a group of three workers. It is a reenactment of an earlier "action" by Santos and an attempt, he later explains, to learn to play the piano as if it were a new instrument. It is also yet another metamorphosis of the piano into a performative sculpture, an act of splintering and anonymization that materializes the conceptual framework of Santos's relationship to the instrument. The film's rapid and syncopated montage moves from the piano to the production process of Miró's late public sculptures, which contain mostly found materials that are then manipulated in the studio by a team of assistants. Binding the process of creation and destruction in this way, Santos and Prévost enact a reading of Miró's work that is faithful to the violence with which he treats the sculptural medium and that is part of Santos's acknowledged inheritance.[77]

Santos's destruction of the piano as a musical technology is relevant in the context of Europe's cultural identifications. The piano was

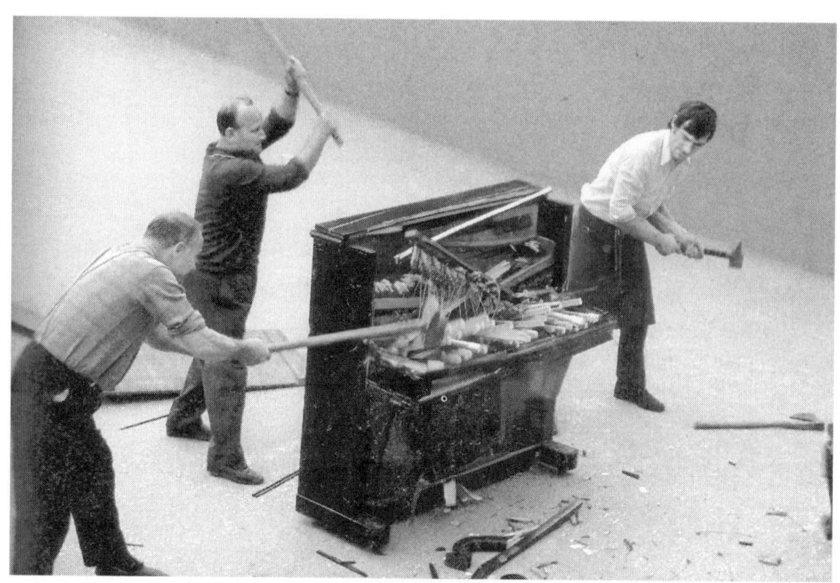

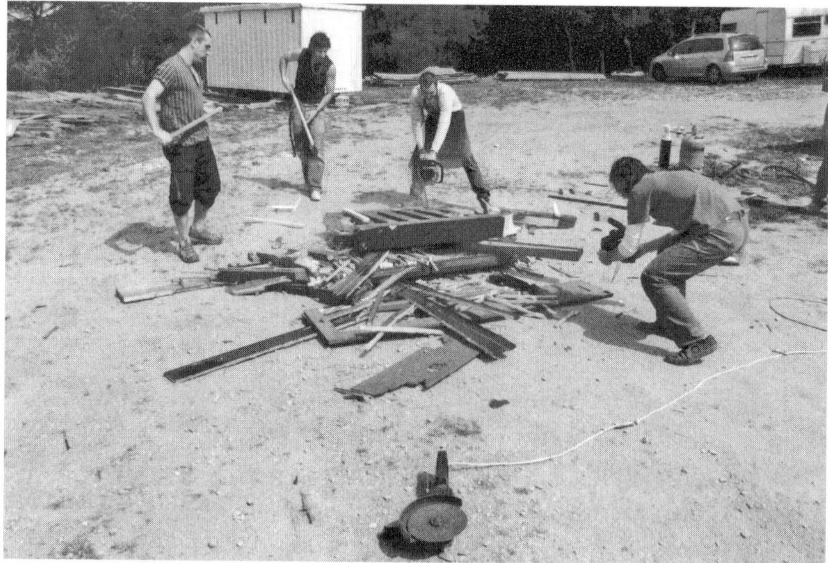

Clovis Prévost and Carles Santos,
Miró sculpteur, 1973. Film stills and performance documentation. Courtesy of ACTAR.

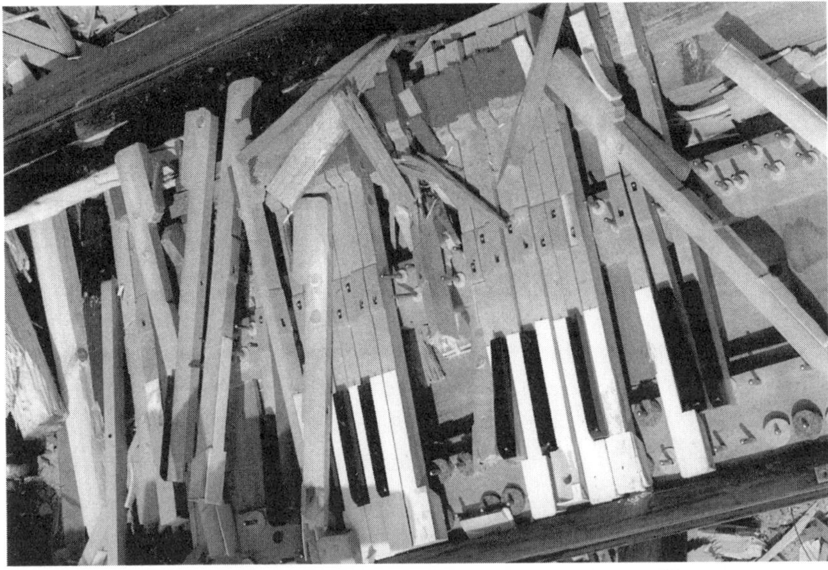

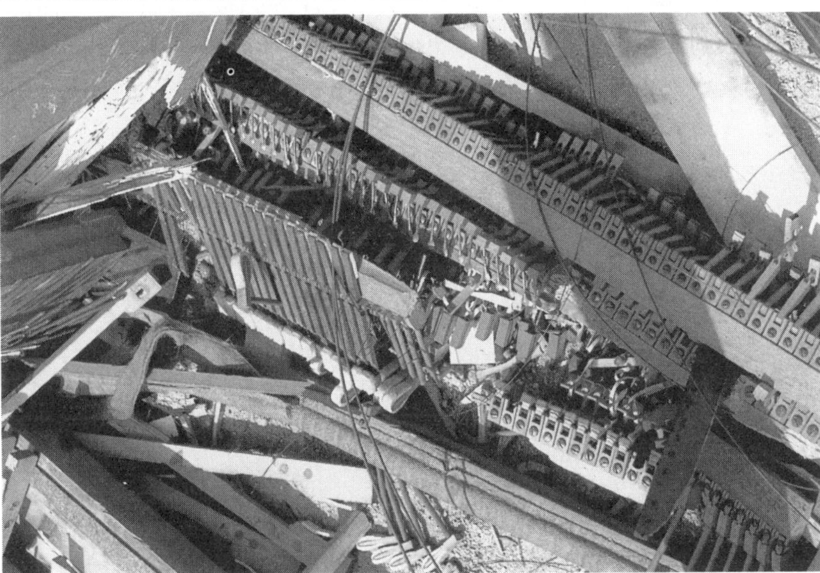

not only the favorite mode of musical reproduction for the emergent capitalist bourgeoisie, it also represented the promises and failures of a class that once considered itself revolutionary. If we return now to the legend of Mendelssohn's discovery of Bach's *Saint Matthew's Passion*, it is clearly not enough that Mendelssohn "discovers" Bach; he must play Bach on the instrument that defines the cultural habits of the bourgeoisie: the piano. The privatization of the piano as a technology plays a crucial role as a mode of cultural reproduction for the bourgeoisie in the development of capitalism and the acceleration of commodification, which will eventually become the structuring social relation in capitalism's *fabrica mundi*. Indeed, the material assemblage of the piano itself, its technical complexity, which Aden Evens calls the "analytic instrument par excellence," embodies the entire conceptual organization of capitalist labor: "Horizontal for pitch and vertical for dynamics; black keys and white keys organized according to the well-tempered twelve-step octave, asserting the priority of Church modes based on the major diatonic scale; a logarithmic presentation of the whole range of the orchestra, laid out within the reach of a seated performer who commands the entire instrument."[78]

Together with the hegemony of the piano, a uniquely European instrument, the emergence of the orchestra is also connected to the rise of the bourgeoisie and its industrial economy. Because harmony as a musical form of abstraction is related to number, the question of the score as an algorithm and of the musician in an orchestra as a worker whose part has been mathematically allocated and whose time has been measured and regulated becomes extremely important. It parallels the factory as capitalism's preferred site. Indeed, the piano keys that are the trademark of cultural and social class in nineteenth-century Europe depend on the violent colonial extraction and trade of ivory on the coast of Central Africa and of ebony in the forests of the Congo. Forced labor, capitalist extraction, unequal trade, and the mathematization of sound prove to be interdependent. Piano keys are often referred to as "bones," and the question that resonates here is: Whose bones?

Inheritance: Chosen and Unchosen

> Nobody has yet heard Mozart, Beethoven or Bach as they truly call, name, teach. This will happen only much later, in the fullest after-ripening of these and all great works.
> —Ernst Bloch, *The Principle of Hope* (1959)

> Cultures make music through a violent assault on the sonic universe. The resultant music then makes more.
> —James R. Currie, *Music and the Politics of Negation* (2012)

Ultimately, the fantasy of a complete mathematization of sound is perhaps possible only in the abstraction of an economic equation through the logical equivalence and quantifiable value of capitalist plunder, a representation restricted to the visual and economic formulations of an economic reality. Ironically, the European Union is fundamentally an exclusively economic form of government: pure administration, with no relation to democratic representation, in which the market has taken over the state without eliminating the nation. Its efforts can be summed up as a harmonization and fine tuning of uneven national economies. Pythagoras's dream of absolute harmonization, endlessly rearticulated as a persistent mirage, is finally encapsulated in the banking algorithms of a disintegrating Europe, rather than in music.

Nevertheless, the immateriality of the musical contains a compositional multiplicity of differentials that can serve as a model for a new conceptual organization. Both Santos and Portabella are as interested in questioning the commodification of Europe's musical legacy as they are in underscoring the compositional potential of the musical and even the inescapable relation between the two. What they propose is a discontinuous transmission of Europe's cultural capital that highlights its differentials, a transmission where the figure of the wolf would no longer be a disharmony to be avoided, but the place from which to build a different kind of harmony, one that is not predicated on the equality of the tones, but on the extraordinary fact that geopolitical realities and musical tradition always contain dissonant sounds and that we must train our ears to listen to them anew. Europe's cultural legacy and the memories encrypted in it—in this world among other worlds—can survive only if it is continually tampered with and understood as the unfolding of a multitemporal performance that is as fragile as it is relevant.[79] Following Adorno, Gerhard Richter puts it clearly: "this inheritance of world—and of the idea of world as such—takes place in relation to a work of art that inscribes itself in a tradition precisely by calling into question the precepts and premises of that very tradition, thereby rendering the legacy that suffuses that tradition a contested matter of perpetual reinterpretation and renewed examination."[80]

Acoustic dislocations and displacement function as indices to complex worlds, to geopolitical configurations that cannot be fully represented or fully signified. Aesthetics and politics emerge as two incomplete orders of visibility that cross over each other like the hands of an interpreter of Bach at the keyboard; their complicity points toward the experience of a belief in the shared experience of collaboration and its acoustic resonances. The situations presented by Santos and Portabella are made of incomplete parts that connect through their incompleteness. There may be a place in these works for a harmony that cannot always be heard but that can be practiced: a collaboration, attunement, and transit between different spheres of knowledge and experience. This collaboration is based on the structural incompleteness of music, cinema, and politics and calls for a transport between these different spheres, as well as a resituation of them. It relies on the anticipatory structure of the acoustic in which one sound always announces the next, as well as on its composition of difference in which no sound is ever identical to another.

In the context of Europe's ongoing crises, where the pitfalls of its postpolitical and neoliberal alliances have proven unyielding to the refugee crisis, to genocide, or to social contracts of any kind, the expression of wounded aspirations and unfulfilled political promises resonates anew. It is unable to hide the current round of discontent. In Catalonia's fraught political present, in the aftermath of a failed renegotiation of its sovereignty, Europe is once again and more than ever before the name of a yet-undefined promise because the assumptions that held it together have been hollowed out. Europe has come to signify pure political expectation because it is now meaningless, a voided idea that is nothing more than a resonating chamber for everything it is not.

Portabella and Santos interrupt the signifying impositions to which Bach's legacy has been subjected and empty them out of the representational myths that reconfigure their form as content. Their interventions rely not on the content of the artwork, but on the yearning for and the movement toward a content. They are the expression of a political demand that takes the form of a void and this because the artwork, like the political, is always structurally unfinished and incomplete. Possibilities emerge because the speculative space of the political can occupy the void the artwork uncovers by understanding absence and silence as sites of possibility. Aesthetic experience is never about identification or belonging, but instead about displacement, strangeness, and nonnormative violence. It is about multiplying the resonances of the wolf, letting their reverberations expand both time and space without respecting borders or enclosures.

That the acoustic is not mimetic but relational, not semantic but syntactical, not concerned with meaning or representation but with the relations established by sound, underscores the potential of the medium in the construction of a shared political performance, one that is based on difference as the prerequisite of any relation. In this way, the relational speaks to a movement of acoustic becoming not bound by signification or identity that can potentially call into being absent or silenced communities. Together, the immaterial and temporal nature of the acoustic underscores the possibilities opened by anything with which it comes into contact. The temporal spacing between a sound and its resonance, the movement of its vibration through space, always brings something other with it. The acoustic is a relational site for encounters, displacements, and counterpoints. As Nancy puts it, "To sound is to vibrate in itself or by itself: it is not only, for the sonorous body, to emit a sound, but it is also to stretch out, to carry itself and be resolved into vibrations that both return it to itself and place it outside itself."[81] Sound forever returns transformed, having folded the outside into the inside and having dissolved the distinction between subject and object. In Santos and Portabella's experimental practices, the acoustic functions as a model for a new organization of the aesthetic, one that is less stable than *mimesis* but more open to the political undertones of a musicalized labor, a performative *poesis*. It is a fully socialized productive force that cannot be instrumentalized because it remains immanent and historical, even if contentless. It is the absence of content that allows for resonance, which is always contingent.

In regard to cinema, Portabella's understanding of the image as a linking mechanism, as a creative and relational movement from and toward the noncinematic, underscores the durational aspect of film as a material labor of time. In this way, the impurity and temporality of cinematic images echoes the dissonant musicality of the wolf because they always begin elsewhere, *outside*. Speaking about Godard's treatment of sound, Badiou explains how the filmmaker "transforms the sonic chaos into a murmur, like a sort of new silence made from the noises of the world." He adds that this silence allows us to hear "a secret the world [is] confiding."[82] In the secret of Santos and Portabella's material impurity—their shared understanding of sound and image—it is still possible to hear Bach's wolf tones, this time untamed and in the form of both a memory of violence and the militant commitment to engage in an endless labor of composition, assemblage, and listening, a labor that, rather than eliminate difference and dissonance, sets them to work together with all the noises in the world and in all the possible worlds it brings into existence.

SECOND INTERLUDE

A Monster in the Ear

> One day, I found out that there was a cellar down below. I looked down and I could see there was an old piano there, so I jumped down because I was taller than all of my friends. I found this pipe and this little rusty axe and I started banging on the piano, trying to destroy it. My sister was taking piano lessons and I used to hate her going *bing, bing, bing, bing, bing, bing, bing, bing, bing, bing, bing, bing, bing, bing*, so that might have been an opportunity to redeem myself from sacrificing this monster that was in my ear, this *ding ding ding*.
> —Raphael Montañez Ortiz, "Conversation with Pedro Reyes" (2010)

> In modernity/coloniality, human beings are not so much wolves, as supremely socialized subjects who target specific subjects and modes of being for elimination, even themselves if they carry the marks of damnation. In this sense, the endless war of coloniality is both, more discriminating and also more lethal than a generalized war in which all human beings act like wolves.
> —Nelson Maldonado-Torres, "Outline of Ten Theses on Coloniality and Decoloniality" (2016)

It is possible to read Montañez Ortiz's over-fifty-year-long piano destructions as relentless and necessarily failed exercises in decolonization, studies of the violent nature of cultural and historical legacies. An attempt to cross the invisible borders that lay at the heart of the Indigenous genocide and America's Middle Passage, these destructions signal not only the barbarity that undergirds all culture, but also the continued need to imagine a counterviolence that will match its force and symbolically materialize and combat its at times invisible, ongoing, everyday aggressions. Montañez Ortiz's highly theoretical articulation of the aesthetic, psychoanalytic, anthropological, and political tenets of his artistic practice must be read as the inscription of the inevitable oscillation and even complicity between bodies and languages, matter and discourse, the real and the imagined. "Art" might even be another name for this intermittent counterviolence in Montañez Ortiz's practice. In his words: "If the cruel and fiendish don't belong in art, I don't know where they belong."[1]

The first official piano destruction takes place in 1962, when the Nuyorican artist was a student at the Pratt Institute. The pedagogical milieu is essential to the action, as is the fact that Montañez Ortiz uses an axe for the first time and will continue to do so in all his subsequent piano destructions. Axes are ancient tools, and unlike the piano, with which they share their materials, are not tied to a particular culture. They are internationalist weapons and instruments that evoke manual labor, the plunder of nature, the felling of trees that initiated the desertification of large areas of the Caribbean, among many other things. They materialize the irrational abstractions of capitalist value and exchange by interrupting the technologies of coloniality and their forms of indebted sociality. Performing as a Latinx art student in New York after having already encountered the systemic racism of a high school selection process that sent Black and Latinx students to study "industrial" arts rather than art or, music despite their talents or inclinations, this piano destruction is the first in a series of disidentifications and displacements that Montañez Ortiz will intensify and multiply throughout his career. Indeed, his "industrial" approach to the piano turns these racialized pedagogical tiers on their head.

In addition, Montañez Ortiz's familial and social genealogies are all threaded with interconnected scenes of violence—Spanish and US genocidal violence, the Holocaust, the Nuremberg trials, the atomic bombing of Hiroshima and Nagasaki, systemic racism, and state violence. Montañez Ortiz's mother came from Vieques, an island that was transformed from a plantation economy into a US Navy bombing range and from its status as a Spanish colonial territory to an "unincorporated" US territory after the Spanish-American War of 1898. The artist addresses Spain's colonial violence head-on; the title of one of his 2019–2020 assemblages in the Museo del Barrio collection reads: "The Memorial to the Sadistic Holocaust Destruction of Millions of Our Ancient Arawak-Taino-Latinx Ancestors Begun in 1492 by Columbus and His Mission to, With the Conquistadores, Colonize and Deliver to Spain the Wealth of the New World no Matter the Human Cost to the New World's Less Than Human Aborigine Inhabitants." Additionally, his father was a Second World War veteran, and references to concentration camps appear in Montañez Ortiz's paintings from the 1960s, as in his *Monument to Buchenwald* (1961) and his *Children of Treblinka* (1962). We can also add the Vietnam War, the Civil Rights movement, and the Puerto Rican Young Lords movement. Violence is everywhere, and with Montañez Ortiz, it becomes a means of artistic production.[2]

Reconfiguring Latinx art's relationship to the Western colonial archive through an iconoclasm that relies on the percussive as its means and rhythmic core, Montañez Ortiz not only performs the severing of ties with a European tradition he never chose but expands and multiplies the range of that tradition by becoming part of it, by insisting that it experience the force of the diasporic, the colonized, and the exterminated. In this way, the "beat" of his axe becomes polysemic. As James Baldwin puts it, "Music is our witness, and our ally. The 'beat' is the confession which recognizes, changes, and conquers time. Then, history becomes a garment we can wear, and share, and not a cloak in which to hide; and time becomes a friend."[3] The layered temporality of the beat, its polyrhythmic unfolding, is fully anchored in history, even as it resists the violence of this history.[4] It is also an acoustic form capacious enough to condense and contain the complexity of coloniality's "metaphysical catastrophe"[5]—metaphysical because it affects at once the concepts of being, relation, knowledge, time, and space.

The percussive, however, is also key to the piano. At a distance from the hands and fingers that activate them, hidden hammers hit interior strings of different thickness and length whenever one of the eighty-eight piano keys is pressed. After each hit, the hammers rebound and return to their original position, ready for the next hit, constructing a fantasy of reversibility. Piano players literally resist their instruments with parts of their bodies. Music is the acoustic outcome of these oppositional forces and tensions. Montañez Ortiz's shamanic metamorphosis of the piano into a sacrificial object is a return to its inner structure and a violent topological unfolding of its hidden enigmas, among them an irreversible colonial violence. Syncopation is both the rhythmic structure of violence and its acknowledgement and symbolization. It is a wolf that, inhabiting the very medium that would eliminate it even as it nourishes it, exposes the ruinous but militant elements *within* musical tradition itself, dividing it, fissuring it, blasting it open in order to transform it. It is also a reminder that from across the Atlantic, Europe has always been experienced as a shipwreck.

Nevertheless, Montañez Ortiz's piano destructions must be repeated over and over again, confirming that the destruction can never be fully completed—the piano, like its interior hammers, always bounces back to its original position. His performances also alter the tradition and repertoire of the instrument in subtler ways. The fact, for instance, that Montañez Ortiz dedicates his televised piano destruction in the *Tonight Show Starring Johnny Carson* to Glenn Gould is not a simple irony, but a framework through which we can view his performance in a lineage of unorthodox musical innovation and experimentation. Moving beyond Fluxus-inflected gestures, his destructions, which also include chairs, sofas, and found film footage,[6] are harbingers of alternative forms of violence that expand its polysemy through layered temporalities moving in multiple and scattered directions in order to short-circuit the colonial state's monopoly of violence. Forms of iconoclasm designed both to destroy and to produce images of coloniality like the aftermath of a shipwreck, extending from the past into the present and hovering over the future. As Rocío Zambrana puts it, in coloniality "the present *is* the past."[7] It is also a war of attrition that hides its violence in the everyday.

Putting uncertainty back into coloniality as an unchosen legacy and choosing unpredictability and randomness over the false certainties of the given, Montañez Ortiz's performance is as much an activist gesture as an aesthetic one. A destructivist gesture that uncovers rather than destroys the inner workings of a cultural icon of value, it is transformed here into a displaced sculptural object that challenges the production of value that has elevated it into an icon in the first place. It can even be read as an archaeological exploration of Western culture as a debris field that can be properly examined only once it has been splintered and lies flat on the ground. Montañez Ortiz's "counter-anthropology"[8] — one that explores the violence of what he calls the "archaic sapiens" — is also a counter-archaeology of the objects and fabrications that supposedly separate us from atavistic violence. His destructions are exploratory voyages of discovery into the inner workings of a colonial project that has found refuge and continuity in culture and that will continue to do so until it comes to term with its complicities. The separation between infrastructure and superstructure ceases to be operative once the piano's raw materials are splintered on the floor: a variety of woods (spruce, mahogany, ebony, Brazil woods), ivory, high-carbon steel, copper. Unequal trade and debt economies literally uphold the piano as an object, as a cultural signpost.

After conducting anthropological research in Puerto Rico, Montañez Ortiz's 1969 founding of El Museo del Barrio in New York City in a classroom at P.S. 125 in East Harlem should be seen in continuity with his piano destructions and not in opposition to them. The pedagogical and counterpedagogical elements of his performances force his audiences to engage with the instrument otherwise, to decode it in a communal act of voluntary and symbolic counterviolence that evokes another deeper and unspeakable violence through experimentation so that volatility and fungibility can become emancipatory tools. The discomfort these destructions invite underscores the role of perplexity in the critical engagement with unacknowledged violence through the fungibility of objects as sites of resistance made singular through a violent inscription so that their impermanence doubles as fugitivity. Similarly, his Museo del Barrio understands pedagogy as a site of collective critique, of a shared historical reckoning, and of production, rather than preservation or fossilization. This "barrio," which originates rather than follows the institution of the museum, should be read in the context of Puerto Rico's exceptional position as an unincorporated territory under the strange juridico-political status of being "foreign in a domestic sense," an emblematic label that signals the bond and complicity between the nation-state, capitalist exchange, and the logic of the border. By contrast, the shifting borders of "el barrio," which exists in any major US city, contain not a territory but the very experience and environment of coloniality, forced economic immigration, institutional racism and inequality, and also counterhistories of resistance. It is a liminal space, a threshold, that does not cease to shift and redefine itself with a fluidity that belies the logic of the border and colonial exceptionality, the doubled situation in which it emerges and against which it articulates its refusal—a refusal that matches the tempos of Montañez Ortiz's militant beats.

PART TWO

Acoustic Relations: Allora & Calzadilla

Beyond Sacrificial History

> The idea of the Archipelago is not that of a return to origins,
> but rather that of a counter reply to the history-destiny of Europe.
> —Massimo Casciaro, *L'arcipelago* (1997)

> What concept of the political can attend to the memory of unlegacy?
> —Alberto Moreiras, *Infrapolitics: A Handbook* (2021)

In the early 1940s, the Spanish Republican exile María Zambrano finds refuge on the island of Puerto Rico. She transforms the island into an exceptional trope, even a philosophical myth, that encapsulates both the promise and failure of the political, caught midway between the ruination of Europe and the fractal possibilities of an archipelagic composition. Zambrano's diasporic and economically precarious exile, what Édouard Glissant might have called her "rooted errantry,"[1] lasted close to forty years. (She returned to Spain only in the 1980s.) Her long itinerancy took her first to Cuba, Mexico, and Puerto Rico and later to Italy, France, and Switzerland. For the larger part of it, she was accompanied by her sister Araceli, who had suffered repeated interrogations at the hands of the Gestapo and whose partner, the Republican politician Manuel Muñoz Martínez, had been executed in Spain after being extradited by Vichy France. The violence of war—one that for Republican exiles such as like Zambrano lasted from 1936 to 1945 and still ended in defeat—and its enduring aftereffects were a constant presence in her life, constituting the background against which her political and philosophical thought unfolded.

Zambrano arrives in Puerto Rico as a victim and refugee, escaping the wolves of European fascisms only to discover there that

Europe itself is a wolf that through "the nightmare of empire" has bequeathed her a legacy tainted with the brutal colonial violence that traverses the Caribbean archipelago.[2] Her exploration of Europe's relationship to violence and ruination (both experienced and perpetrated) finds its counterpart in the archipelago as an articulation of a fragment not entirely consumed by mourning and nostalgia. Assuming Spain's colonial guilt, itself a sign of European ruination, amounts to the uncovering of the memory of an erasure, which in turn becomes an indictment of the logic of force and domination, what Zambrano calls a "sacrificial" understanding of history.[3] Such an understanding of history as violence has been the continent's signature, as well as what, during much of her exile, must have seemed a likely source of its unraveling. Zambrano's effort to delineate the conditions for a nonsacrificial history, a history that will no longer be the result of victories and defeats, demands a different kind of thinking, a (perhaps impossible) thinking without inherited thoughts, a profound undoing of the certainties of the Western sovereign subject on which sacrificial history and imperial politics depend.

Zambrano's novel definition of democracy as the interruption or suspension of a sacrificial and tragic understanding of history, one predicated on a sovereignty that divides the world between victims and perpetrators—she calls the latter, evoking Nietzsche, "idols"—calls for a reconfiguration of the political in the direction of a poetics, one that is more uncertain, fragmented, and risky, but also more plural, heterogeneous, and mobile, capable of establishing a relationship with a world it no longer attempts to dominate or plunder. In Zambrano's mind, only poetic reason has the potential to undo the Schmittian logic of sacrificial history, to interrupt the structuration of the world into conquests and defeats, the rulers and the vanquished, the sovereign and the subjugated. In her writing, she announces the need for a new, nonsovereign subject of a nonsacrificial history, deconstituted by loss, fallen apart, riven, born out of insufficiency and emerging as a nonautonomous entity that can survive only through a relationship to the world's exteriority, exterior because it no longer depends on the sovereign subject as its center. Zambrano's longing is already both diasporic and archipelagic.

This withdrawal of the sovereign self is also a disavowal of Europe's legacy and of the philosophical tradition of a metaphysical subject, a disavowal that announces a second beginning born out of the fragmentation of archipelagic ruination, once the "desmoronamiento" (crumbling) of a sacrificial world order has taken place.[4] Europe's ruins are not simply sites of mourning for Zambrano, although they are that, as well, and poignantly so; they are above all the trace of a shattering that clears the ground and allows us to glimpse and imagine a different politics, no longer grounded in the inheritance of sovereign subjects.[5]

Zambrano transforms the distance and uprootedness of exile into the condition for this new beginning and the Caribbean into a figure for the ungrounded, subjectless, and deconstituted locus where "nothingness works as a possibility. Nothingness gives birth, brings into the world."[6] In this way, the groundlessness embedded in the Spanish word for exile, *destierro*, becomes an existential non-place, a Null Island, from which to begin anew, differently, without relying on Europe's shattered politico-philosophical legacy. It is also a vexed evocation of the "terra nullius" (no one's land), a concept in Roman law that was also used to describe abandoned properties, wild animals, and lost slaves, which could be seized because they had no legal owner. This same doctrine was the key for European colonization during the sixteenth century and in particular for the establishment of Spain's transatlantic empire through the myth of the discovery of the New World under the false claim that American land was "res nullius," thereby erasing Indigenous populations.[7]

It would seem that Zambrano criticizes European violence even as she simultaneously reenacts it through her language—at least rhetorically, and perhaps unwittingly. As we will see, she is not interested in Puerto Ricans or Cubans, but rather in the island as a philosophical myth. However, she is not the only one to fall under the spell of the island as a politico-philosophical figure. Deleuze's brief text on islands, for instance, echoes her sentiment almost verbatim when he writes: "Dreaming of islands—whether with joy or in fear, it doesn't matter—is dreaming of pulling away, of being already separate, far from any continent, of being lost and alone—or it is dreaming of starting from scratch, recreating, beginning anew."[8]

If Zambrano's philosophy is increasingly transformed by poetic figuration, it is because her Caribbean exile prompts a rethinking of the tenets of the Western philosophical tradition and a deeper understanding of its legacies. It requires a new language that stretches beyond the philosophical. Zambrano's unlearning and scattering of the European subject and its philosophico-political legacies moves from mourning and homelessness into an understanding of politics not anchored in sovereignty through a language that is stubbornly allusive, aporetic, and ungrounded, that refuses to reach land, that always stays at sea. Zambrano's texts are driven by the motility of metaphors and figurations because they are constantly disturbed by the violence of history, the exteriority of world phenomena, and the global entanglements of capitalism. As she puts it, "reality—historical, social, and political—is not a rational thing."[9] Her encounter with totalitarianism unveils the rationalized deception that lies at the core of Europe's guilt and domination from the very beginning.

Likewise, Zambrano does not equate the defeated political project of the Second Spanish Republic with sovereignty and the law, but rather with the uncertain movement of a shared and affective experience of time for which history has no name yet and that "democracy" only partially names. It is revealing that despite her public support for the Republic, Zambrano renounces party politics and remains unaffiliated, beyond partisanship, her entire life. Following her logic, it would seem that democratic experience must remain both unfinished and unnamed if it is also to remain political and establish a relationship with justice. As she puts it, "nothing is more fertile than the partial failure of those not committed to a complete failure."[10] Later, in her 1955 *El hombre y lo divino*, she writes: "The historical reserve of the vanquished . . . what was defeated, what never made it to reason or what went beyond reason," becomes "the seed of future reason."[11] This future reason, which would have to be poetic, constitutes an alternative to Europe's amnesic violence by extracting resources from what may have appeared like an unredeemable defeat. As she tells us in her 1945 *Agonía de Europa*, reacting to the myth of European identity that fascism is fully instrumentalizing at this time, "without a doubt, Europe has ceased to have a face; without a doubt, it has come loose and its previous firmness has softened. Without a doubt, something hidden in the roots of the principles that gave it life have slowly corrupted these very principles."[12] Her indictment of the violence that structures Europe could not be clearer: "Europe was constituted in violence, a violence that encompasses all of its manifestations, from the root, and as a principle. Violence is present in every aspect of its life."[13] For Zambrano, the violence of Europe is the violence of history.

While Europe's violence finds its counterpart in the fragments of the archipelago, the latter remains a rather enigmatic source for a different organization of the political through the poetic. Her "razón poética" (poetic reason), the concept that articulates her philosophical trajectory, is embodied, multiple, and heterogeneous, caught between the finite and the infinite, firmly grounded both in the senses and in the imagination: "the thing of the poet is never a conceptual thing of thought but the exceedingly complex and real thing, the phantasmagoric and dreamt-of thing, the invented thing, the thing that has ceased to exist and the thing that will never be."[14] Similarly, she writes of Cuba, her second Caribbean refuge and the site of what she describes as her second birth in exile: "I felt Cuba poetically, not as a quality, but as substance itself. Cuba: now visible poetic substance. Cuba: my secret."[15] In the end, Cuba, Puerto Rico, and the Caribbean archipelago as a whole remain concealed and hidden in Zambrano's poetic imagination. If we do not really know what an island is, it is because to see an island is in fact to remain outside it, offshore. For Zambrano, this means that the island must stay a secret, preserve its reflective distance.

Puerto Rico's insularity is for Zambrano "the footprint of a better world."[16] Her sojourn in the island coincides with the period she tellingly calls the "catacombs" of her exile.[17] If the island belongs in equal measure to the past and to the future, stranded somewhere between nostalgia and hope, it is because Europe has already demonstrated it has no future, because it cannot escape its dependence on force, capture, and domination—its dependence on mythic violence and the establishment of the law of the border.[18] The trope of the island is, above all, a figure of resistance against the decay of the continent. In the end, "Europe" is another name for relentless conflict and strife: "When speaking with a European, one speaks with a conflict, with someone who lives in order to alienate himself from his life."[19] Alienating oneself from life amounts to negating a condition that is "dark, blind, and absolutist," where "everything has the color of empire."[20]

Zambrano's 1940 essay on Puerto Rico for San Juan's *El Mundo*, which would not be republished elsewhere for another fifty years, becomes a vehicle for a suspended, interrupted, or anachronic temporality that haunts the European present in the form of a remainder, of an island as a fragment or ruin, but also (and somewhat uncomfortably) as a "gift." The island is understood as an excess, a surplus that cannot be captured by force, but must instead be freely offered and freely taken. For Zambrano, the insular remnant should be accepted as an expression of nostalgia for what never existed that is simultaneously an enunciation of hope that escapes the political order of her times. While the Europe of the 1940s was a landscape of loss, the island becomes in turn the lost object that inscribes itself in the loneliness of Europe's refugees "in the terrible hour of the present." In this sense, even though Puerto Rico "is more than an island"[21]—its generosity toward refugees and exiles is a symptom of its exceptionality in the midst of the scarcity of Zambrano's European political present—it is hard not to see her "Isla de Puerto Rico: Nostalgia y esperanza de un mundo mejor" (The island of Puerto Rico: Nostalgia and hope for a better world), the title given to her essay in *El Mundo*, as an attempt to separate herself from the structures of European thought and history rather than as an effort to engage with the realities of Puerto Rico's coloniality.

While the acknowledgment of loss and violence distances Zambrano from the utopianism of the island as paradise, she still participates in it rhetorically. While the charge against Spain's colonial exploits is precisely its amnesiac relationship to the crimes and failures of the past, Zambrano's language betrays the legacies of this very amnesia—if Puerto Rico is a "gift," it poses the question of who its recipient will be. This is especially significant in the contexts of the 1940s and 1950s, because the birth of a new political structure is literally under discussion in Puerto Rico as the island moves away from Spanish colonial control, only to enter into another version of that same subjugation with the United States. Following the Spanish-American War of 1898, the US purchases the island and its corporations colonize its workforce.

In 1952, Zambrano becomes one of the editors of Puerto Rico's constitution. Just as her encounter with totalitarianism unveils the rationalized deception that lies at the core of European political sovereignty, the compromised sovereignty of Puerto Rico's constitution also announces that equivocation and denial will be the heart of the relationship between the United States and Puerto Rico. Paradoxically, Puerto Rico's constitution ratifies its status as "foreign in a domestic sense" through a legal sanction for the US colonization of foreign territories.[22] Through the logic of territorial nonincorporation, the US Supreme Court argues that Puerto Rico is simultaneously foreign and not foreign. It is subject to sovereignty of the United States in an international context, yet it is foreign to the United States in a domestic context because it remains unincorporated to the union. This intentionally ambiguous definition is at the core of Puerto Rico's exceptional status and results in unequal access to constitutional rights. The continuation of coloniality and capitalism structures the implementation of US manifest destiny in the Caribbean and entrenches Puerto Rico in a sort of political exile that, like Zambrano's, was not chosen, but imposed by a sacrificial understanding of history.

Roman Coda: Ruins and Cats

Zambrano's deepest reflections on ruins appear in *El hombre y lo divino*, a text with a long gestation period that she begins writing in La Habana in 1945 and only finishes a decade later in Rome. She even returns to it in 1971, to edit and expand some of its sections. In the book, Zambrano connects ruins to her elaboration of the secret through the figure of the Pythagoreans and their cult of the *logos*—as music, interval, and number. As she puts it, for them: "The Universe was a texture of rhythms, a noncorporeal harmony"[23] of the hidden and sacred, of what remains irrational within the *logos*, because, she reflects, it relies on discontinuity, on the harmony between opposites, and it is rooted in "nonidentity" and the multiple. For Zambrano, Pythagoras is the defeated and buried hero of ancient Greek philosophy, and she connects his fate to the discovery of the ruins of a neo-Pythagorean temple in Rome during the construction of the Rome-Naples railway in 1917. The temple lay buried near Zambrano and her sister's apartment in Rome.

In Zambrano's thought, what is hidden is also protected and sheltered, a secret that travels unseen and encrypted in the fragment and the ruin. Secrecy was no stranger to the Pythagorean cult. However, what may have been their biggest secret, the discovery of irrational numbers, somehow escaped into the outside world. This particular secret, the irrationality of the *alogon*, carried within it a crisis capable of undoing the order of the *logos* and its measures. The legend tells of a Hippasus of Metapontum, a Pythagorean who demonstrated the irrationality of numbers but failed to keep the secret protected within the cultism of the sect. After

Hippasus was punished and ousted from the sect, he is said to have perished in a shipwreck, itself an allegorical figure of the upheaval he had unleashed in the world of numbers and measures by introducing chaos in the precision of calculus. Michel Serres quotes an anonymous scholiast in his *The Origins of Geometry* who writes: "The authors of this legend wanted to speak through allegory. Everything that is irrational and deprived of form must remain hidden; that's what they wanted to say. Should some soul want to penetrate this secret region and leave it open, it will then be swept away into the sea of becoming, it will drown in its relentless currents."[24] The relentless currents of the sea, once again, stand as markers of the disorder the land must keep at bay. The archipelago reappears here to shelter and protect what the mainland will not tolerate, unless it hides in a ruin. As in Zambrano's work, the legend's secrets are related to the inevitable violence of the sacred and its laws, which are always sacrificial, but also to a becoming and metamorphosis that challenges the ipseity and insularity of what is most secret.

Curiously, in her first interview for Spanish television after forty-five years of exile, Zambrano recounts her stay in Rome by alluding to another secret she and her sister kept close to them during that time: animals, and in particular, cats. Famously, the two women had been threatened with eviction because they housed and fed *too many* cats—some at home and many more strays in the street. It was the undetermined *number* of cats that made their rescue and care mission both irrational and dangerous to their neighborhood, not the nature of their behavior. As Zambrano points out, the street cats they fed were the ones that did not live in Rome's many ruins—those she tells us were well fed by the tourists and somehow protected by their status as guardians of ancient history. During the interview, she even hints at transspecies relays when, going back to the cat's Egyptian origins (it is worth remembering here that Egypt was often cast as the opposite of Greece, representing religious mystery against the logic of reason), Zambrano claims that these felines carry within them all the knowledge of the Egyptians. However, because of our human limitations, she explains, we are not privy to their wisdom. She concludes by saying she has not yet learned enough from them. In this way, Zambrano transforms the cat into a secret philosophical animal, a marker of the limits of human reason that echoes Derrida's claims in *The Animal That Therefore I Am* that the animal is the "border crossing" that marks "the abyssal limit of the human."[25]

Humboldt's Dragon

> Already within us, outside of ourselves, the most unexpected, the most disquieting metamorphoses are taking place.
> —Suzanne Césaire, *The Great Camouflage* (1941)

> Culture is the precaution of those who claim to think thought but who steer clear of its chaotic journey.
> —Édouard Glissant, *Poetics of Relation* (1997)

> Between my world . . . and any other world there is first the space and time of an infinite difference, an interruption that is incommensurable with all attempts to make a passage, a bridge, an isthmus, all attempts at communication, translation, trope, and transfer that the desire for a world . . . will try to pose, impose, propose, stabilize. There is no world, there are only islands.
> —Jacques Derrida, *The Beast and the Sovereign* (2011)

If Europe is experienced as a catastrophic shipwreck, as a being torn asunder by the colonized, it is because it transforms the sea into a burial ground and the land into a perilous quicksand—a landscape of cargo convoys for human and nonhuman capital, mines, *encomiendas*, plantations, immigrant detention areas, and military training and weapons-testing sites. The Caribbean archipelago is one of Europe's, and later the US's, calamitous colonial encounters, one of the many places to which it exports its violence and borders, incurring an unpayable debt that still shapes the islands' present, like the dead weight of an anchor that refuses to be raised.[26]

The Atlantic archipelago already appears in texts from Greek and Roman antiquity—from Homer to Horace, from Plato to Plutarch, Ptolemy, and Pliny the Elder—under the name of Isles of the

Blest or Fortunate Islands and often in relationship to the legend of Atlantis, the phantom and ill-fated island empire. Fiction and the archipelago have long been entangled. We could even say that those who see it from afar never encounter it for the first time since it already exists in the European imagination in the form of a reverie. When, after traveling to the "equinoctial regions of the new world"[27] from 1799 to 1804, Alexander von Humboldt speculates on an Arabic etymology for the Antilles, claiming it comes from the word *Al-tin* or *al-Tennyn*, meaning "the dragon," the biogeographer and botanist also partakes in these ancient reveries.

That the etymology takes us to Arabic is in itself revealing of the border logic that articulates the relationships between Europe, North Africa, and the Middle East. The dragon's foreignness at the source of the mythical threat it represents is double—an otherworldly creature speaking a foreign tongue that has come to signify the other of Christianized Europe. In the Sea of Darkness of old Arabic Andalusian legends and maritime charts, dragons are the guardians of a limit that must not be crossed. They serve as a warning against exploring unknown territories, terra incognita. On the antipodes of this myth, but still deeply connected to it, stands the old Iberian legend of the island of Antilia as a place of shelter. The legend tells of seven Visigothic bishops who escape the Muslim conquest of the Iberian peninsula by taking refuge in the island of Antilia.[28] After burning their ships to ensure their break from the continent will be permanent, that there will be no return, they erect seven settlements. The main source for the legend is an inscription in a 1492 Nuremberg globe by Martin Behaim, exactly when Columbus begins his first voyage to the Caribbean.

All maps inscribe stories of domination, conquests, and fear of the unknown on their surfaces. Regarding those who inhabit the archipelago, however, maps are less clear about the borders that would enclose them, and the stories surrounding it are infinitely more complex and fractal. The shared but fragmented experience of colonial violence is the historical undercurrent that binds and scatters the archipelago in visible and invisible ways. It forces a dynamic understanding of space and distance that can no longer be measured precisely or notated in a map. In Glissant's words, it is "there and elsewhere, rooted and open, lost in the mountains and free beneath the sea, in harmony and in errantry."[29] The legacy of Europe's fragmentation of the Caribbean is a continued sense of impermanence, motion, and a relentless political and economic uncertainty, all of which, in turn, trigger an intensification of contingencies, encounters, and diasporic drives, or what Deleuze and Guattari might have called "rhythm" and Glissant calls "relation."

The Caribbean archipelago, and more precisely its meta-archipelago, is also a conceptual and performative trope that uniquely represents the networks of ecological and historical relations that constitute it.[30] Each island in this heterogeneous assemblage mutually constitutes each of the others as a member of a never fully determined group. To this day, the territorial and cultural borders of the Caribbean have remained blurry, and attempts at static partitions continue to fail to apprehend and comprehend them — are the Guyanas part of it, for example? Or Central America? Mexico and Colombia? Whatever the answers may be, the Caribbean seems to follow a logic of aggregation and accumulation, of the many becoming many more, but remaining strangely indeterminate and uncountable. The region's infinitely complex geography delineates relational patterns, attunements, and combinations, continuities and discontinuities, and improvisations and refractions that behave like autopoetic assemblages or compositions. The archipelago becomes as much a poetics as a mode of relation — a mode of coexistence and of the intermittence of togetherness and separation.

The Caribbean meta-archipelago emerges from its violent splintering as a disjunctive nexus of biodiversity, languages, erased histories, temporalities and cosmologies, revolutions and counter-revolutions.[31] A constant aggregation of properties and modalities, this assemblage behaves with an aquatic plasticity. In his *Repeating Island*, Antonio Benítez Rojo puts it beautifully when he lists the symbolic and ecological undercurrents of the Caribbean as "unstable condensations, turbulences, whirlpools, clumps of bubbles, frayed seaweed, sunken galleons, crashing breakers, flying fish, seagull squawks, downpours, nighttime phosphorescence, eddies and pools, uncertain voyages of signification."[32] The only constant in this list is movement itself and the perpetual circumstance of being always at sea.

Movement, then, is constitutive of the archipelago; it is both its affect and its modality of being. One can hear in this passage the words of Thales of Miletus, the archipelagic natural philosopher whose cosmology reminds us that water is not simply the origin of all things, but also a container for life—proof of the continuity and resilience of all matter. We could even say that in this fragmented land of volcanos and hurricanes, all matter behaves like water, and because of this, it perseveres in a state of endless transformation.

Indeed, the meta-archipelago seems to function like a cosmic constellation. Benítez Rojo again puts it elegantly: "If someone needed a visual explanation, a graphic picture of what the Caribbean is, I would refer him to the spiral chaos of the Milky Way, the unpredictable flux of transformative plasma that spins calmly in our globe's firmament, that sketches in an 'other' shape that keeps changing, with some objects born to light while others disappear in the womb of darkness; change, transit, return, fluxes of sidereal matter."[33] This comparison to the complexity of a sidereal constellation is also a reminder that, as Suzanne Césaire writes in her *Great Camouflage*, antagonism and binaries are conceptually too simple to describe the Caribbean conflagration. Together with her, a long list of Caribbean poets and thinkers—Glissant, Kamau Brathwaite, Sylvia Wynter, Derek Walcott, Nicolás Guillén, and Jamaica Kincaid, among many others—underscore the archipelago's relationality and motility, its potential for creating new assemblages, its compositional acuity. Creativity and criticality go hand in hand in this archipelagic transnational coalition, demanding a heightened attention to change and transformation. The archipelagic configuration complicates and multiplies relations between islands and islanders through an embodied and performative approach to a singular geography defined by migration, by the constant movement across borders, languages, histories, and temporalities. It transforms anyone who enters its elliptical orbits.

The Vulture and the Flute

> It would not be a matter of "giving speech back" to animals, but perhaps of acceding to a thinking, however fabulous or chimerical it might be, that thinks the absence of the name and of the word otherwise, as something other than privation.
>
> —Jacques Derrida, *The Animal That Therefore I Am* (2008)

> I had almost forgotten that the task of philosophy is not to inform, but instead to slow down, to slip out of tune, to hesitate. To slip out of tune in order to find other ways of being in tune. To seek a change in direction when the road ahead is too straight. To be caught up by different forces. To give facts a power that we do not ourselves have and that we will need to learn to construct alongside them, that *of making things happen*, of producing effects and unexpected effects.
>
> —Vinciane Despret, *Living as a Bird* (2021)

The behavior of the acoustic as a site of encounters—at once a medium and a trace, an echoic propagation of waves through space that, when organized through rhythm and tone, is also culturally and politically inflected—functions as a model or dispositif that traverses Puerto Rico–based artists Jennifer Allora and Guillermo Calzadilla's entire artistic practice. Since the beginning of their career, the artists have amassed an archive of the violent acoustic traces of the ecological and colonial exploitation of the island of Puerto Rico and often have used this vantage point to address, among others, the musical legacies of European imperialism, the arrogance of humanism, as well as the evidence of Europe's ruination. This ruination is also the deep inscription of a catastrophic futurity into a European archive and the violent political, historical, and economic flows that have long acted as forces of demolition. By making a catastrophic future manifest through an archive of sound, Allora & Calzadilla treat acoustic multitemporalities as composite sculptural forms that, at times slowly and quasi-imperceptibly, unfold as orchestral events. Rather than find coherence and unity in style or in a variety of artistic media, the two artists have consistently investigated sound as a hybrid organism that traverses both the biomorphic and the biopolitical as genealogies of matter and metaphor that encrypt the unexpected and often violent metamorphosis of the relation between humans and nature and within nature itself.

Inventing and performatively staging new forms of coexistence among different modes of being, Allora & Calzadilla consistently resist metaphoric transport or analogic thinking in favor of archipelagic undercurrents that operate beyond the perceptible or recognizable and that the artists do not intend or cannot fully control. What we encounter here is, above all, a withdrawal of the artists as agents or initiators of the artwork. They are assemblers, composers, and even hosts, and, indeed, for the artworks to function as intelligent organisms that can potentially produce unexpected or uncontrollable outcomes, the artists must first exit the scene. This withdrawal may in fact be the most performative and calculated aspect of their practice. Similarly, the kinds of expertise their works demand call forth a range of multiple collaborators without which the piece could not unfold, none of whom, in turn, ever act in isolation. This dependence on external forces — technological, biological, human and nonhuman — highlights the fact of the embeddedness and composite nature of agency itself, as well as the amalgamating sociality of the artwork, whose autonomy is born out of heteronomy and whose intelligence is an assemblage of heterogeneous, always incomplete forms of knowledge, labor, and experience.

The acoustic functions as a transient and transformative medium that turns sites into events and objects into performances. It behaves as a multiple and spatiotemporal phenomenon that unfolds topologically through resonance and reverberation and that defies both physical enclosure and the constriction of beginnings and ends. Allora & Calzadilla's continued expansion of the acoustic as a model for aesthetic procedures finds expression in a compositional approach that takes its cue from a musical understanding of duration and of the dynamics of call and response. Because of this, the acoustic functions both as the channel and the trace of a relation between different modalities of existence—a sound that already contains its echo, that is always a reverberation. Sound is a connector that enables contact between organisms and entities that lose their self-enclosure by becoming resonant themselves, instruments traversed by acoustic waves, at times perceptible to human ears and at others imperceptible. It is a reminder of Stanley Cavell's insight: "our primary relation to the world is not one of knowing it."[34]

In *Moby-Dick*, Herman Melville refers to what he calls the "vulturism of the earth"[35] to signal the violent encounters and mutual interferences that inevitably structure the relationship between the species and modalities of being that share the planet and to highlight life's continuity with death in a world filled to the brim with remains. Melville sees this "vulturism" as a characteristic both of nature and of humans and their cultures. In his words, "we are all killers, on land and on sea; Bonapartes and Sharks included."[36] Melville's extraordinary 1851 narrative is particularly apt in describing the undertones of Allora & Calzadilla's close to three-decades-long collaborative practice. This practice is intent on staging and at times simply hosting encounters across different modalities of being that share an inevitable relationship to violence and strife and that speak of coexistence and enmeshment in a web of connections across time and space. As Jane Bennett reminds us, "Humans are always in composition with nonhumanity, never outside of a sticky web of connections or an *ecology*."[37] This composition with nonhumanity is not a harmonious ecology, but a locus where copresence defies a unified worldview in favor of a proliferation of worlds, or maybe islands in an archipelago, that are as entangled as they are incomplete and uncertain. Rather than an interspecies reconciliation or harmonization, we are presented with the undeniable fact of coexistence through unlikely compositions articulated around ephemeral and highly staged performative encounters — encounters that reconfigure each component and treat relationality as a transformative force.

While the use of live animals in iconic pieces such as Jannis Kounellis's 1969 *12 Live Horses* or Joseph Beuys's 1974 *I Like America and America Likes Me* may come to mind as precursors to the work of Allora & Calzadilla, those artworks still imply and activate a certain metaphorical transfer — Kounellis conceived his piece as a painting, and Beuys saw the coyote as a shamanic and therapeutic symbol. Allora & Calzadilla resist both the metaphorical and the symbolic in favor of the surprise and opacity of mere existence that is always also a coexistence. Metaphors belong to sacrificial history because they detach us from the world of matter and phenomena, engulfing us in a language that is always at risk of being instrumentalized and abused in the name of knowledge, meaning, or culture. In contrast, the artists' nonideational language functions like an imprint of one existence upon another, and in this way, it is always the trace and the archive of an encounter, an event. The artists' emphasis on phenomena and presence, instead of on representation or figuration, signals an attempt to acknowledge, rather than to know; to listen, rather than to tell, cognizant as they are that humanism and its tropes belong to an anthropomorphic calculus that can only be sacrificial. In their work, vultures, bats, turtles, elephants, dinosaurs, and parrots point to a sensorium of phenomena that exceed the limitations of the human and challenge ontological borders. In my reading, this assemblage of a veritable bestiary of liminal organisms embodies the many metamorphoses of the wolf, a perennial ontological refugee.

The distinction between knowledge and acknowledgment is extremely useful here, because it hinges precisely on a disavowal of skepticism. It suggests that accounting for what exceeds the self and its limitations is still possible in the absence of knowledge, language, and presence. As Cavell succinctly puts it: "Acknowledgement goes beyond knowledge."[38] Yet, he continues: "I am filled with this feeling of our separatedness, let us say — and I want you to have it too. So I give voice to it. And then my powerlessness presents itself as ignorance — a metaphysical finitude as an intellectual lack."[39] If we remain at the level of intelligibility, knowledge becomes a reminder of our insufficiency, isolation, and fear. However, if we dare acknowledge both finitude and exteriority — and the two are experientially intertwined in their opacity — our intellectual lack becomes the source of our relational dependence, of a broad sociality. It is when our self retracts that we can connect to the exteriority of the world and of others.

This is why the retraction of Allora & Calzadilla in their work is not necessarily a nonanthropocentric stance, which is a lofty goal that is difficult, if not impossible, to achieve completely but is instead a reminder that the nonhuman is constitutive of the human and contiguous with it. Rather than declaring an allegiance to a humanist or a posthumanist standpoint, they acknowledge that in their artworks, the human and nonhuman do not exist in isolation from one another and, as importantly, are engaged in an incomplete understanding of one another. A retraction is not a renunciation; it is an acknowledgement of the composite, relational nature of agency, of the many forces at play in the artwork as a hybrid organism. As philosopher Thomas Nagel affirms in his essay on bat phenomenology, simply "to deny the reality or logical significance of what we can never describe or understand is the crudest form of cognitive dissonance."[40] The works confirm that the limits of ethological knowledge amplify and multiply the limits of various languages and discourses. This deficit in knowledge signals the shortcomings of a humanist solipsism and is the point of departure for many of Allora & Calzadilla's artworks — and especially those that engage with a bestiary invested in an expanded sensorium that moves beyond the alphabet and the figural, beyond word and image.

Their 2012 *Raptor's Rapture* is a wonderful instance of their commitment to a nonideational understanding of copresence as the ground zero of interspecies contact and relation. The video begins with an extreme close-up of a vulture's extraordinary feathers, unruffled by any wind and so eerily quiet that we wonder if it is asleep. The camera then slowly moves along the bird's long and curved neck and stops at the beak and face. It presents the bird in all its wondrous strangeness as a majestic, alien, and mysterious being. The bird remains quiet, only stirring a bit when it delicately moves its head. When we finally see a full shot of the vulture perched on a tree stump, it is now clearly alert, but still very quiet, looking cautious, observant, even meditative. The next shot consists of a pair of female hands searchingly and softly touching a flute made of long and thin bone, carefully perforated at regular intervals. The quietness of the film, together with the dark and somewhat abstract surroundings, invite a heightening of our attention. The surroundings themselves, which evoke the idea of a cave rather than a cave itself, give a contemplative quality to the film, as if we were getting ready to witness an elaborate and controlled experiment whose goal remains unknown to us. We are attentive, yet ignorant, expectant, but open, suspended in a groundless abstraction, a speculative atmosphere that mimics a scientific experiment, but has none of its goals, expectations, or intentions. As we will see, this experiment will insist on remaining an experiment, prolonged and open-ended, refusing deduction, judgment, or interpretation. We are reminded here that art is not science, but rather it is the intensification of experience in a world of phenomena, an autopoietic sensorium for what escapes analysis and understanding.

The first sounds we hear in the film, with an eerily acute precision that would be impossible without sophisticated technological enhancements, are the movements of feathers as the vulture begins to groom, followed by the percussive sounds of a flute as the musician-scholar repeatedly tests the regular perforations in the instrument before attempting to play it by putting it to her lips. From then on, the interplay of her breath and the soundings of the flute will

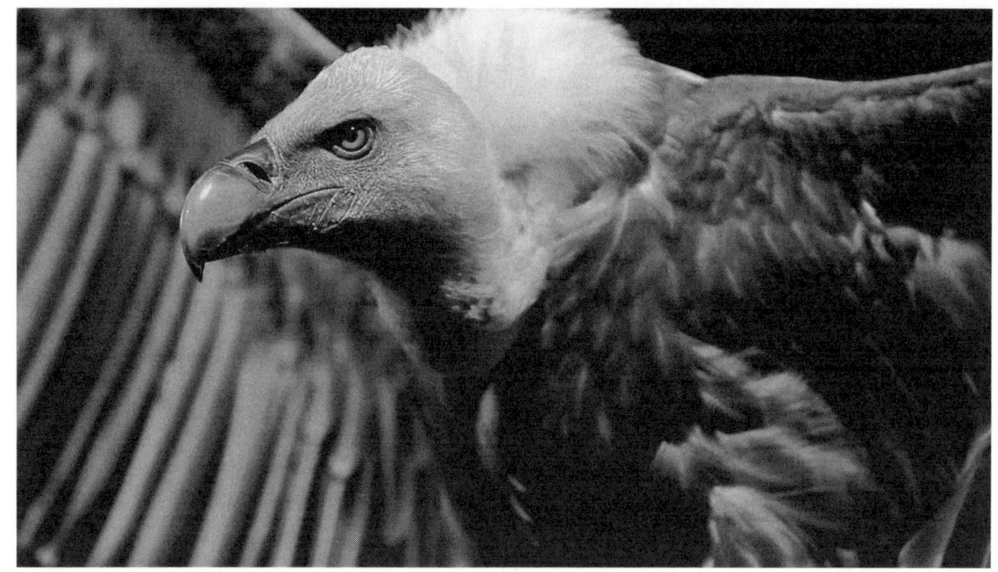

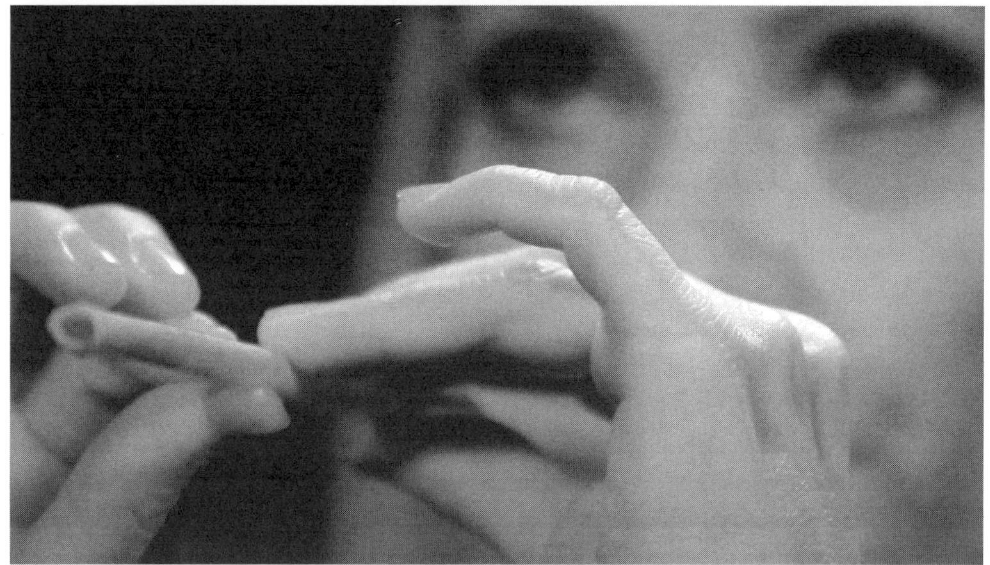

Allora & Calzadilla, *Raptor's Rapture*, 2012.
Video stills. Courtesy of the artists.

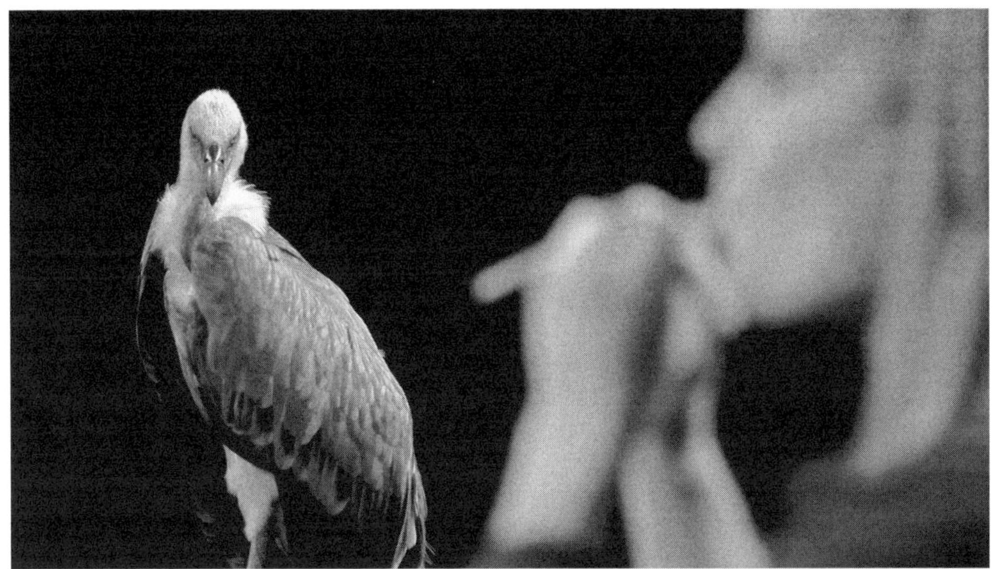

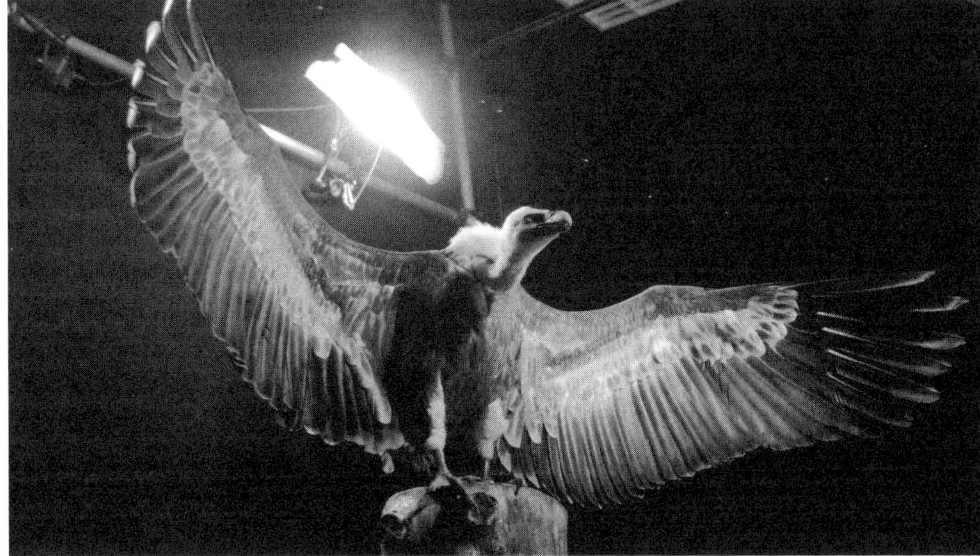

punctuate her speculations into the ways this prehistoric musical instrument might have been played thirty-five thousand years ago.[41] The camera will also begin to alternate between shots of the Griffon vulture and of Bernadette Käfer, a flutist specializing in prehistoric instruments. Each of them is aware of the other but they show no signs of recognition or interest and never appear together on the screen — unless one of them is completely out of focus, thus retaining the logic of separation, even in what appears to be the close quarters of a minimal studio setting. The musician's numerous attempts at extracting notes out of the flute in a variety of ways, which visibly requires a great deal of effort on her part (at times, she appears to be almost out of breath) become increasingly recognizable as music. Toward the end of the film, once the bird has spread its over-two-meter wings to their fullest extension, an uncanny sight in such an enclosed setting, we get a glimpse of the studio lighting apparatus before the film ends with a silent, black screen.

Describing an artwork is decomposing its elements in an attempt to understand its logic, as if it were a matter of simple aggregation. However, because every component, both perceptible and imperceptible, functions only in the simultaneous temporal unfolding of its relation to every other component, the exercise fails to capture the internal logic of the artwork, just as it cannot disclose the enigma that the artwork unveils without resolving. In this process, however, something rather extraordinary happens: the vulture is allowed to be simply a vulture. That is to say, it remains an enigma that is simultaneously a marker of an unbridgeable difference — present because of the limitations of human cognition — as well as of the undeniable fact of coexistence.[42]

As the film unfolds, however, a surprising refraction and metamorphosis begins slowly to take place: the vulture becomes a placeholder for skepticism. The vulture takes on the cloak of philosophical skepticism without even trying, effortlessly, by doing nothing but stare. However, the vulture's "skepticism" reverses that of the philosopher. It does not cast doubt on the existence of the world as an exteriority, but on humanism and its purported privileged relation to knowledge. In the eyes of a vulture—or a wolf, or a bat, or a snail—humanism's discursive arrogance simply vanishes into thin air. We cannot escape humanism on our own. We can only succeed in extending it through a logic of emphatic disavowal *unless* we are made to face an animal's gaze.

Our received perception of the world has been subtly altered, one wing flutter and one whistle tone at a time, making the gap between language and phenomena perceptible, even if fleetingly. Acknowledging our deep ignorance of the world makes space for other forms of life and consciousness, organisms with which we coexist but that remain separate from us. Our limitation, paradoxically, expands the world, even though "we begin to feel, or ought to, terrified that maybe language (and understanding, and knowledge) rests on very shaky foundations—a thin net over an abyss."[43] It should be clear by now that this abyss is none other than the abyss of the animal.

Raptor's Rapture portrays at once an entanglement and a deep divide and takes the form of a controlled exercise or a speculative time capsule. The Upper Paleolithic flute Käfer attempts to play is carved out of the wing bone of a Eurasian Griffon vulture, bringing together the trace of animal remains with a form of prehistoric music. The gesture of putting the dead to our mouths, just as vultures do, reminds us that we never cease to be in their company of their remains. Discovered in 2009 at the Hohle Fels cave in southern Germany, in what is now a UNESCO Heritage Site for the Ice Age, the flute is the oldest musical instrument found to date and is evidence of the central role of music in prehistoric communities.[44] As part of Allora & Calzadilla's orchestration, the piece was originally installed in the Weinberg-Bunker in Kassel, a civilian air-raid shelter from the Second World War. The performance is traversed by historical and temporal layers but does not always openly display them. But what we see in the video is not the shelter but a somewhat abstract and cavelike dark background, a performative erasure of contextual information, a lack of situatedness and a retraction of Germany's political history and of war. The unlikely encounter between the vulture and the flutist is characteristic of the artists' work, a political fabulation or experiment that invents its own conditions of possibility. By superimposing the bomb shelter onto the prehistoric cave, the artists also force a reflection on what dwelling entails. While the prehistoric cave protects its inhabitants from the natural elements, the bomb shelter is a precarious refuge from violence, from war as a hostile environment that has been entirely calculated and manufactured by humans.

Given the scavenging habits of the vulture, the fact that humans used the bird's remains to fabricate musical instruments, the question, in an echo of Melville's vulturism, is of course who the scavenger is, or rather, who is not a scavenger of some kind within an ecosystem that always includes the living and the dead. The sounds of the flute bind the dead to the living, the absent to the present, the buried to the unburied, not through an act of mourning but through the simple acknowledgement of their contiguity and copresence. Griffon vultures are the largest bird species to have survived since prehistoric time. For a long time, the absence of bird fossils, due to the fragility of hollow avian bones, made natural historians assume that this could not be the case. Together with an extremely intelligent sense of location, a capacity for thermoregulation, energy-efficient flying methods, and a sensorial acuity far superior to that of humans, vultures are essential for the recycling of waste and for controlling the spread of pathogens in their ecosystems. In addition to the key role they play in their environment, we may wonder if vultures may not be the only ones that actually know what an Upper Paleolithic flute sounded like, especially if, as Zambrano would have it, they carry a prehistoric memory to which we humans have no access.

Caves; or, The Humming of a B-flat

> What I would like is to build is a cinema in a cave or an abandoned mine, and film the process of its construction. The film would be the only film shown in the cave. The projection booth would be made out of crude timbers, the screen carved out of a rock wall and painted white, the seats would be boulders. It would be a truly "underground" cinema.
>
> —Robert Smithson, "A Cinematic Atopia" (1971)

> My dreams are not *me;* they are not Nature, or the Not-me: they are both. They have a double consciousness, at once sub- and objective. We call the phantoms that rise the creation of our fancy, but they act like mutineers and fire on their commander; showing that every act, every thought, every cause, is bipolar, and in the act is contained the counteraction. If I strike, I am struck; if I chase, I am pursued.
>
> —Ralph Waldo Emerson, "Demonology" (1877)

In one of the scenes in his 2010 documentary essay *Cave of Forgotten Dreams*, Werner Herzog's characteristic voice-over describes the thirty-two-thousand-year-old traces of a child and a wolf perfectly preserved in the Chauvet cave system. The filmmaker, long fascinated with the mysteries and limits of the human, speculates over their meaning. We hear him reflect, "In a forbidden recess of the cave, there are the footprints of an eight-year-old boy next to the footprints of a wolf. Did the hungry wolf stalk the boy? Or did they walk together as friends? Or were their tracks made thousands of years apart? We will never know." Herzog's rhetorical questions clearly operate within the logic of an anthropocentrism that the Chauvet prehistoric cave paintings themselves belie, as he himself suggests at other moments in the film—paintings that, in fact, would be better described as immersive environments: enmity, kinship, and chronology speak of borders, of a vertical order to life forms, and of a linear understanding of temporality. Here, too, the wolf makes an appearance. Every time a border is erected, even in the Holocene, and maybe particularly then, there is a wolf. And indeed, the most fortified border in Western culture may be the one that separates human and animal. Curiously, in his 1955 essay on Lascaux, Georges Bataille also turns to the wolf when he points out that Upper Paleolithic humans "abandoned upon earth . . . make one think of those young humans who are now and then brought up by wolves."[45] For both Herzog and Bataille, prehistory is the time of the wolf, and that evokes a world where beings have not yet been organized into hierarchical strata — where the wolf has not yet become the figure of a wolf and of all the representational weight this figure will be made to carry.

Bataille and Herzog's shared fiction of an artistic origin depends entirely on the expulsion of the wolf from within, in a feat of externalization, exclusion, and separation that marks the beginning of the human. The caves of Lascaux and Chauvet are made to enact retroactively the erection of a border in a distant and decisive point within the linearity of chronological time. The cave's traces, markings, and paintings become inscriptions of a separation that may not have existed when they were made, but that once installed, frames everything before and after. This severing from the wolf and from everything with which the wolf is contiguous may succeed in making these inscriptions less haunting and inscrutable and inevitably, less alive and fugitive in their glimmering and enveloping spectrality.

Yet as if by contagion, both Herzog's and Bataille's texts oscillate and flicker between their humanism and the conceptual challenges of a prehumanism or posthumanism, perched as they are over the abyss of the animal and its encrypted inscriptions in the cave. The movements of their speculative essays are movements borrowed and refracted from the environments they seek to understand and capture. Their words and images are themselves touched by and resonate with an alien atmosphere that countersigns them from an unimaginable distance across time and space, where the sacrificial logic and the great divides of Western history have not yet conquered and organized bodies and minds into strata. When Bataille describes Lascaux as an "infinite symphony of animals secreting furtive humanity," he foregoes the primacy of the eye as a gateway to knowledge in favor of the expansive resonances of a layered space-time nexus.[46] Here we find the boundless musical amalgamations of forms of life that remain porous to one another, where the human is a secretion of the animal, its furtive secret.

However, other nonhuman secretions are also at play. The force of the projected and refracted light of the cave, as both Bataille and Herzog underscore, complicates the nature of the cave both as an artwork and as a border between species and modalities of being. Light itself cannot be grasped or immobilized. It keeps changing, and it changes everything it touches. The motility of the filmmaker and the writer's approach is a direct aftereffect of the reflected and refracted light that mediates their gaze. Like the cave artist who lets the shape of the stone direct his or her hand, they, too, share their agency with the inanimate implements that allow them to see in the dark—a scene projection reveals another projection that supports the first, as well as an invisible refraction embedded within it, and so on, in an unbroken contiguity that traverses the different moments contained in this multitemporal environment.

We could even say that the demand for an experimentalism that can match their compositional complexity originates in the caves themselves, as spaces of profound ontological density that exceed human understanding, of a layered and mobile accumulation of the different organisms that make up and live in the cave—at once situated and in flux, grounded and volatile. Even Bataille points to the difficulties of documenting Lascaux, describing the cave painting as a "mirage," suggesting, as Herzog does, that an optical trick, a trick of the "uncertain glimmers of faint light," is an essential element to the paintings themselves.[47]

The centrality of light, of its flickering and glow, and of the extreme contrast it creates, recurs in all accounts of visitors to the cave. Even though Bataille's text is illustrated by the first color images of Lascaux, in his brief foreword to the book, Albert Skira describes the metamorphosizing effect of the light on the images and the frustrating inability of the camera to capture them in all their vividness:

> Any number of times we came away feeling that at last our work was over. But each time, having developed our plates and checked the results, we decided to make a fresh start, for what the eye sees is not necessarily what the camera registers. The truth is that the Lascaux paintings mysteriously shift and change. They are not painted on a uniformly flat surface and cannot always be viewed from a normal angle, from squarely in front a few yards away, like ordinary pictures. These cave artists took every possible advantage both of the uneven surface of the rock wall and the perspective in each of the various rooms. At every step things change, almost beyond recognition. A bull looks squat and hunch-necked; shift your position and the same animal acquires an elongated body and the head of a giraffe. What is the ideal point of vantage? Each visitor will have the one he prefers; the men of Lascaux must have had theirs, and this we strove to make our own. The pictures at Lascaux literally defy the camera.[48]

The Chauvet paintings that Herzog attempts to document also defy filmic capture, as had those of Lascaux or Altamira before him, and demand a sophisticated 3-D camera that can match their dynamic volumetric complexity. Even then, the capture still fails because the camera cannot quite mimic the fully embodied and yet somehow spectral, almost dancelike motion these animal figures solicit from the viewer. Cinematically echoing Cavell's "empathic projection,"[49] in the cave, as Bataille puts it, "something touches us, we are stirred by it, as though in sympathy with the rhythms of a dance."[50] Indeed, Herzog resorts to *Swing Time*'s "Bojangles of Harlem" number when he inserts a scene of Fred Astaire impossibly trying to catch up to three large projections of his own dancing shadow. Cinematic temporality, as much as the sound and light that materializes it, cannot catch up with its own shadow. It is a form in flux, and more importantly, an expression of its constitutive and not exclusively optical spectrality. The scene is further complicated by Astaire's blackface. While the dance is an homage to the tap dancers John W. Bubbles and Bill "Bojangles" Robinson and, as such, the acknowledgment of a debt, the racial caricature quickly reinscribes the violence, exploitation, and dispossession that Astaire's debt carries within it. In this way, wittingly or not, Herzog introduces sacrificial history into a portrait of a time beyond history, once again revealing the pitfalls of a humanist stance when attempting to understand an alternative to it, an alternative for which we have neither words nor concepts.

When Bataille remarks on the "inhuman strangeness" of the caves, he, too, alludes to a certain animism that escapes the grasp of the human by aligning itself with the animation of life, with the animism of animation itself. It is worth recalling here that the word "animation" stems from the Latin stem *animatio*, literally, the "bestowing of life." This liveliness remains inscribed in cinematic animation as the medium of the moving image. This alignment of the cinematic machine, of an "intelligent machine," as Jean Epstein would put it, with the prehistoric cave speaks of an archaeology of the present, which may entail the beginning of another approach to time. This archaeology, as we will see with Allora & Calzadilla, amounts to imagining a present from which the human has been subtracted in an attempt to be more attentive to the sensations, materialities, and endless metamorphoses that compose our shared environments.

Despite Herzog's and Bataille's meditative wonderment and conjectural approach to the cave paintings, they fully participate in a humanist mythology that Cavell calls "the romance of the hand and its apposable thumb" and "of the upright posture and of the eyes set for heaven."[51] The romance of the hand takes precedent over the mystery and loss that surrounds the *Umwelt*[52] from which these cave paintings emerge and whose disappearance they continue to inscribe, an incommensurable world that we cannot grasp with our opposable thumb — that small appendage that here functions as the synecdoche for a worldview that is exclusively human.[53] The virtual absence of human figures among the horses, bison, bulls, lions, and rhinoceroses would seem to confirm that this mythical separation from nature has taken place: the human is the identifiable maker of the pictorial traces and, with a gesture of the hand, is forever divided and split from the animal world.[54] Such loss or even sacrifice permeates the affective force of these haunting images whose aim seems to be not to capture the animals themselves, but their aliveness and movement in ways that echo Étienne-Jules Marey's chronophotography. If the depicted animals feel strikingly singular and alive, it is because the hypnotic wonder they once inspired is preserved across millennia; the pervasive feeling they arouse is one of irretrievable loss. These depictions are at once a time machine and an archive of the forgotten and the dead, an entryway and a closure. Through them, something has been extracted from the limestone of the cave and its accidental shapes, cracks, and protrusions; something has been taken and given away. Something has died in the act of committing the images to an external time, to the memory of others, and to the effort to prevent a loss of experience, the experience itself. Preservation always implies a certain violence and destruction.

The process that permits us to think that these "pictorial" depictions solicit our gaze is speciation, the emergence of the human as a distinct species. Speciation is first and foremost a mode of estrangement, a violent enclosure into a sameness that announces a wider violence to come, against those who will take the place of an externalized nonself — with "nonself" being another word for nature in Emerson. The "painters" of the cave, for lack of a better word, are enigmas producing other enigmas, both encrypting and encrypted, sealed in a world that we can register only reductively, as the beginning of a long disconnect and as an extension of the loss we register in the tracings on a limestone wall. As Gerhard Richter beautifully puts it, channeling Heidegger:

> For the early human being who steps into humanity for the first time by creating a world in which works of art exist, the fashioning of the work cannot be separated from the intimations of his finitude. The work, created by the living, will outlive its creator, and, in fact, has no need of him, even while he is still alive. It functions in his absence. To construct a world by making a work of art is to render oneself superfluous, even if by creating the work one has opened another world. Here, life and death are once more no longer so radically separate.[55]

In Richter's humanist reading, which also belongs to the romance of the hand, it is the human artist that becomes expendable, whose finitude the artwork both inscribes and transcends. Yet it might also be possible to claim just the opposite: that the artwork provides the prehistoric painter — or painters, because these depictions might involve retracings by multiple hands and across time — with a means to kill the human animal in ways more permanent than any physical violence could ever achieve, so that humans will leave and outlive the cave only insofar as they leave something behind. It is the same "abyssal limit" Derrida speaks about and that is, above all, the breaking of a bond with nature and the beginning of projection as an infrastructure of the human imagination, with its drive to see, know, and represent.

The polysemy of the term "projection," one that Giulana Bruno carefully unfolds in her *Atmospheres of Projection*, brings us back to the instability of a flickering light. Bruno returns to Pliny the Elder's *Natural History* and to the myth of Dibutades, the Corinthian maid who, in order to preserve the likeness of her departing lover, invents representational drawing by relying on projected light to trace the figure of her beloved on the wall.[56] In the story, projection exceeds the optical from the very beginning and is entangled with loss, longing, and desire. After tracking the many pictorial retellings of Pliny's myth, Bruno comes to a conclusion that, in the context of our discussion here, is rather extraordinary: "As a transitive medium whose cultural construction crosses fields, projection offers the potential to link diverse temporal, formal, and disciplinary elements together, transforming boundaries in forms of active kinship and connective contamination."[57] In other words: the very medium that speaks of separation becomes a mechanism that sutures and binds what has become detached, so that boundaries become areas of contact and touch.

Bruno's relational, processual, and dynamic understanding of projection as a medium capable of traversing organisms and their *Umwelten* behaves like an environment, ambiance, or atmosphere and "in the widest sense as an ecology: a mutual compenetration of the body and the body of things, of the human and the nonhuman, in hybrid mixture."[58] However, and somewhat surprisingly, she attributes this kind of atmospheric and projective medium to a "modern" sensibility that resonates with the psychological structures of the self. However, these environments of light, sound, and ambiance cannot be ascribed to any given temporal organization because, like islands in an archipelago, they create and materialize their own temporality in the form of air, moisture, smell, sound, or hue. In her words,

> Atmosphere and projective media create their own elemental environment, in a constant process of change that engages the margins. They are sites that surround us, or border us, producing a state of flux or a sense of becoming. Though somewhat intangible, they do appear to possess material qualities, and this surrounding effect can be felt as enfolding and enveloping, as a sense of connection and even relatedness to other beings and forms. As environmentally charged modes, projective media, like atmospheres, are sensitive to such elements as light, which they transmit, yet they convey as well the shadowy, the nebular, and the vaporous.[59]

If projective media, with the proviso that all media are inevitably projective to a certain extent and all light is both reflected and refracted, produce environments that change from one second to the next in perceptible and imperceptible ways, they demand a certain retraction of the human as a privileged source of agency. The human must retrieve and renounce its place at the center to become one more element or undercurrent among many others in the ever-changing ecologies of a composite and polyphonic environment. The recognition and acknowledgement of this plural materiality must precede any compositional effort in the direction of a new ethology, of a new relational ontology that expands through aggregation and pluralization rather than by exclusion, division, and domination.

* * *

Having somewhat schematically presented the stakes of such a proposition, namely, the composition of environments not fully subjected to human sovereignty, I would like to turn to Allora & Calzadilla's *Puerto Rican Light (Cueva Vientos)* to speculate further on what a nonanthropocentric attempt to acknowledge the incalculable mechanisms that animate the immersive topology of their Puerto Rican cave might look like. In my reading, the piece exists alongside prehistoric caves, instead of "after" or even "beyond" them, in an expansive contiguity that unfolds in an unpredictable temporal and spatial loop that belies both developmental temporality and Euclidean geometry. Allora & Calzadilla's artistic intervention in *Puerto Rican Light (Cueva Vientos)* carries an ontological proposition, one whose experimentalism and risk only an artwork—as an assemblage that is always in motion and thinks with matter—could even begin to manifest and materialize. And this because it can deploy the critical autonomy of an invented and nonnormative language to reveal the heteronomy of a world composed of contiguous life formations that do not and cannot exist in isolation from one another. Rather than reinstate the borders with which we operate in the world as it is now, their installation presents us with the possibility of experiencing multiple thresholds and portals across different temporal scales and modalities of being and their polyphonic environments.

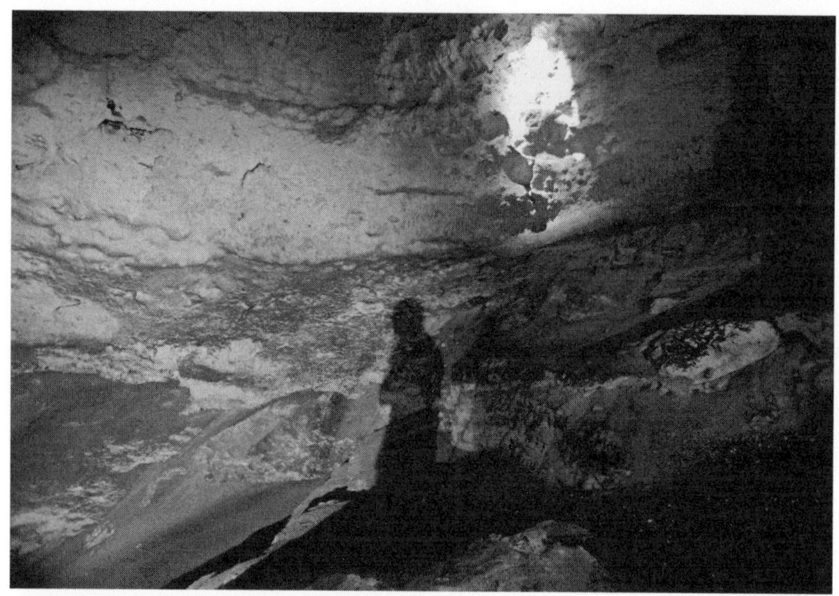

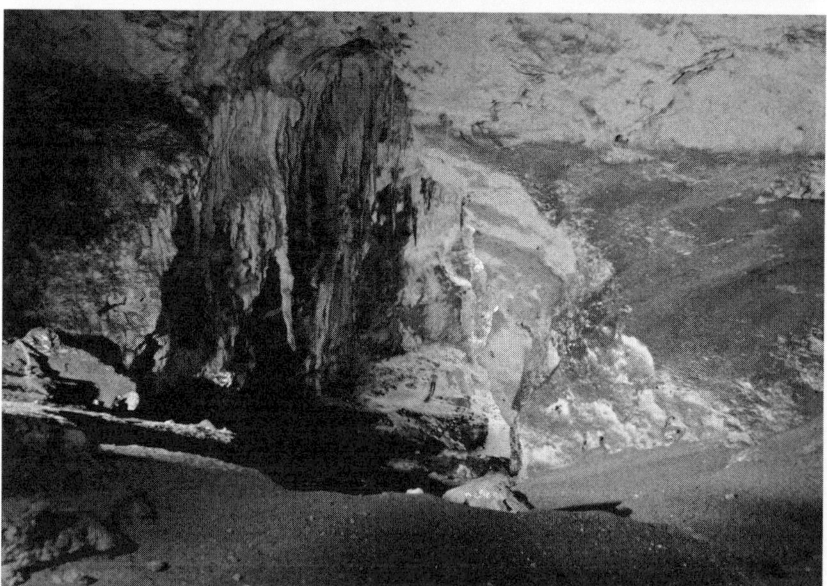

Allora & Calzadilla, *Puerto Rican Light (Cueva Vientos)*, 2015–18. Installation documentation. Courtesy of the artists.

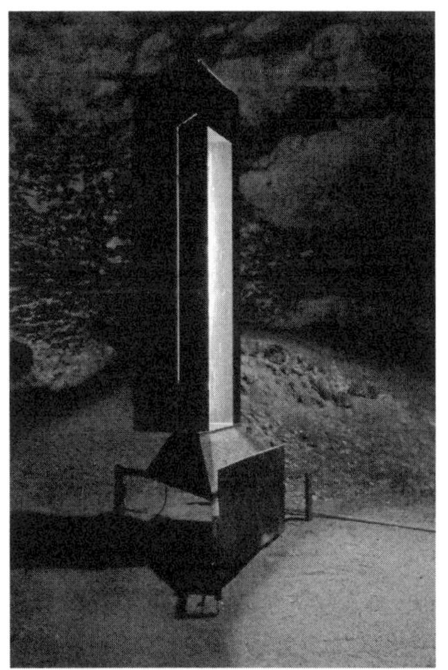
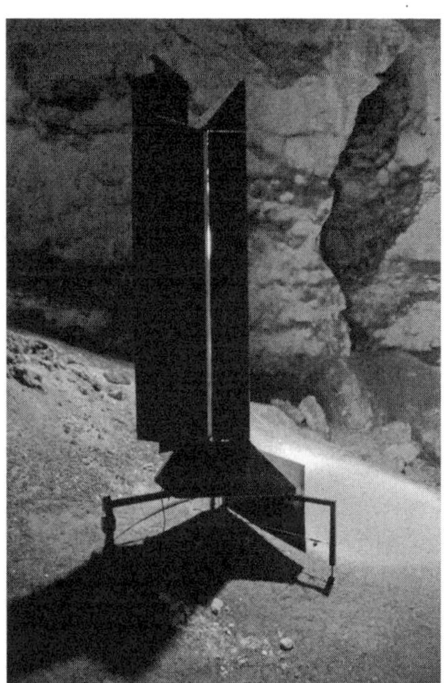
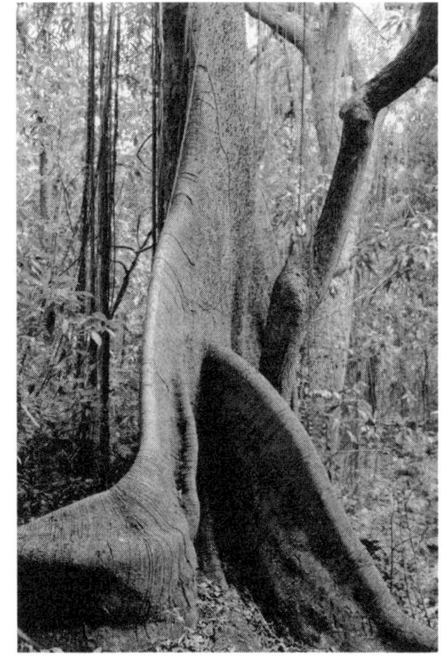
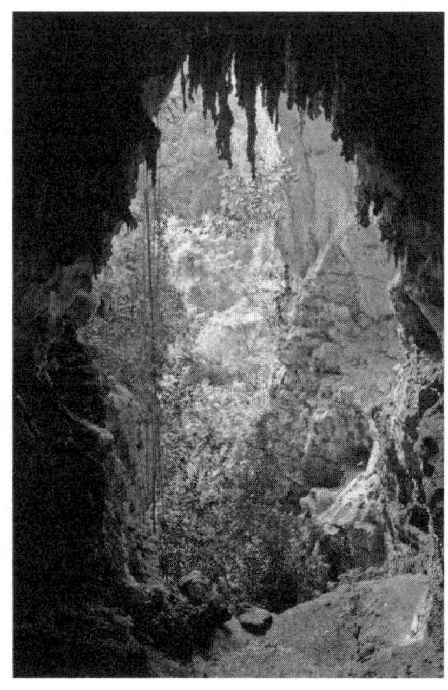

Puerto Rican Light (Cueva Vientos), a long-term, site-specific Dia Art Foundation commission in Puerto Rico, takes on the architectural trope of the cave and relocates Dan Flavin's 1965 light sculpture, *Puerto Rican Light (to Jeanie Blake)*, inside a 30-million-year-old porous and reverberating limestone cavern. The installation was on view for two years, from September 23, 2015, to January 31, 2018, inside one of the caves that are part of the subtropical cave system in the Convento Natural Park Protected Area in Guayanilla, one of the most impoverished and heavily polluted of Puerto Rico's municipalities due to the emissions of the nearby oil-based thermoelectric plants. As is characteristic of their practice, here, too, coloniality functions like a climate and atmosphere, a characteristic of the air that Puerto Rico breathes in and out, daily and without pause. The durational, transductive, and meditative experience of *Puerto Rican Light (Cueva Vientos)* requires that we understand this particular artwork as a resonant undertone or afterimage that runs through all of Allora & Calzadilla's production. It is one of their many constructed confluences and encounters, often premised on the very incongruity of their happening, artistic experiments that take the form of an unlikely coincidence in time and space.

A Taíno origin myth regarding the Cave of the Jagua (Cacibajagua) connects the beginnings of human life to the persistence of the past as a living organism. According to the pre-Columbian legend, the Taínos emerged from the cave to populate Puerto Rico but continued to acknowledge the presence of the dead ancestors that remained there, taking the form of bats, birds, and stones. In Zambrano's reflections on cats, animals, as well as other organisms, are the carriers of a memory that humans have lost long ago, the memory of a nonhuman intelligence that shelters and guards the dead. Europe's genocidal violence, as well as the attendant diseases carried by the Spanish colonizers, decimated the Taíno population in the Caribbean, but in the animism of the Cave of the Jagua, the dead metamorphose; they endure rather than simply disappear. The cave preserves a world not yet organized around antagonisms, between the living and dead or the victors and the defeated. Not simply an originary dwelling for humans and animals alike, the cave is a complex metabolism of expanded temporal scales and life forms—geological, prehistorical, biological—that overlap and coexist without harmonization. The architecture of the cave does not function as a space of enclosure and isolation but rather as the gateway into the resonant continuum of aggregated organisms and their sounds. It is an assemblage and a composition, instead of a static architectural structure or a calculable geometry.

Puerto Rican Light (Cueva Vientos) conflates several genealogies, ranging from the art historical to the decolonial and from the geological to the architectural, all of which function as a circuitry or undercurrent that powers a complex environment of light, sound, and allusion. Working beyond the legacies of American minimalism and land art, Allora & Calzadilla's compositional take on differential dynamics—among them, human, animal, mineral, political, ecological, geological—proposes an anachronic upheaval, a layered approach to temporality understood as geological matter. The entire assemblage is preceded and mediated by relations, scales, and resonances that expand well beyond the cave as a dense nexus of encounters and extensive mediations.

The piece also echoes the artists' own myth of origins: their continued interrogation of art historical legacies, their attention to the history of uneven exchanges between the United States and Puerto Rico, and their attunement to the sonic and political dimensions of the environments that are activated and in turn activate their work. A first intervention on Flavin's *Puerto Rican Light* was exhibited in the Americas Society in New York in 2003 and once again in the same year at the Tate Modern in London for a show entitled *Common Wealth.*[60] Allora & Calzadilla used solar panels in Puerto Rico to collect energy, which was then stored in a series of batteries, placed in a plywood crate, that traveled from San Juan to New York to power the fluorescent lightbulbs of *Puerto Rican Light (to Jeanie Blake)* for the duration of the exhibition.[61] Flavin's piece is invisibly transformed through an intervention into its energetic means of production, which are outsourced to a nonincorporated territory in ways that replicate the extractivism and debt economy that characterizes Puerto Rico's relation to the United States. Allora & Calzadilla complicate this colonial structure by mobilizing it through oscillation and suspension. Flavin's minimalist sculpture becomes the infrastructure, the support, for Allora & Calzadilla's operation, which in turn materializes and sustains its light source. It is an occupation of the light, the glow, the atmosphere, as an unfolding volume that exposes and implicates an exponentially larger geopolitical and even cosmic network — national, political, colonial, ecological, solar — disrupting the stability both of initiation and ownership (since sunlight is unlimited and "free"). As Yates McKee describes it, "Flavin's work requires various chemical and electrical systems, extending from the gas of the tubes, the gallery wiring, the city grid, power plants, resources fueling those power-generating machines, and ultimately, the feedback loops between the deep times of geology and biology through which organisms are compressed into fossil fuels ('buried sunshine,' in the parlance of the industrial revolution)."[62] The piece does not reduce light to an optical phenomenon. Instead, it enacts and performs its energetic refraction, its transductive capacity, to traverse and transform objects well beyond the notion of surface illumination.

It is worth noting here that Flavin's own naming of the piece, and particularly his dedication to the Puerto Rican art assistant Jeanie Blake, already speaks to the diasporic homesickness carried by an afterimage and its reflected glow to another affective modality of "buried sunshine." Blake had told Flavin that the colors of the sculpture reminded her of her native Puerto Rico and of the Puerto Rican Day parade in New York City. The longing of a Caribbean memory and its web of social and historical forces is already embedded in the original piece. The first glow of Flavin's sculpture shines, having already traveled across borrowed time and space, fully mediated by an invisible trace that the name of the piece only partially notates.

However, *Puerto Rican Light (Cueva Vientos)* is clearly not a simple iteration or relocation of Allora & Calzadilla's 2003 installation but a new work that builds on, intensifies, and complicates its conceptual premises, expanding the architectural boundaries of the earlier piece. Ironically, in *Cueva Vientos*, the two artists play a role that is closer to that of Flavin in their *Puerto Rican Light* as they retract their agency in favor of the complex material environment of the cave, reconfiguring the causal relationship between artist and artwork into the specifics of a material and compositional arrangement suffused with an enigmatic uncertainty they cannot fully control.

Puerto Rican Light (Cueva Vientos) could be likened to a slowly developing film apparatus that documents geological processes that we will not live long enough to see. And this because the temporality of these processes is no longer human but at once organic, chemical, and geological. This Puerto Rican cave itself becomes a "phenomenal" camera and darkroom that closes the gap between the production of a film and the film itself, collapsing one into the other, because the product is never fully detached from its process, just as matter is never fully detached from phenomena. The acoustic and visual environment of this subtropical cave enacts, and also deepens, Robert Smithson's imagined cinema because it presents us with the display of the heterogenous and changing components that, once they project and reverberate onto one another, allow this geological apparatus to unfold as a slowly developing film that, recording its own spectral becoming, the human eye cannot see.[63] The natural light that enters the cave from above interacts with the light of Flavin's sculpture, in turn powered by that same solar energy, creating a loop where the visible is fueled by the invisible and vice versa, rendering the distinction between the two inoperative.

Transporting Flavin's sculpture across temporalities and locations, the light of the sculpture itself becomes a form in transit, a mutable afterimage, an echo of another time and space. Literally, and thus ironically reminiscent of a minimalist strategy, reading

Flavin's acoustically inflected description of the piece as "a quiet cavern of muted glow," *Puerto Rican Light (Cueva Vientos)* reveals and amplifies the sonorous quality of the sculpture and adds a "cavernous" element to it.[64] The generators, powered, again, by Puerto Rican solar energy, emit a continuous hum, a single and vertical note, a B-flat. The note, which would hardly be noticeable in isolation and certainly remains more muted in a gallery setting, engages the reverberation and echoes of the cave's complex metabolism and polyphonic score: the flapping of the bats' wings, the buzzing of insects, the crawling of reptiles, the movements inside the guano mound on which the sculpture stands, the slow motions of geological fault lines. Amid these undercurrents of life, Flavin's technologically obsolete fluorescents speak of the evanescence of human history as an experience of finitude embedded in the extended flow and duration of other kinds of matter. The fluorescent sculpture becomes an archeological remnant of modernity, not unlike the abandoned copper, salt, and cement mines that Smithson wanted to turn into cinema caves[65] or the derelict sugar plants in the area surrounding Flavin's sculpture. Ontology, phenomenology, and an economy and culture that cannot be detached from its colonial violence go hand in hand in Allora & Calzadilla's cave apparatus as it enacts the coexistence of different but contiguous and refractional modalities of becoming that touch and affect one another.

The architect Frederick Kiesler had already described the architecture of the cave as a figure for the extensive relation between humans and their environment, as a long-forgotten prehistoric memory inscribed in human ethology and wrapped around the body in the form of the natural world—a kind of "magic architecture" that humans carry around like a cloak, incorporated and invisible, yet protective and nurturing.[66] Kiesler coined the term "correalism" to refer to the continuity between humans and their environment and to the recognition of architecture as a living organism that metabolizes the human experience of dwelling in the world. As he describes it:

> The cave is only a small detail of the world as a whole. It is its innermost cell. One by one the other layers of natural environment grow: trees, rocks, mountains, rivers, the ocean and the sky. They are all part of man's "shelter." They are the architectonics of the great structure of the seen and felt universe. They envelop one's body continuously. The intertwining growth of branches, lianas and leaves of the jungle shield him with endless caves of lattice-work; they form floors, walls and roofs; they are soft and elastic and yield to pressure.[67]

Kiesler's argument questions and expands the boundaries of the human body by integrating it fully within a much larger organism—an organism that keeps growing and expanding, moving from trees to the sky above them and beyond. The body here is not a separate entity but a nexus of relations. If the cave is another name for a human ethology based on a relation to the natural world in which it is integrated and that makes human life possible to begin with, for Allora & Calzadilla it also emerges as a reminder of a broken bond with nature. This broken bond, in turn, forever entangles the natural with the political and the biological with the sacrificial. Take, for instance, the pungent mound of bat guano onto which the Flavin has been perched. In the context of Puerto Rico's colonial history, the guano trade, which had originated in response to the exhaustion of European soil in the nineteenth century (itself an effect of what Marx calls a "metabolic rift" with nature), speaks to the extractivism of racial capitalism as much as to the inevitable chemical and biological transformation of matter. As we saw with *Raptor's Rapture*, Allora & Calzadilla continue to compound and implicate discourse and matter, historicity and natural processes, in their performative and dynamic unfolding of the cave as a site of encounters that expand well beyond its architecture.

Of these encounters, it is perhaps the one enacted by a colony of bats that inhabit Cueva Vientos that better materializes the complexity of the temporal, discursive, and ecological loops that spiral and cross over one another in Allora & Calzadilla's composition.

The El Convento Cave System is the home of a colony of ten thousand cave bats (*Brachyphylla cavernarum*), the largest colony in southern Puerto Rico. Their existence there is itself the result of another fortuitous encounter and transformation—one that involves gorges, caves, and hidden streams. While Guayanilla and Peñuelas are in Puerto Rico's most arid southern region, the effects of El Cedro Gorge, the perennial underground brook of Quebrada de los Cedros, and the Convento Cave System completely transform their surroundings with a combination of moisture and shade that provide a microhabitat for species not found anywhere else in the area. The rich fauna and flora of this delicate ecosystem, a limestone subtropical forest, include more than two-thirds of all the birds endemic to Puerto Rico—some of them, such as the Puerto Rican Nightjar (*Caprimulgus noctitherus*), are now an endangered species.[68] The selection of this cave among many others, based on the specifics of this particular site, has been carefully considered by Allora & Calzadilla, and to a large extent, part of the agency of the cave's environment has been delegated to the bat colony, whose sheer number of individuals upstage the artists' human intervention. After all, bats make up one-fifth of the mammals on earth, with a diversity of fourteen hundred species, and carry as much symbolic weight as wolves when it comes to their place in the human imagination, especially as relates to questions of mortality and spectral remnants and to the crossing of boundaries between the living and the dead.

One could say that these nocturnal animals are more than just collaborators for Allora & Calzadilla. In collaboration with insects, bacteria, and chemical reactions, they are the agents behind the guano mound that organizes the internal architecture of the cave and the organic "pedestal" that elevates the Flavin to an ironically monumental height. With the batting of their wings, they also control, to a very large extent, the temperature and atmosphere of the piece and are by far the most numerous and sustained audience for the piece. While human visitors may struggle with the darkness of the cave after the sun sets or be unable to perceive the various register of sounds that reverberate in the cavernous space, bats are uniquely equipped to interact with this strange relic of industrial capitalism and American minimalism that has landed in their midst. One could even say that bats are better suited than humans to experience the piece fully. Their ultrasonic calls bounce off the sculpture and echo back, and when comparing the outgoing pulse with the returning echoes, bats can gather precise information on their surroundings and the changes that take place in them. This process allows them to detect both prey and predators in darkness. The question is, to return to Herzog's reflections with which I began this section: Do these cave dwellers hear the sounds of Flavin's sculpture as evidence of a prey, a predator, or neither? Will they remember this strange artifact when it is gone?

This last question brings forth another one: Is it possible for the human visitor to determine precisely where *Puerto Rican Light (Cueva Vientos)* begins and even when it ends? In the shared environment of the cave, time and space unfold in topological shapes that do not correspond to any calculable geometry, measurable perimeter, or linear time frame. Like Chauvet or Lascaux, the work itself defies filmic and photographic capture and far exceeds optical perception.[69] The ebb and flow of its shifting atmosphere of light and sound suggests another kind of associated intelligence altogether, a slow but continued transformation of given and anthropomorphic spatial and temporal premises in favor of a continued topological unfolding. The spatial and temporal beginning and end of the artwork demand to be reconfigured, because fixed markers cannot contain the logic of expansion and incorporation that animates Allora & Calzadilla's composite environment—an environment in which they are partial agents alongside other partial agents. Recognizing that agency is always shared and inevitably compromised, never fully bound or concentrated in one single entity and never fully unfolded or even known, always changing, the artists engage in a modality of collaboration that is a fact of existence we barely acknowledge, trapped as we are in a human sovereignty over nature that diminishes us and our environment alike. In Allora & Calzadilla, the ethico-political must be both ethological and incalculable, not enclosed within the limits of the human individual. Only when economic, technological, social, and ecological forces are considered as reverberating, echoing, and traversing one another can we begin to join in a process of becoming in which we play a part, but never fully control. This form of activist artmaking relies on the multiplication and aggregation of diverse and partial agencies, each one of them multiplying and aggregating in turn. It might be that Marx's associated producers will thrive only when they include both the human and the nonhuman, the Me and the Not-Me.

Variation Two: The Bats Already Know You Are Coming

After driving though an arid landscape punctuated by abandoned sugar-processing plants, petrochemical complexes, and impoverished rural towns, you park the car and begin your hike. As you walk along the wide trail, you become engulfed by a cacophony of sounds, smells, colors; your skin feels the cool moisture of a lush and shady forest. You become more alert, aware of your body as your senses awaken in ways they are not used to, enveloped by the exuberance of life all around you. Yet you are a visitor and may not belong there at all. You see a boa wrapped around the branch of a tree, sleeping; vertical lines of lianas attached to the soil everywhere; birds singing with seemingly boundless energy; insects, frogs, and lizards share the path with you. You begin to feel you are approaching the cave even before you get there — a drop in sound and temperature, a quietness. The first things you notice as you step inside are the pungent smell of guano, the softness of the soil, your feet sinking and your imprints deep, the stalactites on the wall, the dust particles in the air, touched by light and reflecting it back. The atmosphere swerves. You notice a small aperture at the top of the cave and then the alien red glow of an incongruous object on top of a guano mound. You then begin to hear the vibration and humming of an electric generator. After a while, you notice many other, softer frequencies — coming from the walls, the soil, and even the cool breeze in the cave. Everything moves and breathes. Even the pile of guano seems to shift and creak ever so faintly. Nothing is quiet. A few bats begin to flap their wings, then all of them move at once, filling the air. It is feeding time. The temperature cools noticeably as they bat their wings. It then starts to rain, heavily, loudly. Everything darkens, and the sounds of the cave are drowned by the water falling outside. The cave is now a refuge for you, too. Time passes; you eventually leave. But do you? Once only a visitor, you are now the guardian of a memory, an afterimage, an undertone. You are part of the cave, and the cave is part of you.[70]

Napoleon's Elephants

We say monument, although it was only a rough model. But this model itself, a marvelous sketch, the grandiose skeleton of an idea of Napoleon's, which successive gusts of wind have carried away and thrown, on each occasion, still further from us, had become historical and had acquired a certain definiteness which contrasted with its provisional aspect. It was an elephant forty feet high, constructed of timber and masonry, bearing on its back a tower which resembled a house, formerly painted green by some dauber, and now painted black by heaven, the wind, and time. In this deserted and unprotected corner of the place, the broad brow of the colossus, his trunk, his tusks, his tower, his enormous crupper, his four feet, like columns produced, at night, under the starry heavens, a surprising and terrible form. It was a sort of symbol of popular force. It was sombre, mysterious, and immense. It was some mighty, visible phantom, one knew not what, standing erect beside the invisible spectre of the Bastille.

Few strangers visited this edifice, no passer-by looked at it. It was falling into ruins; every season the plaster which detached itself from its sides formed hideous wounds upon it. "The aediles," as the expression ran in elegant dialect, had forgotten it ever since 1814. There it stood in its corner, melancholy, sick, crumbling, surrounded by a rotten palisade, soiled continually by drunken coachmen; cracks meandered athwart its belly, a lath projected from its tail, tall grass flourished between its legs; and, as the level of the place had been rising all around it for a space of thirty years, by that slow and continuous movement which insensibly elevates the soil of large towns, it stood in a hollow, and it looked as though the ground were giving way beneath it. It was unclean, despised, repulsive, and superb, ugly in the eyes of the bourgeois, melancholy in the eyes of the thinker.

—Victor Hugo, *Les Misérables* (1862)

On March 23, 1798, two Sri Lankan elephants were brought to Paris as part of Napoleon's military loot, spoils of France's imperial wars. They had been captured in 1785 and donated to William V, Prince of Orange, by the Dutch United East India Company and then transported to The Hague. Once the Netherlands became a protectorate under the French Republic, the two elephants, one male and one female, were transported to Paris. The captive elephants became an immediate attraction for Parisian revolutionary crowds and even had poems dedicated to them. The citoyen Vignier, for instance, wrote in his *Epître aux éléphants de la ménagerie nationale* (Epistle to the elephants of the National Zoo):

> Vous que le citoyen admire en sa patrie
> Ma muse veut chanter votre rare industrie;
> Assez d'autres, jadis, prodiguèrent l'encens;
> Ils l'offrirent aux rois, je l'offre aux éléphants.
>
> You whom citizens of all lands admire
> My muse sings of your diligent ways;
> Many in the past offered gifts of incense;
> They offered it to kings, I offer it to the elephants.[71]

The poem invites a hierarchical upheaval and uses the elephants to inspire the republican and revolutionary values that had integrated the former Jardin du Roi and Ménagerie Royale de Versailles into the Muséum National d'Histoire Naturelle.[72]

That same year, on May 23, fourteen musicians from the Conservatoire, together with their flutes, bassoons, oboes, and violins, performed a concert in the Jardin des Plantes for the two pachyderms, Hanz and Marguerite. (Before being renamed upon arrival in France, the female elephant had been called Paraqui.) Among the pieces played were an air from Christoph Willibald Gluck's *Iphigénie en Tauride*, Pierre-Alexandre Monsigny's "O Ma Tendre Musette," an adagio from the opera *Dardanus*, and the Revolutionary anthem "Ça ira." This private concert for the two captive elephants was part of a speculative project in keeping with the Enlightenment's investment in the production of knowledge—an experiment organized by the scientists at the neighboring Muséum National d'Histoire Naturelle. The event was ostensibly devised to observe the animals' reaction to the music "in and of itself" as a nonlinguistic medium detached from representation or meaning. When the elephants swayed, became either agitated or calm, and moved and reacted in various ways to the music, they provided crucial proof of the emotional universality of the aesthetic, as well as of its ties to the natural world. The *Musical Record and Review* published a description of the animals' behavior during the performance. The journal wrote, "These effects, however wonderful they may appear, ought not to astonish us, if we but reflect that the passions of animals, like those of human beings, have naturally an absolute rhythmical character, totally independent of all education and custom."[73] Through a proto-Romantic and anthropomorphic reading of their movements, Napoleon's elephants were enlisted as scientific evidence in the debate over the problem of musical meaning. At a high point in the production of revolutionary political anthems—"La Marseillaise" would be composed at this time—Hanz and Marguerite became the bearers of a scientific and aesthetic universalism intent on limiting the political agency of music by naturalizing it. The very fact that the elephants were in Paris was already the aftereffect of a political revolution transformed into a colonial empire, but this was seen as nothing more than a minor detail in the context of the concert experiment.

The remains of these same elephants are now stored in a subterranean facility at the Zoothèque of the Muséum National d'Histoire Naturelle in Paris, together with thousands of other animal specimens. It is there that Allora & Calzadilla stage the encounter, itself a displaced reenactment of the eighteenth-century one, that structures their 2013 *Apotomē*. In the film, the American vocalist and composer Tim Storms sings a subsonic version of the music played in the Jardin de Plantes and addresses it to the skeletal remains of the two elephants.[74] His voice is recorded by extremely sensitive devices—the same devices used in the detection of earthquakes. The event is, once again, presented as a private concert for Hanz and Marguerite and for all the other animal remains that have multiplied and now constitute a veritable crowd living in a spectral and subterranean underworld.

The film begins and ends with medical imaging of Storm's thyroid gland, which takes the form of a strange butterfly, expanding and contracting with each breath. Before we see the elephant bones, we are given an eerie tour of the museum's extensive collection of taxidermy animals, each specimen carefully labeled. We see, among other animals, lions, leopards, panthers, seals, swordfish, zebras, horses, donkeys, bears, wolves, rhinoceroses, monkeys, and bats. All of them, positioned sometimes in groups that suggest families or packs, are presented in ferocious or predatory poses—the camera focuses on their teeth, claws, and glass eyes. As the film progresses and we move through this library of remains, with the film often cutting to close-ups of Storm's face, we arrive at a storage section containing bones and fragments of fossils. At this point, the musician begins to touch the bones, then to caress them, and finally to hold and carefully turn them in his hands—at one point, he holds a single hollowed vertebra as if to signal a missing link. One of the bones bears the name "Marguerite" inscribed on its surface. These remains carry the memory of life—after all, elephant's brains, the largest among mammals, store a prodigious memory.

The subsonic frequency of Storm's voice and of the musical notes it carries is so low that only animals as large as elephants can hear them. Nevertheless, because of the sophisticated recording technique used in the piece, viewers of the film in a gallery or museum experience his singing as involuntary reverberations in their bodies, as staccato or syncopated intervals that resonate in the stomach's flesh, very much as it does in large pachyderms or even whales. The linking mechanism between the notes, the hidden melody of the compositions, is missing, or more precisely, cannot be heard. The silences and guttural sounds echo the intimate sound that only

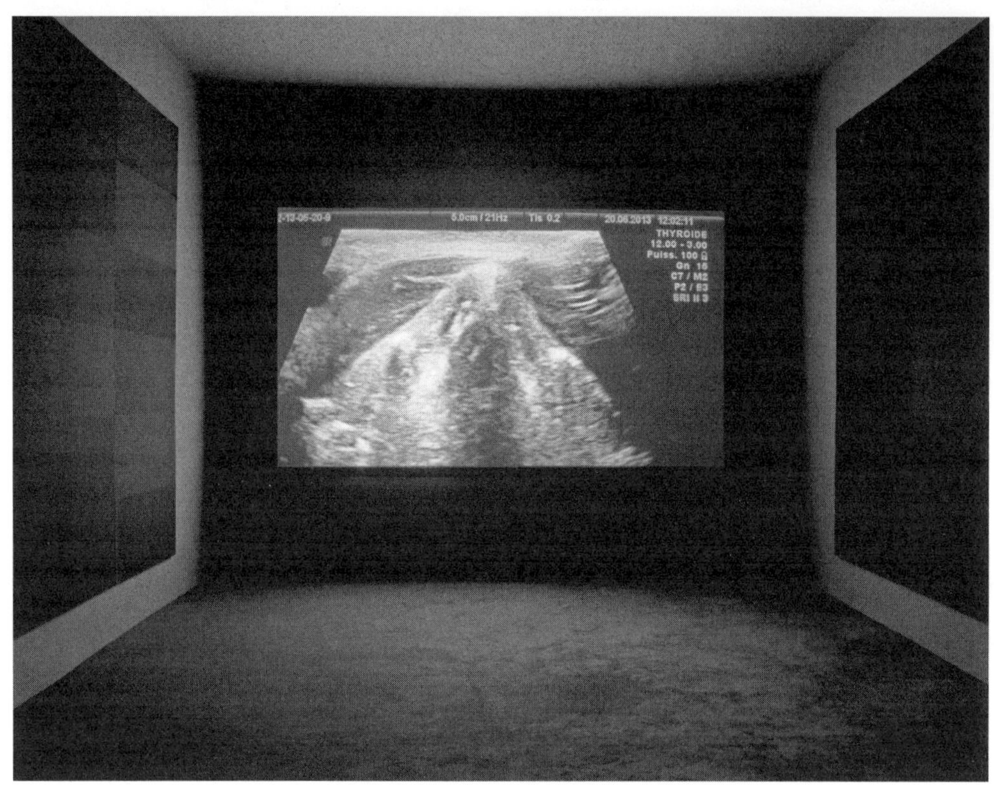

Allora & Calzadilla, *Apotomē*, 2013.
Exhibition documentation and video stills.
Courtesy of the artists.

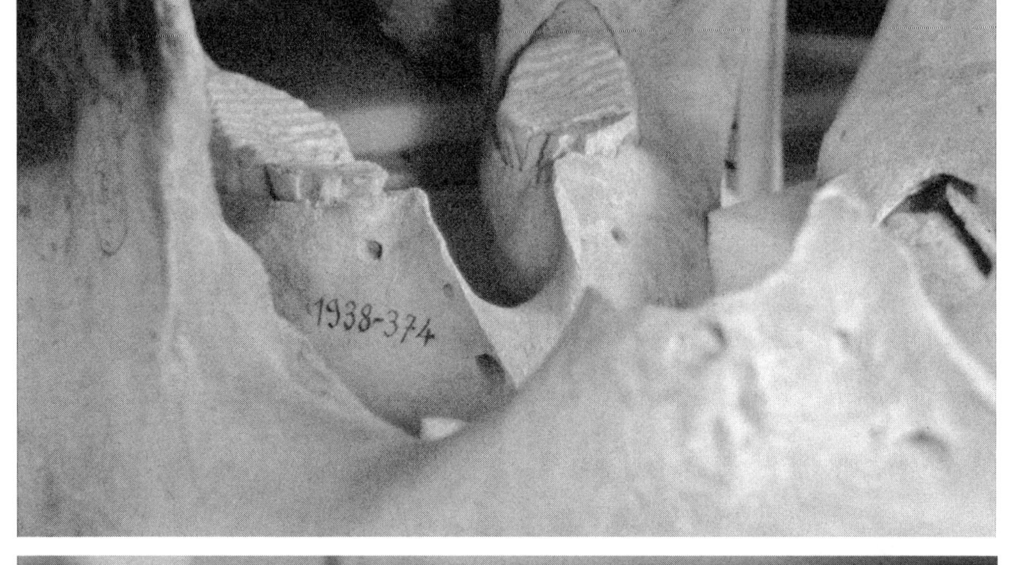
1938-374

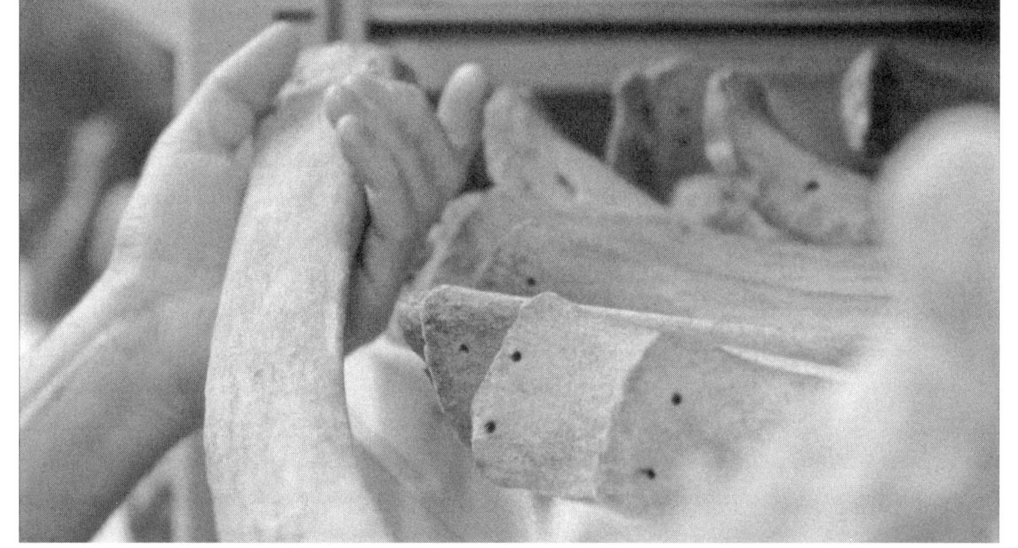

elephants would be capable of hearing in their bones, muscles, feet, and tympanum, if they were alive. But, in this instance, the encounter demonstrates that this reenacted experiment is even more speculative than the first, since, addressed to the remains of the two elephants, it is instead a performance of the impossibility of an encounter with them.

Allora & Calzadilla set up the scene only to dissolve its premises in the silence of a sealed basement. The missed encounter between Storm and the elephants is echoed in the fact that we are not privy to the sounds of the singer's voice. Our ears cannot hear them, but they still reach us as the silence of the animals' absence, as another version of their being, and again, as a reminder that all beings have a sound, that organisms do not cease to reverberate.[75] Storm's voice, the vibrations of his breath, touch us as they touch the bones of the two elephants. We remain acoustically suspended somewhere between the exteriority of the world as an unknown and the limitations of our finite bodies and minds, our limited hearing and our cognitive boundaries. In this way, Allora & Calzadilla refrain from synthesis or analogy in favor of the deferment of acoustic suspension, understood as contiguity, rather than continuity, by allowing contact and intimate proximity to take precedence over the narrative causalities that undergird the production of knowledge and meaning.

Filming the piece at a museum of natural history, a privileged locus for the Enlightenment's ideals, Allora & Calzadilla reanimate these philosophical and political speculations and calculations. However, rather than keeping *Apotomē* at the level of culture critique, the artists return to another form of calculus. The Greek term *apotomē* indicates the interval of a semitone in the Pythagorean scale, an exercise in arithmetical precision that refers to the remainder of a musical tone. Very much like Pythagoras's legendary fifth hammer, *apotoma* mark the gap between the sensible and the intelligible and here between the human and the nonhuman, between art and ethology. At the core of the piece, then, there is an impossibility: of ever fully hearing, of knowing, or of representing.

All we have is the break — and that is where Allora & Calzadilla choose to stay. Something remains immeasurable in the intervals of sound, forever escaping the calculus of measure — but with all the resilience and memory that Hanz's and Marguerite's bones encode as carriers of this second missed encounter.

Their bones indeed remain, but the twenty-four-meter Napoleonic monument of an elephant, a commemoration of military victories and colonial exploits that would be made from melted captured cannons, does not. Between 1813 and 1846, "The Elephant of the Bastille," a full-scale plaster and wood model for a bronze monument conceived in 1808, stood on the site of the former Bastille prison. As the trunk fell and the monument decayed, it was overgrown by plants and overrun by rats; it became a refuge for the homeless and for street children. When the crumbling monument was finally demolished, Hanz's taxidermy had been completed, and Marguerite had been carefully dissected by the renowned zoologist Georges Cuvier.[76] A Paris newspaper wrote: "*Marguerite*, the elephant of the Garden of Plants, at Paris has been dissected.... It is regretted by the baker, the green-grocer, and the hay-merchant, who supplied its food."[77] Not all of Napoleon's elephants were mourned in the same way.

Demolitions

> We are in a ship that necessarily will shipwreck.
> —Jan Patočka, *Plato and Europe* (1977)

> What is a bell? Is it a directly struck idiophone percussion instrument? A herald of the hour? A body, complete with shoulder, waist, mouth, lips, tongue? A call to prayer? If idiophone means, from Greek, "self-sounding," can idiophones also be tools for the collective?
> —JJJJJerome Ellis, *The Clearing* (2021)

In 2008, the Palast der Republik, an architectural icon of the German Democratic Republic, was demolished. The building had housed the Volkskammer and had been erected to replace the Stadtschloss, which had itself been demolished in 1950, after being partially damaged by Allied bombs during the Second World War. The decision to raze the baroque imperial palace was not without controversy. Despite the structural integrity of the building, the only section that was preserved was a portal of the balcony from which Karl Liebknecht had declared the Free Socialist Republic on March 8, 1918, during the German Revolution that followed the Spartacist uprising. The Stadtschloss carried enormous symbolic weight; it had been the residency of German emperors and kings of Prussia after the German unification in 1871 and it was an emblem of Prussian militarism. The Weimar Republic transformed it into a museum in 1918. The modernist building of the Palast der Republik was begun in 1973 and completed in 1976 and it hosted East Germany's parliament until 1990. It was also a multipurpose cultural center that included restaurants and a bowling alley and whose glass façade implied transparency.

On September 19, 1990, the building was sealed off to the public because of asbestos contamination. On October 2, East Germany's parliament was dissolved and the building fully vacated. Even though the asbestos had been removed, in November 2003, the Bundestag voted to demolish the Palast and reconstruct the former Stadtschloss. East Germans largely opposed and protested the decision, led by the Volkspalast (People's Palace) movement in an effort, once the dictatorial state apparatus of the GDR had collapsed, to salvage the communal project of socialism.

In February 2005, an art installation featured giant illuminated letters on the façade of the abandoned building, spelling the word *Zweifel* (doubt). It was a piece by artist Lars Ramberg entitled *Palast des Zweifels*, and it had been six years in the making. Demolition of the Palast started in 2006 and, after some delays, was completed in 2008. Construction of the Stadtschloss, mostly known now as the Berlin Palace, started in 2013 and was completed in 2020, with three sides of the building carefully replicating the original baroque façade. The building opened to the public in 2021 as part of the Humboldt Forum.

Allora & Calzadilla's *How to Appear Invisible* was filmed at the end of 2008, during the final days of the dismantling of the GDR's Palast. The historic density of the site, a baroque serialization of erasures and reinscriptions, appears here with the impersonal force of bulldozers, cranes, diggers, saws, and hammers. Among the rubble, noise, and muddy terrain, we sporadically see isolated workers, miniaturized by the scale of the demolition site. At times, a crane appears as a strange mechanical insect, perhaps a humorous take on René Descartes's "animal machine," delicately nibbling at the tall cement building. Splatters of mud are a reminder that history is not a solid foundation, but a soft, porous surface traversed by multiple tracks that overlay and cross over one another.[78] The crumbly cement and the dust that spreads over the terrain further suggests that this rather desolate landscape is moving and that the ground is shifting. Berlin is presented here as a no-man's land, but

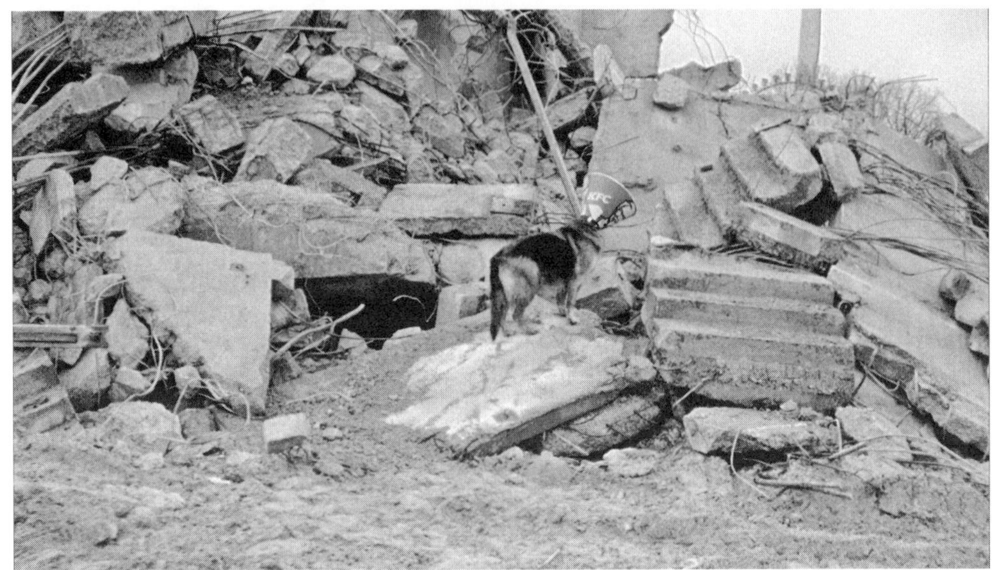

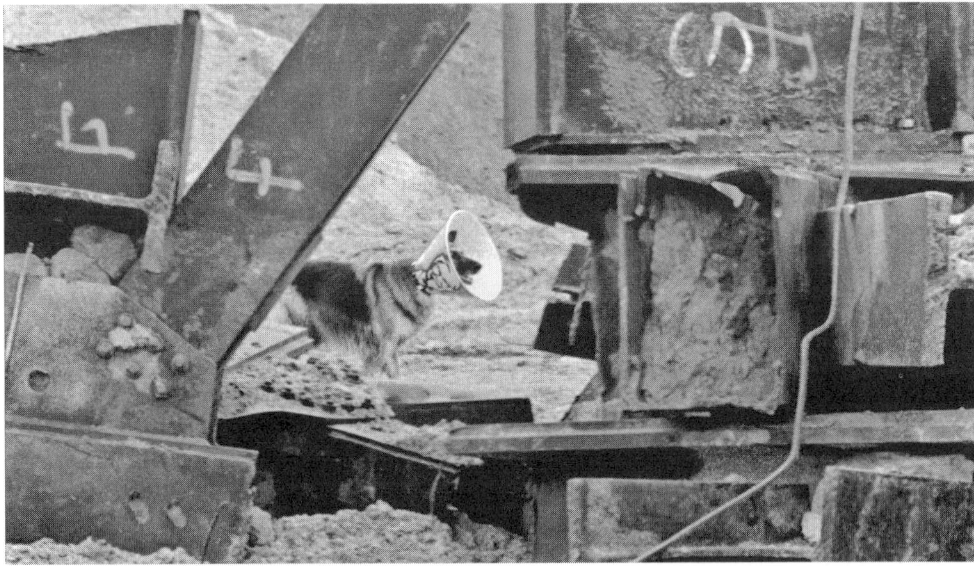

Allora & Calzadilla, *How to Appear Invisible*, 2008. Video stills. Courtesy of the artists.

one whose future has been carefully mapped out, carefully calculated for effective consumption and symbolization. These are, after all, the trenches of real-estate speculation that will overtake the city, complicit with the rewriting of national narratives—indeed, fully intertwined with them and revealing once more the solidity of their alliance. In the film, the hollow shell of the demolished building behaves like a gigantic and eerie wind instrument, animated by the ghost of a past, by the invisibility of historical memory and its layered erasures. A graffitied phrase, "Ulbrist was here," is the one lonely inscription that reminds us of the former human occupation of the site.

After we see brief traces of red paint on the gray cement wall, a German shepherd appears. The dog's head is shielded by a large red cone, a kind of Elizabethan collar—the cone-shaped device use to prevent dogs from licking wounds or stitches—made from a bucket of Kentucky Fried Chicken, with its franchise logo, Colonel Sanders's face, clearly visible on its surface. While we never see the dog's face—like much in the film, its appearance speaks about invisibility—the bearded face in plantation attire that we do see encrypts globalized racial capitalism, brutal industrial farming practices, and unfair labor practices amid what will be a sumptuous monument to cultural consumption. The conspicuous vulgarity of the KFC logo, an acronym that echoes the GDR but also the USA, is not casual. It is a reminder of the economic and social inequalities hiding in plain sight, sealed within the grandeur of high culture and its own franchising.

The German shepherd prowls the site like a wolf, or maybe a guide dog, somewhat incongruous in a desolate urban landscape surrounded by baroque imperial architecture, monuments, and tourist attractions.[79] In the mostly muted gray surroundings, red will remain the only distinctive color in the film. But this red, caught in an ideological no man's land, is not only shared by state Communism and KFC, but also encapsulates the transit between socialism and capitalism enacted by the demolition. Amid the

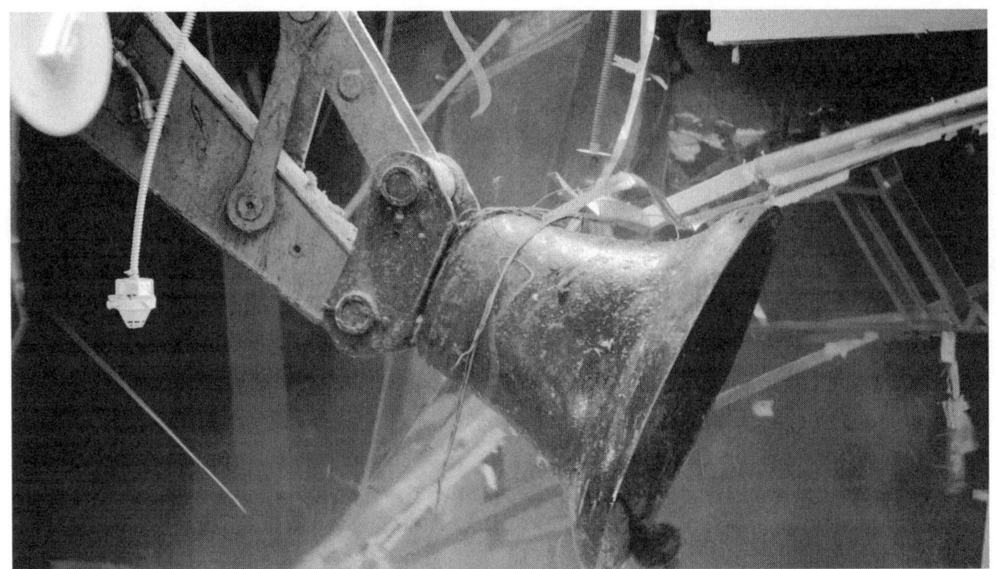

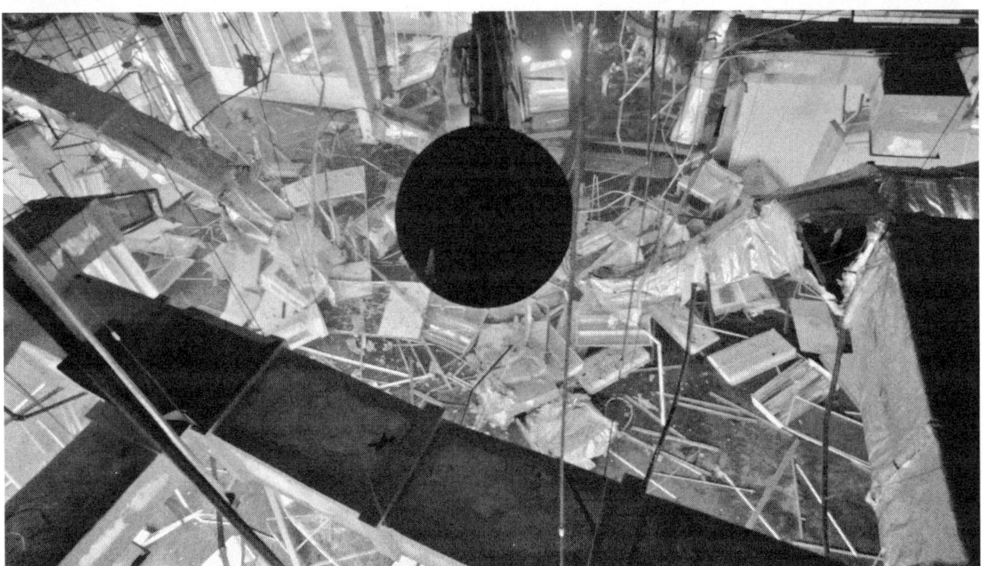

Allora & Calzadilla, *The Bell, the Digger, and the Tropical Pharmacy*, 2014.
Video stills. Courtesy of the artists.

bulldozers and cranes that continue to dismantle Berlin's socialist past, the doubly marked dog takes over the film's itinerary. From now on, he is our guide. He wanders around, searching, resting, and mostly smelling the grounds. Out of this composite site, an iconic and ever-changing landscape, a performative monument of a European history, past and present, slowly emerges. It monumentalizes Europe as a demolition site—one that Europe has for centuries continued to multiply and expand beyond its borders.[80]

While the dog is our guide in this strange itinerary through history as demolition, there seems to be no direction to his movements. What are we to make of the animal's wandering? In this instance, the dog, supplemented by Colonel Sanders's hardly veiled neocolonial enterprise, reverses the Deutsche Grammophon and later RCA logo of a dog looking into a phonograph's conical horn.[81] In a hybrid assemblage with the KFC cone, he also appears as a silent bell, sounding the double invisibility of a forgotten history contained in the soil of a no-man's land in the dead center of Europe.

Six years later, in 2014, Allora & Calzadilla return to another demolition site with *The Bell, the Digger, and the Tropical Pharmacy.* This time, we witness the relentless production of colonial rubble. A construction digger has been modified so that the scooper is now a cast-iron bell.[82] Inside the now closed, but still fully equipped GlaxoSmithKline plant in Cidra in central Puerto Rico, the digger relentlessly proceeds to break windows, dropped ceilings, tables, equipment, walls, electrical installations, and laboratories.[83] The noise of this destruction becomes the score of this violent contact. The entire building shakes, animated by the force of a manufactured earthquake, tornado, or hurricane. Indeed, the broken glass, shattered walls, and hanging and exposed tangles of electrical wires register as the aftermath of a natural disaster. The traces of human labor—lipstick, perfume, lockers, shoes, showers, office chairs, or writing on the glass window—suggest a hasty and unexpected departure. Throughout the building, we see overflowing water from open faucets, and the multiple blinking light sources no longer serve any purpose. Because water and electricity are at the core of Puerto Rico's energy dependency, water restrictions and blackouts are a common occurrence. Here we see them wasted with abandon and even with violence. As the bell digger continues its journey, interspaced with shots of empty laboratories, showers, locker rooms, and decontamination devices that go in and out focus, becoming abstract in the process, the bells seem to multiply. As the fragments of debris become themselves pendants, they behave like bells and perhaps pendulums or clocks that call more and more bells into existence, producing both a scattering and a gathering of sound, a clamor and a protest. By the end of the film, the bell becomes a hammer that pounds the floor with a performative violence that calls out the much more insidious and relentless colonial violence that has subjugated Puerto Rico for centuries. This, too, is Europe as a demolition site.

Beethoven's Carcass

Chaos is come again.
—*Quarterly Musical Magazine and Review* (1825)

Benjamin speaks of song, which may possibly rescue the language of birds as visual art rescues that of things. But this seems to me the achievement of *instruments* much rather than of song; for instruments are far more like the voices of birds than are human voices. The instrument *is* animation.
—Theodor W. Adorno, *Beethoven: The Philosophy of Music* (1998)

By the end of the Napoleonic Wars, citizens of Vienna had witnessed peace treaties, renewed fighting, and the hardships of occupation—all within a public sphere closely policed by the state. Music echoed this complex and mutable political culture.
—Nicholas Mathew, *Political Beethoven* (2013)

On the main gallery floor of the Fundació Antoni Tàpies, below a balconied mezzanine, at the center of an exhibition conceived as a polyphonic score or ensemble, stands a Bechstein piano with a precise circular hole cut into it.[84] Standing inside the hole, Luca Ieracitano is playing the "Ode to Joy" from Beethoven's Ninth Symphony, reaching over the front to access the keyboard and pushing the piano around the exhibition space from within the instrument. The acoustic itinerary of the 2018 Barcelona show is articulated around the possibilities opened by this void. The full title of Allora & Calzadilla's 2007 piece, *Stop, Repair, Prepare: Variations on "Ode to Joy" for a Prepared Piano*, harks back to Cage's prepared pianos and experiments in noise and music integration, as well as to Gordon Matta-Clark's negative architectural spaces; it mobilizes the legacies

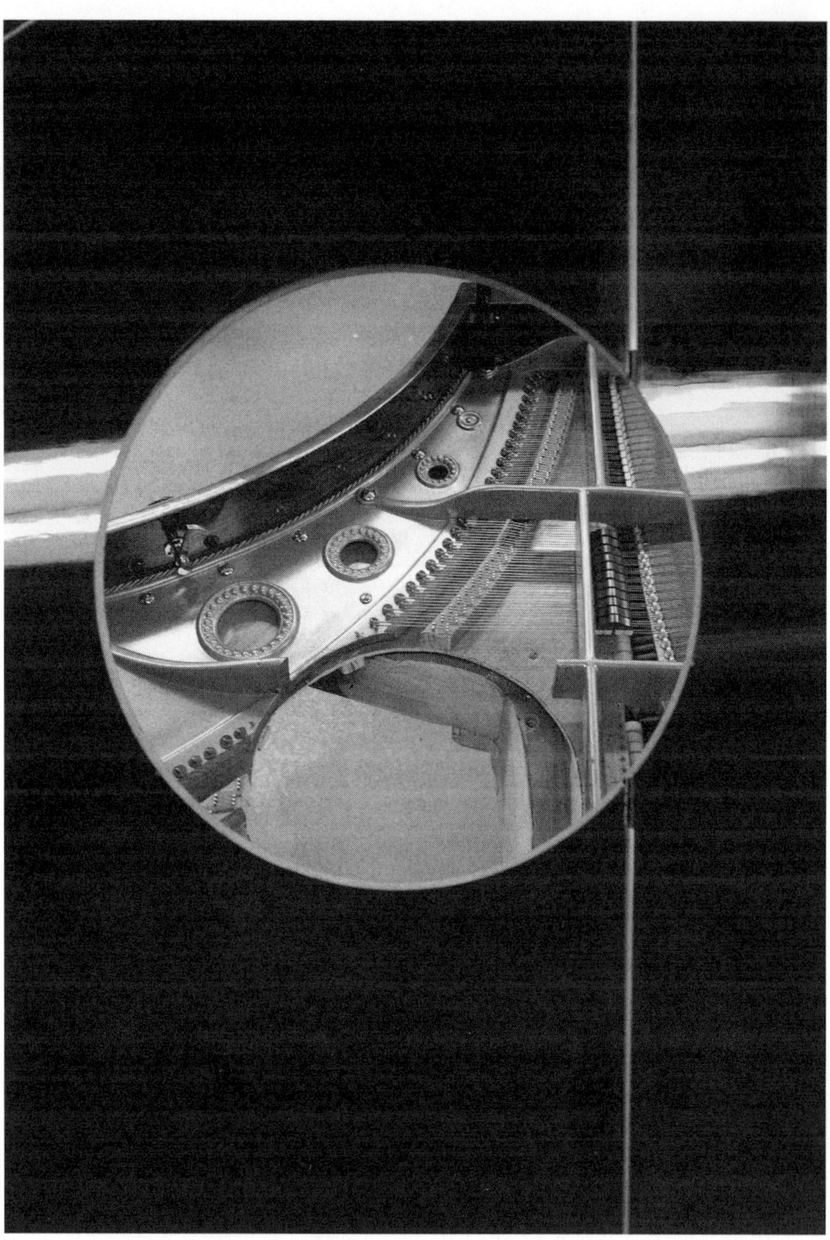

Allora & Calzadilla, *Stop, Repair, Prepare: Variations on "Ode to Joy" for a Prepared Piano*, 2007. Exhibition documentation. Courtesy of the artists.

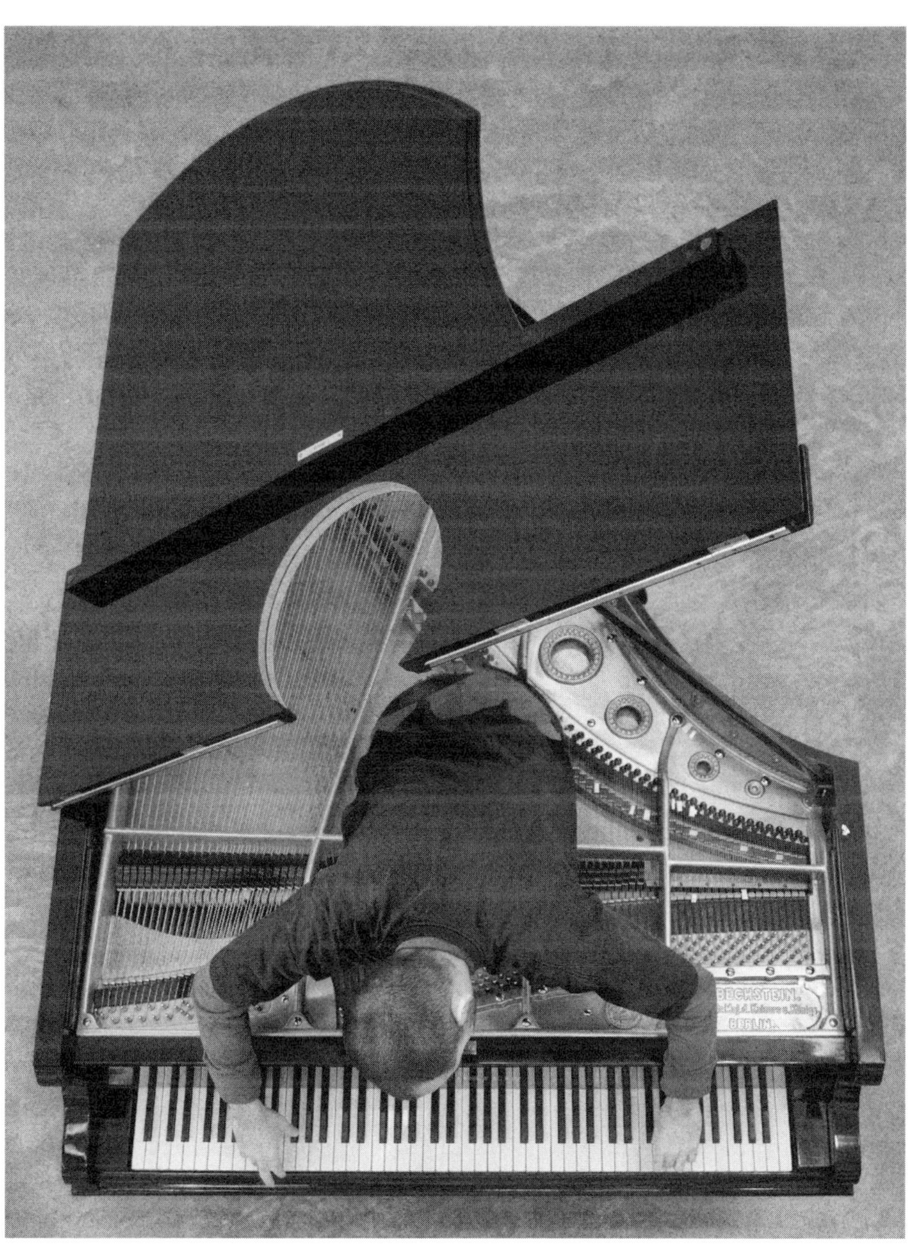
BECHSTEIN.
BERLIN.

of a canonical avant-garde as much as it does Beethoven's musical heritage. For a Barcelona audience, the prepared pianos of Santos and Portabella's *Die Stille vor Bach* also come to mind, creating an even richer and more layered set of historico-political associations through the inevitable complicity and dependency of the musical on the material conditions of the nonmusical. It is also a reflection on music's relationship to the strife and violence of cultural, political, and economic value systems.[85]

The first performance of Allora & Calzadilla's piece in Die Haus der Kunst, as well as the publication that accompanied it, references—as does Portabella's film—the crisis that engulfed Europe after French and Dutch citizens voted "no" to the drafting of a European constitution in a 2005 referendum. Spain had voted "yes" by a large margin earlier the same year. The French vote, and the Dutch vote only three days later, put an end to the transnational constitutional project and emphasized, among other things: the EU as a cultural, economic, and political model; the role and strength of national sovereignties; the nonexistence of a social Europe; inequality within the Eurozone; older EU members versus new post-Communist members; worker's rights and social welfare; immigration, isolationism, and racism; and, more generally, the logic of the referendum as a democratic tool. The fact that France, perceived as culturally central to Europe, cast an ostensibly Euroskeptic vote challenged the elite bureaucratic consensus that a "yes" was the expression of a fragile and somewhat vacuous predetermined European harmony. Eventually, another more complex and slippery reading began to emerge: the "no" was polysemic, dissonant, and a chaotic protest, and because of this, it expressed more accurately than a "yes" would the fraught realities of a collective that still largely depends on an obsolete, hollow, and largely depoliticized cultural myth.[86] This refusal, in other words, was a very loud howl.

Allora & Calzadilla's piece is entirely mediated by their reading of Slavoj Žižek's 2006 essay "Against the Populist Temptation," an influential critical analysis of the European referendum that ends with an interpretation of the last movement of Beethoven's Ninth. As the Slovenian philosopher puts it, the French-Dutch response to the referendum calls out its whole premise as a false choice. He suggests that rather than feel threatened by the outcome, if "Europe is to redeem itself, it should, on the contrary, be ready to take the risk of losing (in the sense of radically questioning) both . . . the fetish of scientific-technological progress" and "its reliance upon the superiority of its cultural heritage."[87] Both the contradictions and the violence contained in the "Ode" as "the unofficial anthem of the European Union" are similarly reconciled in a populist, rather than popular, European kitsch, so they can no longer be heard: "What if we got all too used to it as a symbol of joyful brotherhood? What if we should confront it anew, reject in it what is false?"[88] Allora & Calzadilla take on the final part of the essay as part of the research apparatus for their piece and even reprint a version of it in the Haus der Kunst publication, which illustrates with photographic materials each one of the examples Žižek gives of the ideological use of the "Ode to Joy" as a postpolitical empty signifier. I quote the passage of the essay that lists the heterogeneous appropriations of Beethoven's Ninth in full: it is

> a true empty signifier that can stand for anything. In France, it was elevated by Romain Rolland into a humanist ode to the brotherhood of all people ("the Marseillaise of humanity"); in 1938, it was performed as the highpoint of *Reichsmusiktage* and also for Hitler's birthday; during the Cultural Revolution in China, in the atmosphere of rejecting European classics, it was redeemed as a piece of progressive class struggle; and in today's Japan it has achieved cult status, being woven into the very social fabric with its alleged message of joy through suffering. Until the 1970s, or during the time when both West and East German Olympic teams had to perform together as one German team, "Ode to Joy" was played during the presentation of Germany's gold medal, and, simultaneously, the Rhodesian white supremacist regime of Ian Smith, which proclaimed independence in the late 1960s in order to maintain apartheid, also proclaimed the same song its national

> anthem. Even Abimael Guzman, the (now imprisoned) leader of the *Sendero Luminoso*, when asked what music he loved, mentioned the fourth movement of Beethoven's Ninth. So we can easily imagine a fictional performance at which all sworn enemies, from Hitler to Stalin, from Bush to Saddam, for a moment forget their adversities and participate in the same magic moment of ecstatic brotherhood.[89]

The composition itself, popularized as an anthem through decontextualized quotation, a kind of surgical extirpation not unlike Allora & Calzadilla's circular cut, carries with it a jarring litany of political instrumentalization and ideological projection.[90] Žižek is quick to point out that Beethoven's use of the Turkish march (*marcia Turca*) complicates a unified and self-identical reading of the piece through countermovement, negativity, and critique. While Allora & Calzadilla amplify the instrumentalization of the "Ode to Joy" by performing their piece for the first time at Die Haus Der Kunst, a building inaugurated in 1933 to exhibit Nazi propaganda art and at the time known as the Haus der Deutschen Kunst, with a musical program that also included Beethoven's composition, they, too, call attention to the music's internal dissonance. They mobilize this cultural fetishism as a serialization of erasures while reactivating the memory inscribed in locations that are simultaneously symbolic and material, reminding us that dissonance is always relational. Situatedness embodies a violent history by "staying in place" and refusing decontextualization and universalization. On a more conceptual level, Allora & Calzadilla materialize the negative and critical content in Beethoven's music by fabricating a negative space in the center of his iconic instrument.

When the artists present the performance in Barcelona months after the violently repressed nonbinding referendum on Catalan independence[91] and in the aftermath of hurricanes Irma and María in Puerto Rico,[92] their prepared piano resonates with the plight of collectives that have remained unheard. Puerto Rico and Catalonia's appeals, respectively, to the United States, the Federal

Emergency Management Agency, and the European Union Parliament—as institutions that would protect Puerto Ricans from social and economic devastation and Catalans from political violence in Europe—have been largely ignored. Rather than reproduce the kitsch of the "Ode to Joy" as a failed listening, however, Allora & Calzadilla intensify the internal caesuras in the music through a surgical cut in the body politic of the piece that transforms the center of the piano, the interiority of a Romantic conception of the self, into an echoic hole where the polysemy and polyphony of Beethoven's music is accumulated and multiplied rather than erased—into a site, that is, constantly occupied by the nonmusical. The proliferation of resonances, overwhelmingly violent and conflicted, calls other resonances into being, in this way enacting the real movement of the piece. After all, the guilt nexus of Western music is fully traversed by Indigenous genocide, the Middle Passage, violence against women, and the accumulation of holocausts. Colonial and aesthetic networks travel the same paths. Yet if sound is a multitude, it is an incomplete one. Something or someone will always be missing because the movements and metamorphoses of history do not pause or stop; they persist in their unfolding in time and space.

Allora & Calzadilla also call attention to the material networks, collaborations, and technological infrastructures that make the emergence of "classical" musical media possible to begin with. What Lydia Goehr has called the "Beethoven paradigm," which is the theatrical performance of the lonely creative mind, comes with a hidden assembly, a collaborative structure without which it could not take place.[93] The secular liturgy of the concert hall and its museumification, the chronometric control of the orchestra, and the stabilization of scores through increasingly precise notation are, among many others, the producers and guarantors of musical value and cultural capital. The material networks of colonial global capitalism and musicology emerge simultaneously. Beethoven may have been one of its earlier beneficiaries, at a cost that became apparent only in his posthumous reception. Ownership and authorship are inextricable in nineteenth-century colonial capitalism, and in Beethoven's Vienna, inextricable from war and military occupation.[94] Warlike music, revolutionary and counter-revolutionary patriotic songs, military marches, obsequious occasional compositions, such as Beethoven's *Der glorreiche Augenblick* (one of the composer's homages to masculinist military "heroes" such as Arthur Wellington and Napoleon Bonaparte), are everywhere. It is a music traversed by the experience of war, siege, and profound political instability and violence. We could even say that Beethoven naturalizes and musically formalizes the experience of history as an intermittent war and as the site of political strife. Music, history, and ideology coalesce in wartime compositions. Behind the trope of war there is actual war.

The percussive and militaristic overtones of the "Ode to Joy" are contained in the composition itself in the form of a Turkish march, which the composer also uses in his 1813 *Wellington's Victory*, and are, oddly, followed by a quasi-religious choral passage.[95] Beethoven was not the only European composer to include "orientalizing" military marches in his compositions (Haydn and Mozart had done so, too). However, that his appropriation of Turkish Janissary music has—oddly, perhaps, but also appropriately—come to represent Europe as a distinct cultural entity contingent on defending its borders against Asia and Africa is, as Žižek points out, more than a bit perplexing. Turkish marches were so popular in the nineteenth century that piano manufacturers produced versions of the instrument with a Janissary stop, a pedal that, when pressed, would strike a bell or a padded hammer (and sometimes both) that then sounded like a bass drum or a cymbal. These pianos could have up to six pedals, and their goal was to mimic the cacophonous sounds of a Turkish military band. By the time Beethoven writes his Ninth Symphony, Turkish marches have become outmoded, and his inclusion of them appears as an anachronism, one that he further intensifies in the final choral section. He continued to experiment with piano pedals throughout his entire life, and he owned several pianos with technologically innovative pedal configurations and added resonators that transformed the instrument into a vibrating organism he could sense with his entire body. As his deafness progressed, Beethoven's piano modifications became essential for the continuity of his work. We could even say not that Beethoven never heard his Ninth Symphony, but rather that he heard it differently, through his muscles and bones. It is the rest of us who have never heard the "Ode to Joy" as he did.

Beethoven's use of the piano as a technology and of the orchestra as a media platform, both key modes of reproduction for the emergent bourgeoisie as it defined its cultural values and aspirations, cannot be separated from either colonial capitalism or the multitemporality of an incipient globalization. It is worth noting that Beethoven is a contemporary of Black sorrow songs and of abolitionist hymns. The increased privatization of musical instruments and racial capitalism belong to a capitalist mode of production intent on producing a cultural value that will be exported worldwide as a universal equivalent. One of the greatest victories of capitalism may have been to make art safe, to tame the wolf that always lies within it.

However, the last movement of Beethoven's symphony refuses to unify fully its different voices. In 1868, several years after the end of the American Civil War and the beginning of Reconstruction, an American reviewer wrote that the finale of Beethoven's Ninth "appeared to be made up of the strange, the ludicrous, the abrupt, the ferocious, and the screechy, with the slightest possible admixture, here and there, of an intelligible melody. . . . The general impression it left on me is that of a concert made up of Indian war-whoops and angry wildcats."[96] The racism of the passage is revealing. The puzzlement and even anger at the absence of a unified monolingual and harmonic subject, at the absence of reconciliation, underscores the reviewer's discomfort with the polyphonic clamor of the composition and with the polysemy of its sounds.

This Beethoven is too historical and too political, and above all too enigmatic, for the bourgeois concert halls that will transform him into a monument.

By the nineteenth century, classical music had exposed "the limits of the representative mode of production long before they appeared in [the] material production" of his time.[97] Beethoven provides the bourgeoisie with an expressive realization of their limited realities and their failed revolutionary aspirations that anticipates both their historical realization as well as the possibility of their utter failure. What Daniel Chua, borrowing from Wagner, denotes the sonic regime of "absolute music" calls for the effacement of the extramusical, the *Umwelt* from which music emerges.[98] It is, above all, an attempt to hide the violence and the failures of European history. It is a dysphoric gesture that extirpates history in order to survive as myth—a kind of musical negative theology. It is abstraction as the subtraction of history's material conditions, as an attempt to control the polysemy of sound, which is entirely contextual and social and always the product of an encounter and a relation.

When Allora & Calzadilla cut a gaping hole in the body of the instrument, two octaves remain inoperative, and Beethoven's "Ode to Joy" sounds unfamiliar and broken. The music's oscillation between military authoritarianism and an explosive and revolutionary freedom is more audible than ever. Emphasizing the dissonances contained in the music itself, which did not escape Beethoven's contemporaries, Allora & Calzadilla make it harder for him to represent a universalist Europe that continues to be at pains to suture a shattered social contract, supposing there was ever one, and to hide consecutive rounds of social and political discontent. Disordering Beethoven and recovering his violent musical informality, returning his myth to historical contingency, Allora & Calzadilla counter a reified and rarified cultural monumentalization that, echoing Europe's own cultural and political stasis, hides its accumulation of violence.

The body of the pianist is contained, or maybe trapped, by this hole—as if it were a suit of armor or some strange and cumbersome prosthetic — as he pushes the instrument around the room while playing it in reverse. The effort and skill, even discomfort, demanded by the performance is an essential component of the moving sculpture and proposes an unlearning of a European musical legacy that we can no longer hear because it has ossified by refusing to acknowledge the violence that made it possible. Here, the musician is similarly bounded and constrained, but the music is not. The pianist and his audience are restrained by the memory of a tune everyone knows, and this memory, a memory that interferes with listening to the performance, acts as an analogue to an unchosen and unexamined inheritance. Furthermore, the performers must not only be highly skilled musicians, but more importantly, willing to undergo a process of unlearning that may very well affect their technique more generally. Playing "improperly" is also playing outside the logic of culture as ownership. The piano, a mechanically mediated musical voice that does not need to breathe, is here transformed into a hybrid, maybe monstrous object that walks on six legs — four wheeled wooden ones and two human ones — and that requires the audible breathlessness of a body that plays while pushing a heavy ensemble of wood, hammers, and strings in a free and unpredictable itinerary through the gallery space that accompanies this now also unpredictable music. We witness the reanimation of a carcass grafted with the human body, now a modified organism.[99]

However, the text of the "Ode to Joy" itself is already a kind of graft, the place where Beethoven, Friedrich Schiller, and Immanuel Kant overlap uncomfortably and then leap into a fugue, a passage that is already polyphonic, an aftereffect of the transit among different languages and media, including poetry, philosophy, and music. For his choral finale, Beethoven uses a fragment of an 1805 revision of Schiller's "An die Freude" (originally written in 1785). In the last verse of the choral section, Schiller's modified quotation from Kant reads: "Seek him above the starry canopy. / Above the stars he must live," moving the entire piece in the direction of the inhuman and the supersensible. The music, at this point, joins in, belying any notion of a recognizable, existing human collective. But the most poignant proviso appears a few bars earlier with the lines: "But let the man who knows nothing of this / Steal away alone and in sorrow." What we encounter here again is another false choice since those "who steal away alone and in sorrow" either refuse to join a global brotherhood structured around a logic of domination and sacrificial history (and therefore choose to be exiled as the vanquished of this community) or they refuse the logic of domination and sacrificial history itself, again becoming, with scarcely any difference, vanquished in terms of that logic. In the context of nineteenth-century Europe's fight for imperial ascendancy, these words suggest a historically marked exclusion, a border that keeps the non-European at bay. The excluded here are those who will indeed compose their own sorrow songs and inscribe their refusal into a fugitive musical form that defies both capture and forgetting by integrating into them the diasporic rhythms of Africa, the Caribbean, and the Middle East.

The "poet of freedom," Schiller is as mythical as the "heroic Beethoven" and appears to be equally conflicted; like the music that accompanies it, his poem is anything but conciliatory. It is a force field of contradictions. Encouraging us to listen to the "Ode to Joy" anew — to hear in it an ever-shifting assemblage of voices, united only in their disharmony — Allora & Calzadilla's surgical cut appears as a labor of "repair" and animation, a restitution of opacity and dissonance. In their hands, Beethoven still howls, but with a voice that is not entirely his own, if it ever was. Their negative circular void proves to be a force of inclusion for those who have been excluded, operating beyond the sovereignty of a European identity that remains bound to its sacrificial history.

THIRD INTERLUDE

The Talking Knee

He who seeks to approach his own buried past must conduct himself like a man digging. Above all, he must not be afraid to return again and again to the same matter; to scatter it as one scatters earth, to turn it over as one turns over soil. For the "matter itself" is no more than the strata which yield their long-sought secrets only to the most meticulous investigation. That is to say, they yield those images that, severed from all earlier associations, reside as treasures in the sober rooms of our later insights — like torsos in a collector's gallery. It is undoubtedly useful to plan excavations methodically.
— Walter Benjamin, "Excavation and Memory" (ca. 1932)

I must clear up, once and for all, a fundamental error: that we dead are somehow dead. We are full of protest and energy. Who wants to die? We speed through history, examining it. How can I escape the history that will kill us all?
— Alexander Kluge, "The Talking Knee," (1979)

Shards of history and images of sedimentation, demolition, and rubble permeate Alexander Kluge's multimedia critical approach to Germany's national narrative. Combining film, documentary, video, television, critical theory, literary fiction, and music, Kluge produces a counterhistory in which the past is presented as opaque and foreign, torn from a context that lies forgotten and buried in the soil. He turns cinema into a time machine.[1] The sheer proliferation of all the different worlds that can be experienced within cinema—and its archival capacities to retain fleeting traces of these several worlds—account for the literalization and anonymization that take place in Kluge's filmic experiments, each of which engages in a reparative democratization of history that casts light on a series of procedures that he shares with Portabella and Allora & Calzadilla. We need only turn to Kluge's 1979 *Die Patriotin* (*The Patriot*) to see how the cinematic literalization and materialization of abstract philosophical concepts—together with the anonymization, collectivization, and estrangement of a cultural tradition—can be used as a means of creative critique and reassembly. In the film, Kluge transforms historical information into a sensorium by staging what it might mean to make history a part of oneself, even literally to grasp or digest it.[2]

Die Patriotin returns to a fictional character, Gabi Teichert (played by Kluge's longtime collaborator, the stage actor Hannelore Hoger), who first appeared in the collective 1978 film *Deutschland im Herbst* (Germany in autumn).[3] The "patriot" in the title refers to a committed, searching, often perplexed history teacher who has assumed the formidable task of finding the raw materials for a history that will no longer be one of victors and vanquished or scripted as sacrificial and teleological. The first time we meet Gabi Teichert, she is literally digging the soil with a spade in search of fragments that will illuminate the enigmatic blur of Germany's distant and recent past. As she continues her research into German history—the Mayerling incident, the Royal Prussian Military Railway, and the Spartacist uprising[4] are some of her interests in the first film—she turns to an even more literal and material approach to history in *Die Patriotin*. She not only continues, illegally and at no small risk, to excavate the soil, but she also begins to dissect, cut, and even infuse texts into concoctions she then imbibes (and that make her too sick to teach her classes). In a basement laboratory, and with the help of hammers, drills, torchlights, and test tubes, Gabi Teichert becomes increasingly frustrated and isolated. She is unable to achieve any clarity in her attempts to study and systematize the fragments of history that accumulate on the screen. Among these fragments, we see random everyday objects that have now become treasures: the political history of Napoleon, images of Stalingrad, the acrobatics of the elephant Jenny, medieval illustrations of hybrid animals, the price of geese in 1914 Silesia, a photograph of the Grimm brothers in an excavation, myths and legends, footage of the delegates of the German Social Democratic Party, legal analyses of fairy tales, and a variety of quotations from the history of music, painting, and film. The list is endless, but one of these heterogeneous fragments stands above all the rest, because unlike all the others, it speaks to us directly, although Gabi Teichert cannot hear what it says.

This voice belongs to the Talking Knee of Corporal Wieland, who was blown to pieces in Stalingrad on January 29, 1943. *Die Patriotin* begins and ends with the voice of the dead, the missing link to a history that is deeply buried and that the Talking Knee materializes in the form of a chatty and opinionated voiceover. The fable of the Talking Knee is thus, tellingly, a literalization and materialization of Walter Benjamin's famous lines: "*even the dead* will not be safe from the enemy if he is victorious. And this enemy has never ceased to be victorious."[5] The knee is the joint that makes forward movement possible, we are told, but this particular knee is not attached to a body; it is another isolated fragment detached from a context, in this instance, a body that once gave it the semblance of meaning, that once inscribed it in history as a lived experience, instead of as a relic. Kluge's fictional Talking Knee is also a literal rendering of Christian Morgenstern's antiwar poem "The Knee," a fiction born out of another fiction:

> There wanders through the world, a knee
> It's just a knee, no more.
> It's not a tent; it's not a tree;
> Only a knee, no more.
> There was a man once in a war

Overkilled, killed fatally.
Alone, unhurt, remained the knee
Like a saint's relics, pure.
Since then it roams the whole world, lonely.
It is a knee, now, only.
It's not a tent; it's not a tree;
Only a knee, no more.[6]

The Talking Knee that "wanders through the world" and its history across the millennia knows in perfect detail everything Gabi Teichert is desperately seeking. The Knee is the repository of an accumulated collective and impersonal memory that connects the pieces of a history that has become disjointed and shattered by violence. However, this would-be mediator—between the living and the dead, between the past and the present—never actually meets Gabi Teichert. She has the questions, the Knee may have the answers, but in the end, as in Portabella's *Die Stille vor Bach*, it is the audience that becomes the missing link between the two—but then only to multiply disjunctions and missed encounters, rather than to reconcile them. We are all like Gabi Teichert, trying to put the fragments of the film together, and we are no more equipped than she is, with her shovels, hammers, and test tubes.

The accumulated collective wisdom of the Knee—warning us not to believe that the dead are dead—has multiple and heterogeneous sources, and like Kluge's film more generally, never ceases to amalgamate these sources to strange and surprising effect. At another point in the film, for instance, the Talking Knee quotes from Adam Smith's *The Wealth of Nations*, "Water is vital to all aspects of life. One cannot exist without it. Yet rarely can one use it for purposes of trade. A diamond, by contrast, has no intrinsic value but can be used in trade for all sorts of other commodities." That this same quotation appears in Kluge's 1983 film, *The Power of Emotion*, suggests his sense that the lines—evoking the vicissitudes of value—could not be more pertinent to a contemporary audience. But the question Kluge seems to be asking is whether anyone is listening at all. The resources for a counterproduction of history, in equal measure a labor of dismantling and of rebuilding, already exist, Kluge seems to imply, but the imaginative and critical intelligence that can assemble them into a new configuration has not yet gathered into a collective force.

The role of music in this accumulation of disconnected and contradictory fragments is signaled from the very beginning of the film. The film opens with time-lapse photographs of Frankfurt, appearing with the soundtrack of Eisler's original score for Alain Resnais's 1955 *Nuit et brouillard* (Night and fog). The counterpoint between the two is at once jarring and understated. The colorful and somewhat festive illumination of the urban landscape, proof of Germany's economic "miracle," stands in contrast to the somber music, a fragment of Witold Lutosławski's *Musique funèbre*. This musical prelude is also, rather astonishingly, the *only*, and rather obscure, reference to the Holocaust in a film devoted to German history and its accumulated violence. The rest of the film's soundtrack is a vast collection of anonymized and scattered fragments, quotations, we might say, from, among others, Beethoven, Mendelssohn, Jean Sibelius, Alexander Scriabin, Robert Schumann, Johannes Brahms, and Joseph Haydn.

This dismantling and potential reorganization of classical Western music through fragmentation and quotation becomes central in the final section of the film, entitled "New Year: A Question of Context," and, particularly, in relation to Beethoven's Ninth.[7] This time, we see Gabi Teichert working together with others as she tries to decipher and analyze rather obscure stanzas from Schiller's "An die Freude."[8] A few scenes before, she had broken down, crying bitterly, overwhelmed by the enormity of her militant task. She now pursues her systematic historical study in the company of other fellow female teachers over drinks as they sing to a radio transmission of the "Ode to Joy," likely the traditional New Year's broadcast organized by the Social Democratic Party, which plays in the background. None of them can make heads nor tails of the fragments of the poem, but they all agree that it is "macabre." Their quotations and readings seem to hint at a cup brimming with the dead from which we all must drink. One of the women recalls the saying that to have a talkative person become silent, a stone must be put over a grave. It is a comedic scene, but also an exercise in counterhistory. Schiller's lyrics appear briefly on the screen. They are placed on the same level as all the other fragments that the film scatters and accumulates, as is Beethoven's Ninth. As the music continues, we see a succession of images—a vintage photograph, New Year's Eve fireworks, Christmas lights, a cathedral, and a train—and then a quote from Karl Kraus, "The closer you look at a word, the more distantly does it look back" and, a few seconds later, an overlay of the word "GERMANY" at the bottom of the screen. For Gabi Teichert, as for Kluge, Germany is an enigma—and so are the words, images, and music that make up *Die Patriotin*'s cinematic compositions—an enigma that reaches further and further back the more closely we look at it.

In the next segment, after another montage of engravings, paintings, documentary war footage, medieval illuminated manuscripts, a demolition site, and utopian architectural plans, we see photographs of Lenin's empty apartment, now a museum. As the images of the rooms appear on the screen, the Knee asserts that the question is not just "What Is to Be Done," a well-known title from Lenin, but also, and as importantly, "What Is Not to Be Done"—after all, Corporal Wieland was in the Wehrmacht. After telling us, matter-of-factly and without any hint of affect or regret, that history could have unfolded differently, the Knee confesses to being a remarkably unreliable narrator; knees do not typically speak, and least of all when they are not attached to a body. All the Knee ever wanted, we learn, was simply to survive in whatever way possible. It is at this moment that its words slowly devolve into a rapid amalgamation of quotations in Latin, an ideological verbiage that has at times passed as wisdom. Appearing in a dead language, these textual fragments are survivors, remnants that, detached and nomadic, populate the script of the film as a debris field.

In the film's final scene, Gabi Teichert looks at snow falling through the window and wonders if this new year will bring a new history curriculum, or at least hope for a different beginning.[9] The last quote on the screen reads: "the stars are disorganized in a new house." When Beethoven's Ninth is heard again over the film's credits, we cannot take his music for granted and certainly cannot claim to understand or possess it; instead, perhaps for the first time, we hear the echoes of a disorganization, disorder, and dissonance that harbor the possibility of a different beginning.

* * *

Kluge's cinematic images are traversed by the Western classical musical tradition to the exclusion of all others. Beyond his feature films, he has continued to explore the history that makes music possible—and the history that music encrypts within it—with a diverse and ever-growing number of collaborators across generations, media, backgrounds, and genders. In these works, Kluge proposes an almost infinite number of arrangements, combinations, and compositional approaches to musical archives that he refuses to see as dead culture, insisting instead on transforming and sometimes recycling them into experiential and multisensorial experiments. We get the impression that like Gabi Teichert, the filmmaker cannot possibly have enough time to accomplish the enormous, urgent task he has set for himself. But unlike the solitary Gabi Teichert, Kluge establishes new forms of cooperation and speculation, using technology as a relational platform that increases the chances of multiplication and proliferation.

To reference just one recent example: in 2019, a few months before the worldwide COVID lockdown, Kluge filmed a video triptych in his home, a collaboration with the prolific Filipino filmmaker, poet, and musician Khavn de La Cruz. The two filmmakers already had collaborated in the 2018 feature *Happy Lamento*, and they continued to work together, releasing *Orphea* in 2020. The collaboration significantly expanded Kluge's musical and historical archive. In the video, we see the nonbinary artist Khavn performing their composition on a piano that has been modified in a variety of ways, forcefully renegotiating a relationship to the instrument that resonates with, among many others, Santos's practices. In each of the three videos, Khavn plays different variations of the same melody.

In the first installment, the hammers of the piano have several kitchen and domestic utensils placed upon them (a spatula, a duster, different kinds of knives, a bottle opener, a small metal support, the figurine of a dog). The instrument rattles with metallic tones, and Khavn's playing becomes louder and more percussive. The objects vibrate and become animated with syncopated small movements that, in turn, affect the music being produced. Kluge himself comes to the piano and runs the duster through the keyboard and the hammers and, later, holding a kitchen knife, joins the performance, which becomes a duet. Throughout, we see different kinds of cameras and sound-recording devices—including a static shot of an old movie camera, a reference to early cinema—as well as visual compositions of unexpected objects, rearranged as surreal *nature mortes*, including a duster and a wig resting on the keyboard, a baroque and carnivalesque eye mask, a bottle opener, a spatula, and a meat cleaver wedged between the piano hammers.

The protocol of the "variations" extends to every single element in the video, suggesting an infinite number of different arrangements. These visual compositions indicate that the video is not the documentation of a live performance but a nonchronological montage that is fully mediated by a number of recording technologies. Halfway though the performance, Khavn stands up from the stool and begins to play with a spatula and a meat cleaver. When they return to the seat to continue to play, with their hands now back on the keyboard, we get a better look at the room: we see a cameraman sitting on a sofa, more figurines, a table filled with framed family portraits. When we get a view through the window, the cars and trees look like mass-produced miniatures that echo the domestic objects and figurines filling the room. The anonymity of these mass-produced objects is matched by an entire bestiary of animal representations—on pillows, tables, shelves, and even on the pattern of Khvan's coat, which depicts an extinct species of frog. The room somehow contains an entire world, a world that Kluge and Khavn continue to reassemble in different configurations.

In the shorter second variation, the tempo slows down significantly. The video begins with Khavn playing the melody by tapping on the closed fallboard and then opening it to continue to play on the piano keys. Meanwhile, we see Kluge record the movements of the hammers on a cell phone—we will see these images briefly later in the film. We then begin to see a digital accordion-shaped montage of a series of boats and charts of the Atlantic—moving from England to the Caribbean. As the images later begin to peel off like pages in a book, we start to see the shipwrecks of these same boats, one after the other. The history of European movement across the ocean is presented as a series of shipwrecks and catastrophes—Amerindian genocide, the Middle Passage, the coolie trade, the colonization of the Pacific... the list goes on. These shipwrecks, Kluge and Khavn suggest, are the material infrastructure of Western music.

The third, shortest, and final variation is a fast performance of the same melody. Donning a white wig not unlike the one used by the Bach impersonator in Portabella's *Die Stille vor Bach* and an eye mask with a baroque design, Khavn now plays the melody with the arrangement of a baroque fugue. This fugue is not just a parodic appropriation, however; it is instead a distorted return from the colonized non-European in the form of disorder, chaos, and shattering. What we hear and witness is the violence behind the fantasy of structural consistency and order. Together with Kluge, Khavn—whose name pronounced in Tagalog sounds like a filler word for things whose name one cannot recall—insists, like all the artists evoked in this book, that musical traditions are not cultural property but historic assemblages with which we must continue to experiment, rearrange, and play differently.

PART THREE

Inter Canem et Lupum: Anri Sala's Fictions

Variation Three: One Wall, Three Scenes

¡Tor Auf!

The images that accompanied this command are impossible to forget and are inscribed in the collective mind of a Europe still structured around a promise, a desire, and an indeterminate hope that the very existence of the Berlin Wall had managed to preserve.

On November 9, 1989, citizens of the German Democratic Republic were unexpectedly declared free to cross the city's internal border. East and West Berliners started walking toward the infamous wall. By midnight, the checkpoints that had become sites of terror and impossibility for generations of East Berliners since 1961 were overrun by thousands. By the weekend, those thousands grew to two million, and Berlin became an ecstatic party, its rhythms punctuated by the sounds of "Mauerspechte" ("wall woodpeckers"). Images of the Berlin Wall being chipped at, hammered, bulldozed, and graffitied with jubilant slogans and of the Todesstreife, or "death strip," transformed into a blank canvas onto which the expectancy for a new political future could be inscribed, circulated worldwide. Indeed, the reunification of East and West Germany was made official at record speed, by October 3, 1990, less than a year after the fall of the Berlin Wall. History, it seemed, could also fast-forward, and the experience proved to be dizzying.

The Mauerfall was an unprecedented television event, not only because it was watched by millions and shown continuously in a loop over the course of the next days, but because those images themselves were chipping away, hammering, and bulldozing the ideological armature that had sustained the everyday reality of millions of Europeans, now collapsing like a condemned building.

Shortly after, a reunified Berlin, still one of the poorest areas of Germany—with an abundance of cheap rentals and cheap labor—started to emerge once more as an art capital.

The Vlora

The Vlora, *the name of the cargo ship carrying thousands of Albanian refugees—soon to be called "boat people," a name given to millions of others, before and after—to the Italian port of Bari on August 8, 1991, has come to symbolize the human cost of an ideological collapse that, despite all warnings, could never be fully anticipated.*

After forty years of isolation, an economic, social, and political downfall had left Albanian citizens, already half forgotten by a Europe focused on the hopes and fears surrounding a newly unified Germany, little choice but a desperate leap forward into the unknown. Basing their knowledge of Europe on the images on Italian television, a massive exodus of at least twenty thousand people (in a country of less than three million) arrived on the coasts of the Italian Adriatic. A humanitarian refugee catastrophe ensued, sadly announcing many more to come, as the Italian authorities resorted to confinement in sport stadiums, military transport planes and ferries, and violent suppression. This form of violence would be repeated with little difference, over and over again, in the following decades. Europe's future was catching up with its past, at high speed, and with no end in sight.

The Sarajevo Philharmonic Orchestra

In December 1993, during the escalation of the Yugoslav Wars, defined by savage ethnic cleansing and sexual violence, and during a practice session of the Sarajevo Philharmonic Orchestra, the concert hall was hit by five shells. In the course of the longest siege of any modern war, seven of its musicians had already been killed, and many more had been wounded; the philharmonic musical archive had been damaged, and many instruments had been destroyed, damaged, or lost; rehearsals took place in harsh winter conditions, without heating, in basements lit by candlelight. Yet the orchestra continued to hold concerts, and the audience continued to attend. One musician explained that music is "like a time machine. It brings the audience to another country, another place" and added, "You feel like a free man."

On June 19, 1994, during a brief cease-fire, the Sarajevo Philharmonic Orchestra and the chorus of the National Theater gave a televised concert in the ruins of the City Hall.[1]

I begin this section on the Albanian artist Anri Sala with these three scenes of an ongoing series because, reproduced in different media and contexts, they evoke the much larger set of political traumas that traverse, entangle, and define his generation of Europeans and many more. I also begin with them because they delineate the condition of possibility for Sala's work. Indeed, the artist has filmed in these three locations, Berlin, Tirana, and Sarajevo, and together, these settings, as well as the histories they contain, belong to the political, social, and economic armature that underpins his acoustic and cinematic fictions, the contingencies inscribed in all his perceptual abstractions. If Sala's layered acoustic and visual assemblages are able to include those who Europe has willingly excluded in its selective historical and political leap, it is because he finds in music a gathering force of historical relations that does not think in terms of oppositions, borders, and antagonisms. If generations were separated by a wall, and generations were again separated by a fallen wall, maybe walls can no longer be the answer.

The expression that gives title to this chapter, *inter canem et lupum*, "between dog and wolf," refers to the perceptual uncertainties that can occur in the liminal temporalities of nightfall or dusk, when one may very well mistake a dog for a wolf or a wolf for a dog; or, when, in an exchange between the known and the unknown, between what is familiar and what is threatening, one might perceive a danger where there is none or feel comfortably safe in the face of peril. Sala used the French version of this expression, *entre le chien et le loup*, for a 2003 exhibition at Le Musée d'Art de la Vie Moderne de Paris and for his first published detailed monograph, ostensibly alluding to the fact that a large number of his films until then had been shot at night, utilizing an ominous and crepuscular palette.[2] The phrase, however, also encapsulates aspects of his practice that go well beyond the specificities of a film's lighting, among them: the plasticity and metamorphoses that accompany uncertainty, the role of perceptual and sensorial doubt in our relation to the world and in our reaction to it, and the role of love toward the familiar, as well as the fear and even hate toward figures that seem to threaten the boundaries of the known. Sala's films are elaborate acoustic and cinematic environments where wolves are not only welcomed, but actively sought, guardians of a limitless listening that belongs to no one.

A Cinematic Caesura

> What characterizes inheritance is first of all that one does not choose it; it is what violently elects us.
>
> —Jacques Derrida, *For What Tomorrow* (2004)

Anri Sala's first project, the 1998 documentary film *Intervista (Quelques mots pour le dire...)*, not only marks the beginning of his career, but also carefully documents his becoming an artist (or more accurately, a producer of art). The film encapsulates and unleashes, like a Pandora's box,[3] the motifs and the structural underpinning of all of Sala's later work—the encounters, ellipses, relations, reduced agencies, gestures, and repetitions that anchor the stylistic configurations of his video installations, on the one hand, and, on the other, the personal, historical, social, and political confluences that his images will inscribe, echo, and displace in the direction of a reconceptualization of the relation between art and politics. Furthermore, *Intervista* introduces the logic of inheritance, unchosen, and yet assumed, as the existential, historical, and political condition that determines our restrained freedom in relationship to the past, both personal and collective. The film also marks Sala's ensuing relegation of the linguistic in favor of the musical in his work, which, as we saw with Allora & Calzadilla, is no longer an oppositional system but instead one predicated on the composition of differences and singularities.

Intervista was Sala's graduation project in film direction for Le Fresnoy-Studio National des Arts Contemporains in Tourcoing and signals both a beginning and an end, an emergence as well as a disappearance. Through a caesura that will bring forth a new understanding of the cinematic, Sala's film takes its point of departure

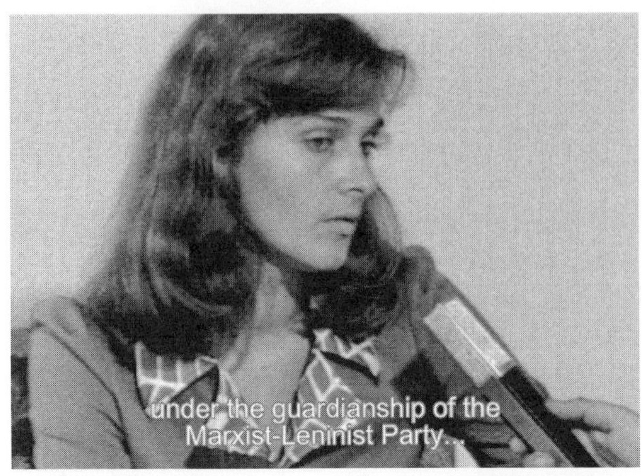

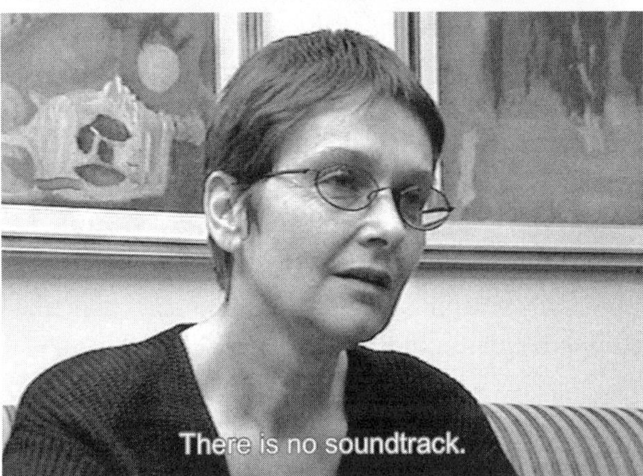

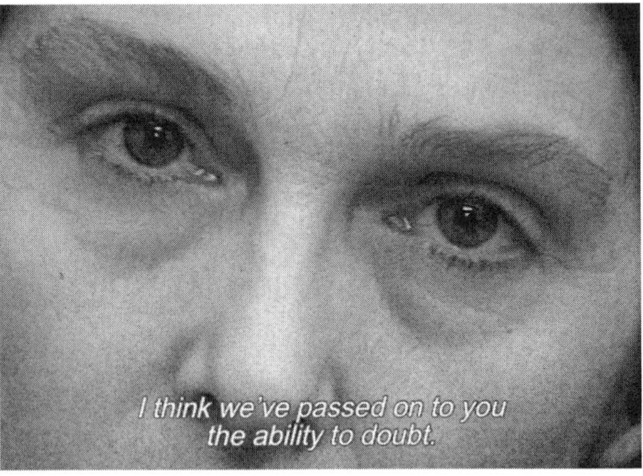

Anri Sala, *Intervista (Quelques mots pour le dire . . .)*, 1998. Film stills. Courtesy of the artist.

from an inheritance, at once maternal and national, encountered somehow by chance and yet inevitably inscribed in the syntax of all his later work. The film opens with a first return, Sala's trip back home to Tirana, and a first encounter, his discovery of an old reel of film that includes footage of his mother at a Communist Youth Party Congress standing with the party elite, with a crowd applauding its leader, Enver Hoxha, and footage of her being interviewed by a local news station. The film begins as a literal "inter-vista," as a film that takes place in between other films. Sala underscores this in his title, and in more than one way. While the Albanian translation of "interview" would be "intervistë," Sala instead chooses the cinematic reference of "intervista," echoing Federico Fellini's late fictional autobiographical feature, the 1987 *Intervista*, a film that is also a reflection on personal memory and national history and that includes references to a variety of other films. Fellini's film famously ends with the director's voiceover equivocally stating, "So the movie should end here. Actually, it's finished." Apparently, the Italian director ends his love letter to film quite uncinematically, yet, like Sala, he also implies that after the emergence of cinema and its effects on our sensorial perception, all the transits between different media are already cinematic, including acoustic ones. Nothing is foreign to cinema.

Sala's parenthetical subtitle, "a few words to say it," further emphasizes a connection between words and all the visual elements of the film. To be more precise, the word "intervista," naming the entire film, joins a particular generic form to every detail or scene in the film (appearing under this name, everything in the film becomes an "intervista"). The title becomes a way to displace what we think we know, to transform what is familiar to us, and to rethink the relation between the particular and the universal, the personal and the collective. Referencing an increasingly large archive irreducible to just linguistic and visual elements, it suggests the enormity of the task of attempting to somehow "say it." These intermedial figures and motifs and his understanding of translation as a form of displacement, between languages, but also between different temporalities and media, are simultaneously a beginning and an end for Sala—something is lost, but something else is found instead, and that something else is an effect of cinema as a technology of production through reproduction.[4]

At the beginning of the film, we see a black screen, hear the sound of cardboard being cut, and then see a sliver of light coming through this cut. Next, we see Sala's face and torso, frontally lit, but with a sunlike beam behind him, emerging out of the opening he cuts into the storage cardboard box, which clearly resembles a darkroom and where the camera has been placed. In this highly artificial setup, we witness Sala rummaging through the box and finding an old film reel that he proceeds to unspool. The found reel and Sala himself belong inside the camera-box and will be incorporated into the film we are about to see.[5] A few establishing shots taken from a moving car immediately follow and depict everyday life in the impoverished city of Tirana (where food shortages had become the norm), and together with the folkloric soundtrack suggest the somehow detached point of view of a visitor who may or may not be Sala, pulling away from the self-referentiality of the film's opening. We are then shown a newly built apartment to which Sala's mother has presumably moved. Sala enters his mother's apartment and declares, "I have a surprise for you," to which the mother immediately replies by saying she is wary of surprises. He then shows her the footage he has discovered. While being recorded for Sala's film, his mother, Valdet, laughs lightheartedly at the silent images, remains unmoved, and has no trouble dating them—1977, she guesses—yet she has no memory of being filmed for an interview and bemoans that the sound has been lost.

The film turns into a quest to find the soundtrack for these found images. *Intervista*'s initial interview leads to multiple other interviews, suggesting the social and political entanglement of Albanians and their degree of complicity with a forty-six-year Communist dictatorship. Throughout the film, Sala interviews his mother multiple times, but he also interviews the original interviewer, Pushkin Lubonja, the former political prisoners Liri and Todi Lubonja, the sound engineer-turned-cabdriver, and the translator at the School for the Deaf. While all the interviewees remind Sala that both the questions and answers of any public dialogue during the Communist regime had certainly been fully scripted beforehand, that all of them were a series of quotations of ideological commonplaces, in the interviews Sala now conducts, we hear about political purges, violence, lack of safety, economic scarcity, and above all, a pervasive fear, a sense of illegibility, and heightened uncertainty about the past and the present. A more scattered form of opacity supersedes a rather uniform and monolithic one. Throughout the film, Sala allows unexpectedly poignant fragments of dialogue to sink in, and one can still hear their resonances in the artist's subsequent projects to this day. When at one point the former sound man, talking about recording technologies, exclaims, "synchronicity did not exist here," it is hard not to hear a comment on Albania's political history in the twentieth century, on Europe as a whole, and on Sala's own future cinematic procedures.

Indeed, Sala's search for the lost soundtrack will entail another formal and expressive quest—the search for a cinema that will be nonmimetic and composed of asynchronous, nonlinear conceptions of time and space, where *bios* and *technê*, the human and the nonhuman, remain in intimate proximity to one another. *Bios* and *technê* implicate one another in Sala's works: the act of filming and recording, of technological reproduction, sets the stage for the intermittent and often surprising emergence of the human, whose sovereignty, autonomy, and "originality" are compromised and restrained. The procedures that organize the entirety of his works are already present in his first film, but while initially presented as problems to be solved, they become structural issues that can never be left fully behind.

With no small irony, and with the help of one of the teachers at a school for Deaf and speech-impaired children, who transcribes

Valdet's words into hand gestures by reading the movement of her lips (in his ensuing work, Sala will often depict sound through movement and gesture), the filmmaker extracts his mother's words from the images.[6] Knowing the script, however, does not make Valdet's words any less impenetrable. When she hears the transcription, she becomes visibly upset at her predictable propagandistic gibberish; she recognizes her own erasure behind ideological platitudes. She becomes a cipher to herself in front of us. By this point, the audience has seen the original footage a few times and at different speeds. Each repetition signals a higher degree of intelligibility in the past, even as it literally becomes a reflective surface onto which to project the fears and uncertainties of Albania's fraught present. Valdet is clearly an intelligent, educated, and articulate woman who, unlike all the other interviewees, has managed to survive apparently unscathed by the transition to a new and unpredictable Albania, now in the throes of violence as it enters the free market after the collapse of state Communism. Even as she admits her family's privilege and relative independence during the Communist regime, she continues to react, to think through her initial disbelief, in conversation with her son. As the scene becomes more intimate and unguarded, a sense of loss—whether of meaning, ideals, or hope—begins to creep into the interview. The film intercuts footage of unfailingly optimistic propaganda films and even a patriotic musical number with scenes of Valdet speaking of being split or broken into two in relation to her past. We can read Sala's work as an homage to this ambivalence about political affiliations—an homage that nevertheless manages to contain and preserve his mother's hopes and aspirations in the fictions he so carefully constructs. It is possible to view his later works as enactments of another way of thinking about political action and its consequences, as a reconceptualization of the possibilities of political indeterminacy through his art.

It would seem that the question of agency that circulates through Sala's entire production originates in his mother as she reflects on whether a commitment emerges within ourselves, or if it is incurred in relation to others, in the form of indeterminate group formations. At this point in the film, Sala turns to Italian and French television news reporting on the what was nearly a civil war in Albania in 1997, a result of the violence that engulfed the country following the failure of a free market that had relied heavily on different pyramid schemes. We then return to Valdet, who now turns to the future, to her fear for the future — for herself, for her children, and for her country. Her last words are worth transcribing in full:

> I have fear because I can't see the issues of the future. I no longer understand what is happening. I'm afraid. Everything is confusing. When I think of the future, I think of everything that is close to me, but also of the destiny of the country. The recent events have shattered many hopes. We could say that a destructive force has swept away all constructive energies.
>
> I'm afraid. I'm afraid for you and for me. What is most important for me is that you and your sister have a future. It is my greatest desire. As great is my desire for a future for Albania. This makes sense since I am not detached from this country. If the country has a future, we will have one, too. But if it doesn't, we won't. As we say in Albania: ask for one thing and you will get two.
>
> I believe I have transmitted a doubt to you.

These moving last moments in the film spell out Sala's inheritance, his filiations, and the contours of the collective experience embedded in his cinematic images where everything is entangled and resonant with echoes of all kinds. The impossibility of separating individual lives from the political conditions of the country and world — and the suggestion that identity is never punctual, never linked to a single moment or place, but instead involves a wide and complicated web of relations, of histories woven together and filled with loss, violence, and all sorts of complicities — will become a constant undercurrent in Sala's work. In his films, the only certainty is that the relation between the past, the present, and the future can never be calibrated in a determinate way, and for this reason, it often takes the form of fear. It is this fear, this uncertainty, that his work attempts to address and give form to without ever fully eliminating it.

Intervista is a compelling investigation of history and memory, and it is distinguished by a few key features that set Sala apart. He refuses to separate the "wrong-headed" Communist past from the democratic market "freedom" of the present. His act of retrospection would have been impossible in the era to which he returns, that is, it can take place only in the present even if it is also a product of the past. And he approaches public history through private memories—and also memory lapses—and in doing so recognizes the impossibility of direct access to the collective and insists that the key factor differentiating the present from the past is the changing use of language, of syntax as a mental scaffolding. As the artist comments in a later interview, "political situations impact and scar syntax"[7] and bring forth a series of entangled ruptures and cuts—in meaning, narrative, belief, and temporality. Sala's work attempts to produce a new syntax that is itself made up of cuts, caesuras, and ruptures and to find a more plastic and malleable form through this act of cutting.

Variation Four: Singing Under Her Breath

Between the trees, a film screen, a window onto another space-time, appears. The screen changes colors — pink, blue, green, white — like a highly artificial time lapse of a dawn, or maybe a sunrise. An intensely emotive and cinematic music, the orchestral part of the first movement of Pyotr Ilyich Tchaikovsky's Symphony No. 6, Pathétique, *begins — and so does the film.*[8] *A young man is sitting down across from it, somewhere in a city park, perhaps waiting. We see the screen again, an orchestra is playing the music we hear, the audience is scattered near the musicians — it's a rehearsal. The next character we see passing the man is a woman, casually singing, and then running to cross the street. We hear birds singing, a dog, a bicycle. Everyday life in a rather tranquil urban setting, it would seem. The woman crosses a second, wider street, again running. As she regains her breath and slows down her pace, we notice walls filled with graffiti, boarded-up buildings, surfaces covered in shrapnel holes.*

The film now cuts to a rehearsing orchestra. The conductor instructs the orchestra to "rest" and to "remain silent" while he quietly directs with his hands before asking the musicians to join him and play a few bars. We cut to the woman again and a medium shot of people running through street crossings, anonymous and collective. She is surrounded by other passersby, all dressed either in black or with very muted colors, like herself. The pavement they walk on is covered in shards of glass. The people walking, stopping to decide when to cross the street, appear strangely statuesque in their stances; they look like actors or dancers absorbed by a mental calculation. They begin to take turns at crossing the street, running, in a slightly choreographed series of relays. We hear a shot. There is no doubt now: we are in Sarajevo, a city under siege. We see sheets, like a precarious movie screen, hanging at the end of the street. We hear bells, water, and enter a courtyard that is eerily quiet — the subtle orchestration of a city suspended.

Sala's longest film, the 2011 feature *1395 Days without Red*—one of the two films resulting from a collaboration with Bosnian artist Šejla Kamerić, film director Liria Bégéja, and with arrangements and additional music by Ari Benjamin Meyer—addresses the Sarajevo siege through a series of displacements and mediations. Red is absent because, bright enough to attract the attention of snipers, it is avoided by the citizens of Sarajevo. The choice of music, played by the Sarajevo Philharmonic Orchestra, is by no means obvious. Finished in 1893 and premiered only nine days before Tchaikovsky's death, the Symphony No. 6 in B minor was renamed *Pathétique*—"Patetitčeskaja," meaning "passionate" in Russian—by the composer the day after this first performance and dedicated to his nephew, Vladimir Davydov, with whom he was very close and who committed suicide a few years later. It was the composer's final composition, and its second public performance was already a memorial of the first.

Cut to the rehearsal room again. The conductor's instructions—"wait," "don't get behind," or "stop here," and later, "one more time" and "tempo"—could be directions for the walkers as much as for the orchestra. The bassoons slowly foreshadow the main theme in E minor. Meanwhile, the street crossings become longer, more demanding, riskier. We see a background of forested mountains. A long shot of a road with multiple lanes and train tracks, the infamous "Sniper Alley," brings to mind a musical staff, the lines of musical notation that allow notes to occupy their place in relation to the linear grid.

We now see a series of static shots of the city: a closed optician's shop, followed by empty, angular buildings, their verticals like intervals that cut the image into blocks with variable measures. We return to the rehearsal room, but it is now empty. Only the music stands and scores are there, as if waiting. When we return to the woman, who's breathless after traversing the alley, she slows down again as her breathing becomes more rhythmic, more musical. The orchestra then arrives in the room and starts assembling, gathering, and tuning. The cue to begin to play will not come from the conductor, however, but from the woman walking and softly singing under her breath—a reminder that all music begins with breath, as well as a sudden transformation of Tchaikovsky's Sixth into a war song of resistance, *a question of life and death. The unfolding of the first movement is literalized but also intensified; emotion becomes a source of motion and vice versa. The "programmatic" nature of the symphony—accompanied with titles or descriptions evoking a mood, a landscape, a scene, a story—is here realized through cinematic images. Music and film complete each other's phrases, not exactly in a call and response but in a series of displacements and substitutions.*

Changing the rhythm or phrasing slightly, modulating to another key, subtly altering the melody and having different instruments play it in succession, as in a game of musical chairs, or doubling (when two or more instruments play a melody simultaneously), Tchaikovsky's music keeps us suspended in a state of waiting. It relies on chromatic sequencing, fragmentation, and suspension, and because of this, its tonal center is hard to locate. The complexity of the composition, with its very slow exposition of themes and unusual tempos, evokes a sense of uncertainty and expectation. The main melody is referenced uninterruptedly, yet sometimes it breaks down into two, in a counterpoint, to come back again transformed, like a refrain that maintains a melodic theme throughout by always changing slightly. At other points, the oboes, trumpets, and violas gather together and against the remainder of the orchestra, with melodies and countermelodies clashing with one another. During the composition process, orchestration, the gathering together of all the instruments, became a source of struggle for the composer. The coming together of the orchestra does not hide the effort it demands. The final and brief coda is a forceful brass chorale, a collective celebration, that fades out. It is also a direct quotation from the Russian Orthodox Requiem Mass, the irruption of an unexpected collective voice that gains new meaning in the context of the complexity of the first movement.

The symphony's Romantic, evocative, and poignant melody has been collectivized into an affirmative act, a defiance amid persistent violence—gratuitous, hidden, and random. The woman's singing is now a shelter, a support, a dwelling, an anchor. Her mouth becomes an oboe, a bassoon, and then a flute, in a doubling of the same melody. She returns to Sniper Alley, but she is now walking unhurried. This Sarajevo binds

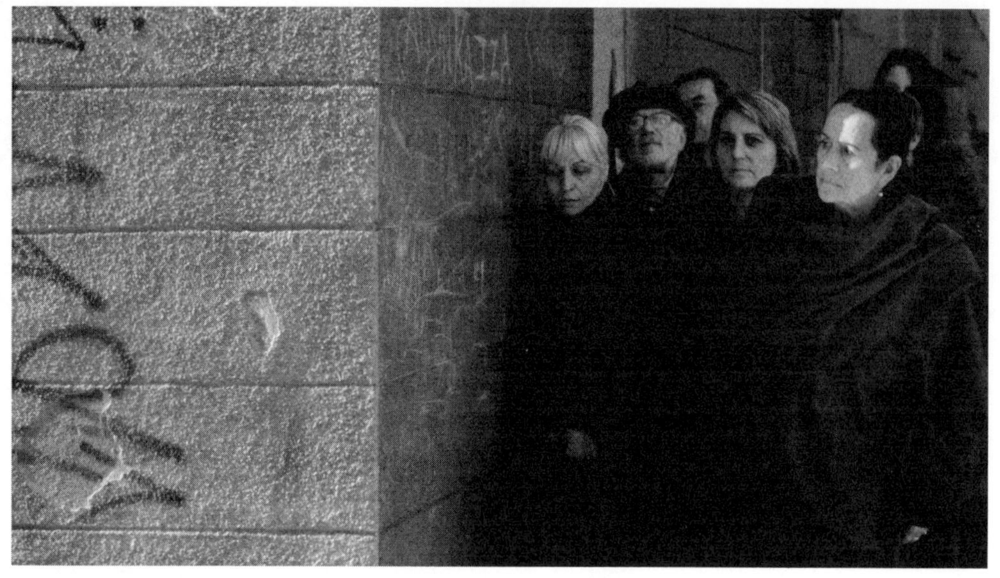

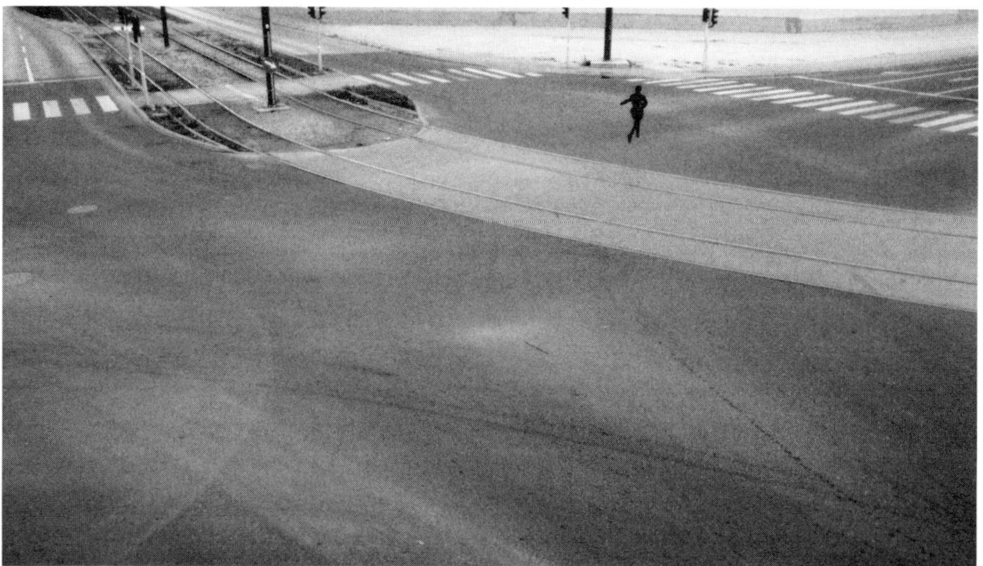

Anri Sala, *1395 Days without Red*, 2011.
Film stills. Courtesy of the artist.

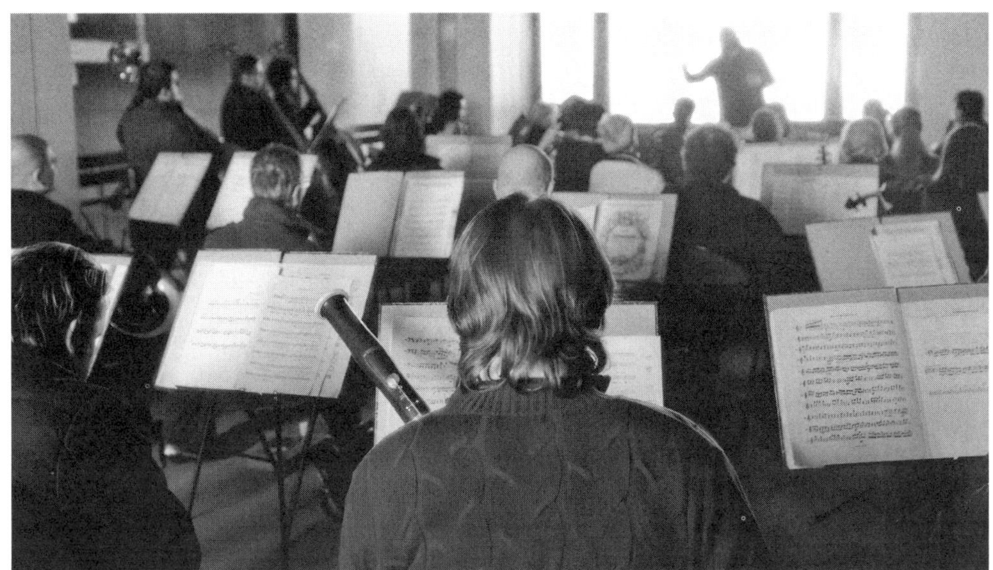

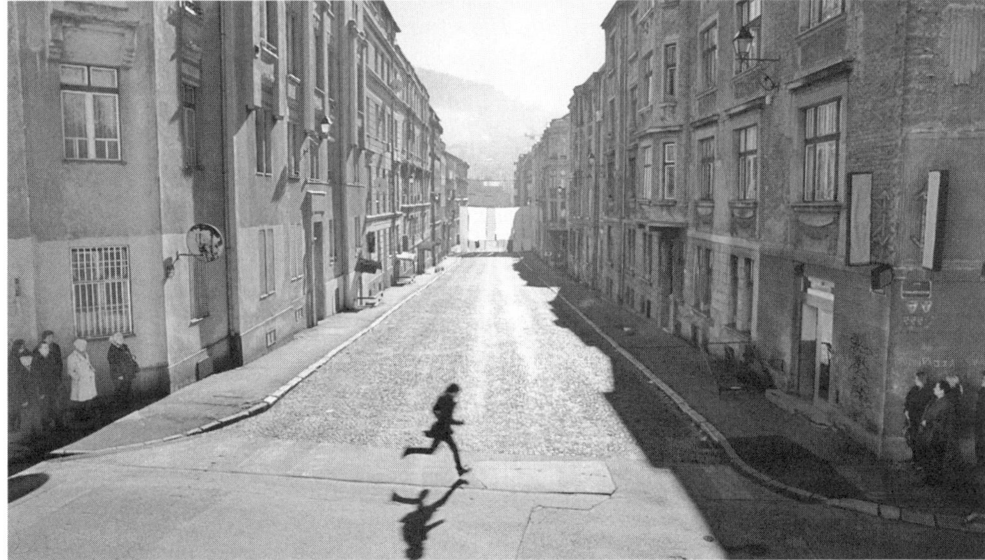

the past to the present and the present to the past, not quite belonging to either. Like the music, it is both a memory and a performance, a sound in the room and in the mind. We see a musician and her clarinet, breathing into her instrument not unlike the singing woman. We see the passersby again, walking at ease, stopping to light a cigarette — they are the same, yet entirely different. Sala has never used this many actors. They, too, are an orchestra that he directs, unseen. The singing woman, played by Spanish actor Maribel Verdú, is intercut not simply with the members of the orchestra, but also with citizens of Sarajevo, survivors of the city's long siege, all enacting their own memories. The choreography of their movements has changed, but it still feels like a dance, maybe even more so. The city has not changed, but we see new constructions in the distance, some façades have their glass intact, but others are covered with newspapers. Past and present Sarajevo overlap. The passersby move toward the rehearsal room, as if called by the music. The woman hums Tchaikovsky's first movement, not missing a beat, and returns to the first street crossing, as does the music. The film's temporality follows the returns and repetitions of the music; cinematic movement is yet another score. We see the woman through her reflection on a shop window. Refracted, she turns. We hear shots again, or perhaps simply the memory of those shots in her head. Time has been contorted, and it is no longer possible to tell. She moves toward the rehearsal building. She has arrived. Directed by the conductor, the orchestra is silent for the last bars. Another requiem is being played, this time silently.

We return to the young man sitting, his face surrounded and tinted by the reflected light from the screen, which is now bright red. The movie fades into a solid red screen. The music, we now know, has been red all along.

Natality and Flight

> This is exactly how the music called *jazz* began, and out of the same necessity: not only to redeem a history unwritten and despised, but to checkmate the European notion of the world. For until this hour, when we speak of history, we are speaking only of how Europe saw — and sees — the world.
>
> But there is a very great deal in the world which Europe does not, or cannot, see: in the very same way that the European musical scale cannot transcribe — cannot write down, does not understand — the notes, or the price, of this music.
>
> — James Baldwin, "Of the Sorrow Songs: The Cross of Redemption" (1979)

> I want to be sung. I want
> all my bones and meat hummed
> against the thick floating
> winter sky. I want myself
> as dance. As what I am
> given love, or time, or space
> to feel myself.
> — Amiri Baraka, "The Dance" (1964)

Sala's 2005 film *Long Sorrow* begins with a glacially slow take of a window in a vacant apartment, with the camera slowly zooming into a mysterious object that at first seems to have been left and forgotten in the windowsill, a residue of the former occupant/s of the space. From the viewpoint of the camera, the subject/object divide does not function.[9] The only other object in the room is a white radiator that mimes, in miniature and off scale, the regular rows of white apartment buildings of Berlin's Langer Jammer — to which this apartment belongs — as if what can be viewed outside the window is already inside the apartment, torn from its more usual context. This figurative breach of the distinction between public and private space corresponds to the fact that for the first few minutes of this initial sequence in the film, it is unclear whether the object on the window belongs inside or outside the space and whether the music we hear emanates from inside or outside the apartment. Because of the camera's slowness, this first movement takes up half of the entire film and forces us to look closely and listen carefully. Sala's camera lures us into an intensity of attention that matches the texture of the sounds we hear but whose source is still not identified. Indeed, music and image begin together, but the source of the sound will remain unclear until we are able to identify the object by the window.

If we are asked at this early stage to linger in this space, to follow the camera's gaze as it moves through the room and approaches the window and as we listen to the music that accompanies this movement, it is because together, these activities provide their own window into Sala's own nomadic multimedia practice. The window's multiple frames appear as excerpts of strips of film, each of which forms part of the window and is in turn captured by the window that the cinematic lens is. The slowness of the camera presents us with a series of stills in which the image of a window transforms a room into a series of framed images. Drawing us into its space, the cinematic image becomes an entryway—a window, a camera's shutter, a strange aperture composed of multiple frames. Arriving at the room's threshold, we witness the transformation of what seemed to be a forgotten object into a head that—moving to the music and joined with a voice whose sounds are unintelligible—is adorned with leaves and flowers. It is only by passing through this window, by experiencing this passage as the conceptual movement the camera articulates, that we can encounter the world we inhabit as a surprise in all its difference and singularity.

As soon as the camera arrives at the window, the music pauses for a moment, allowing us to hear the sound of the wind and of the world outside the room. What immediately follows this brief interlude is a kind of yelp, followed by a series of cries and moans that—interrupting the music while simultaneously becoming part of it—come from the head that has slowly come into view. Wind, breath, voice, and instrument now all join in an alternating rhythm that creates another kind of composition, a call and response that will in turn call forth several others. While the film's slow opening seems rather calm and meditative, we now understand that it works to initiate a complex play of displacement and discontinuity that eventually leads us to a series of unexpected discoveries. The first relational convergence and transformation takes place when the camera frames the window completely and we notice simultaneously: that the now visibly leafy object moves rhythmically to the music; that it is a human head with dreadlocks braided with leaves and flowers;[10] that this head and body are the source of the music; and that the saxophonist is somehow mysteriously perched outside the window, with the window's transom seemingly marking the intersection of the earth and the sky, dividing them. This play between earth and sky is displaced in another form when the musician's braided locks seem to double as a visual evocation of roots, of earth and soil, that give birth to leaves and flowers. The locks function as the first "ground" in a film that will show itself to be ostensibly concerned with the possibility of defying gravity, with different forms of transport and flight. This joining of earth and sky, of grounding and flying, finds its echo in the music, which grows simultaneously more mournful and more experimental.

Arriving at the window, we realize that we have been following the slow-moving camera in an affirmative no return, since we begin to leave the radiator and the room behind us as we continue to move forward. But within the logic of displacement and substitution that is at the heart of Sala's cinematic practice, we do not leave the radiator entirely behind. As we approach the window, we can see in the distance the rows of apartment buildings of which the radiator was already a miniaturized model, a visual echo that creates a bridge between inside and outside.

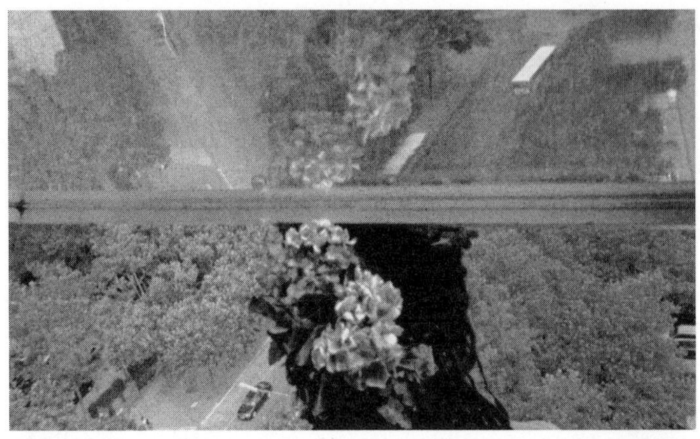

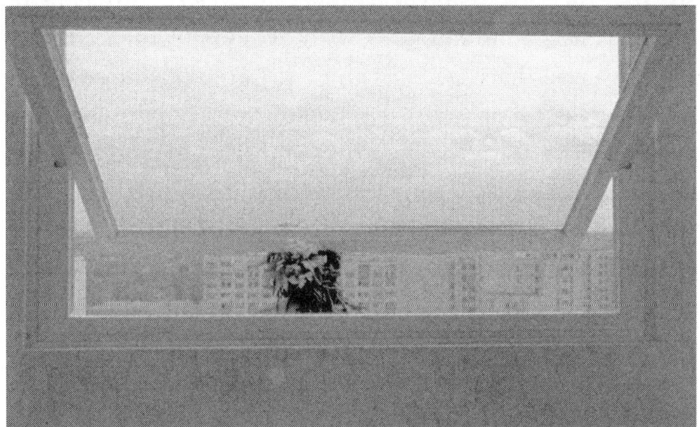

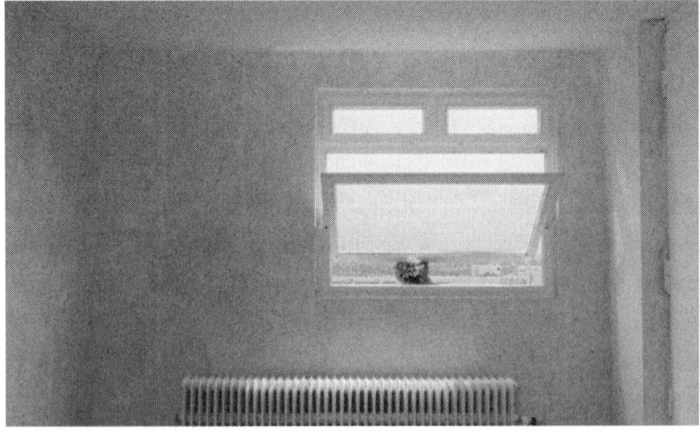

Anri Sala, *Long Sorrow*, 2005.
Film stills. Courtesy of the artist.

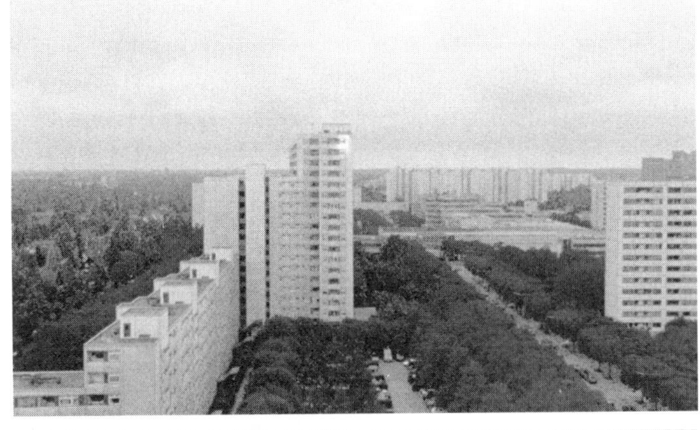
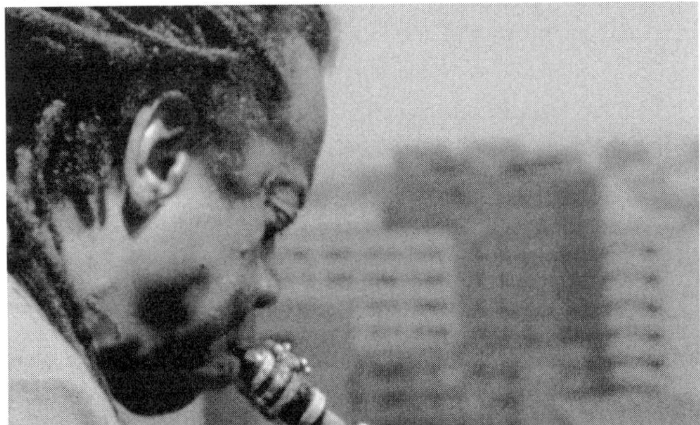
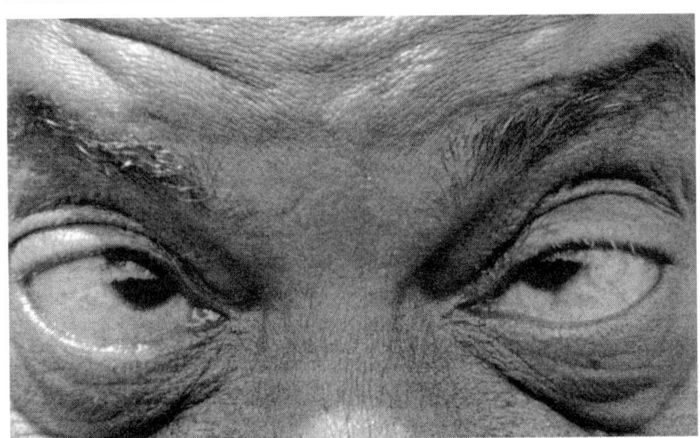

Given Sala's Albanian origins, art historical and critical accounts of *Long Sorrow* have generally stressed the film's historical reference to the Berlin Wall and to utopian architectural rationalism (a topic he already had addressed in his well-known 2003 *Dammi i Colori*). Indeed, the Langer Jammer ("long lament" or "long lamentation"), the popularly named kilometer-long apartment block of about seventeen thousand units with chains of high-rises, built from 1964 to 1974 by the GeSoBau Gesellschaft für Soziale Gebau (the Association for Social Apartment Construction), stands near the west side of the former Berlin Wall. Following the concept of the Bauhaus-designed housing estates of the 1930s, the building bears the traces of the debates over rationalist planning, top-down social experimentation, and modernist urban governance in large metropolises and resonates deeply with Sala's earlier work.

But it is important to insist that *Long Sorrow* is an intermedia duet, a call and response, between Sala and musician Jemeel Moondoc, camera and saxophone, light and sound, belonging to one as much as to the other.[11] It is not an accident that after studying with Cecil Taylor and under the influence of John Coltrane and Ornette Coleman, Moondoc's formative years evolved in another urban architectural and musical experiment soon after he moved to New York, when he became part of the New York loft jazz scene in the mid-1970s.[12] He brings with him the history of these earlier years, including the essential relation he already had experienced between architectural space—infused by issues of class and race, along with the construction and destruction of cities—and the possibility of creating music. When Moondoc is suspended outside the buildings of the Langer Jammer, he evokes Baldwin's description of "the state of being . . . out of which the blues come" as "very, very tricky . . . kind of a fantastic tightrope."[13] The possibility of falling is echoed musically by the possibility of failing—the real danger embedded in Moondoc's "risky" playing is translated by Sala into images that amplify and intensify every sound.

Like most of Sala's work, *Long Sorrow* is a collaboration. But this collaboration is never between just *two* since nearly everything is in relation to something else that already seems to inhabit it in displaced form: rooms double as the interiors of cinema and its apparatuses, windows are another name for the camera's lens, radiators become miniaturized architectural forms, music and wind prove to be related to one another, the voice becomes a musical instrument, a body and saxophone nearly meld into one another to such an extent that each is affected by the other's movement. In Sala's cinematic and acoustic spaces everything can become something else.

Moondoc's saxophone functions as a prosthesis, a supplement to his body, a fact that is most evident in the scenes in which we see his face and eyes moving in relation to the sound and to his exertions in producing it. In these scenes, the prosthetic interface between body and instrument calls attention to the operations of transfer the film depicts, especially the transfers of the agency between subject and object and back. Because of Sala's elliptical filmmaking, it is impossible to determine when and where the transit from one mode to the other has taken place. The logic of subtraction that subtends Sala's camera work stands in oppositional relation to the layered inscriptions present in each of the elements of the film's composition. Moondoc himself, both as a musician and as a body, also carries histories that not only precede the film, but also extend beyond it, signaling a complex network in which Sala's film stands as a momentary convergence.

That Moondoc and his music appear as a transient nexus of historical relations that Sala's film evokes and deploys can be read in the context of his free-jazz improvisations. Sala's decision to translate "Jammer" as "sorrow," instead of the more usual "lament" or "lamentation," resonates deeply and links the piece with the long tradition of African American "sorrow songs." In his 1903 *The Souls of Black Folk*, W. E. B. Du Bois famously writes about the origins, significance, and expressiveness of the sorrow songs.[14] Du Bois's antinomic genealogy of the genre traces it back to the long history of slavery and especially to the possibilities of survival after unimaginable loss, to music understood as a resistant remainder that endures and communicates its pain to the world at large, as survival:

> In these songs, I have said, the slave spoke to the world. Such a message is naturally veiled and half articulate. Words and music have lost each other and new and cant phrases of a dimly understood theology have displaced the older sentiment. Once in a while we catch a strange word of an unknown tongue, as the "Mighty Myo," which figures as a river of death; more often slight words or mere doggerel are joined to music of singular sweetness. Purely secular songs are few in number, partly because many of them were turned into hymns by a change of words, partly because the frolics were seldom heard by the stranger, and the music less often caught. Of nearly all the songs, however, the music is distinctly sorrowful.[15]

Sala and Moondoc reference this long history of Black sorrow, portraying music as both a dangerous and necessary *Trauerspiel*.[16] Moondoc's presence in Berlin reinserts this history into a German and European context, fully complicit in its legacy. His sorrow song is a formally experimental speculation rooted in the echoes of a violent past. This multitemporal convergence brings together a number of histories that prevent Moondoc's performance from being a solo or even a duet. It becomes instead the clamor of many—the long history of the sorrow song and its relation to the even longer history of slavery and racism, together with the genre's incorporation of the memory of the dead. Moondoc's incorporation of African sounds and rhythms into his unique improvisational style prevents his pluralistic musical practice from being confined to a fixed or determinate location. Additionally, his presence in Berlin ties his personal history to Germany's colonial legacy in Africa and the nation's longstanding forms of anti-Black racism, spanning from the nineteenth century through the Wilhelmine era, the Third Reich, and into the present. Since German reunification in 1989, cultural, institutional, fascist, and everyday forms of racism have continued to persist. It is as if he and Sala want to produce a new form of sorrow song, one that might more closely match and distill the multitude of sorrow songs that have yet to be listened to and that, if heard, could perhaps speak of an imagined deliverance from slavery and racism. This deliverance, however, can be found only in film and music and can appear only as a promise, or as we will see, a fictional flight.

This is why the slow movement of the camera in the first half of the film brings us to a kind of birth, to a change in perspective that, allowing us to see what until now we had been unable to see, transforms everything. When we return to the film's nonnarrative unfolding, as we begin to absorb the consequences of the metamorphosis that marks the "first movement" of the film, we register the object as Moondoc's head, and we experience the plasticity that connects and transforms objects into subjects and subjects into objects. After a brief and poignant silence punctuated by the wind, Moondoc's voice interrupts his musical improvisation with a yelp and then a cry that registers as the lament of a newborn and slowly emerges as a call and response with his saxophone. With the emergence of the voice—an emergence that coincides with our arrival at the window and our ability to see through it more fully—we get a clearer image of the buildings that face the window, of their scale and height. The voice is replicated acoustically, if in distorted form, by the traffic and the distant voices of the housing complex and finally by bells tolling. The world emerges with the birth of a voice and the relations that sustain it. We are now in an environment and a soundscape that includes the world beyond the room in which we began. Nevertheless, a film that at first appears as a meditation on absence is interrupted by the emergence and surprise of the new and begins a second time, differently.

In her *Origins of Totalitarianism*, Arendt identifies "natality," the condition of being born, with the capacity to begin. Joining ontology to politics, she links natality to the possibility of appearing in a shared world in a singular way. For her, freedom and choice are rooted in the givenness of birth: "the freedom of man . . . is identical with the fact that men are being born and that therefore each of them *is* a new beginning, begins, in a sense, the world anew," and "the very source of freedom . . . is given with the fact of the birth of man and resides in his capacity to make a new beginning."[17]

She elaborates this point later in her essay, "The Concept of History." There, she writes, through the fact of natality, "the human world is constantly invaded by strangers, newcomers whose actions and reactions cannot be foreseen by those who are already there."[18] The possibility of something new being born is legible in Sala's collaboration with Moondoc—not only in the slow progress of the camera and its arrival at a threshold, an opening, a movement that gives birth to sight, but also in the promise that the arrival of this stranger, this newcomer in Berlin, can take us somewhere we have never been before. The mournful and newly improvised song played by Moondoc appears to give birth to a new sorrow song through a cinematic and sonic gesture that inscribes the long histories archived in his body and music and that helps him take flight. The collaboration between Sala and Moondoc encapsulates Arendt's understanding of birth as a call to action and improvisation born out of the need to evade capture and domination. In Baldwin's words, Moondoc's "'beat' is the confession which recognizes, changes, and conquers time."[19]

Already in 1867, William Francis Allen describes the improvisational and heterophonic chorus of the work song in ways that anticipate Du Bois and Baldwin's readings of the sorrow song and that also echo Frederick Douglass's accounts of music in the plantation setting. Allen writes:

> There is no singing in parts, as we understand it, and yet no two appear to be singing the same thing—the leading singer starts the words of each verse, often improvising, and the others, who "base" him, as it is called, strike in with the refrain, or even join in the solo, when the words are familiar. When the "base" begins, the leader often stops, leaving the rest of his words to be guessed at, or it may be they are taken up by one of the other singers. And the "basers" themselves seem to follow their own whims, beginning when

> they please and leaving off when they please, striking an octave above or below . . . or hitting some other note than chords, so as to produce the effect of a marvelous complication and variety, and yet with the most perfect time, and rarely with any discord. And what makes it harder to unravel a thread of melody out of this strange network is that, like birds, they seem not infrequently to strike sounds that cannot be precisely represented by the gamut, and abound in slides from one note to another, and turns and cadences not in articulated notes.[20]

The "base" is here the collective social and historical infrastructure that makes the song necessary and possible—both musically and politically—as an act of resistance, survival, and encryption. It is also a reminder that all music is choral and vocal, entangled with the rhythms and beats of the body, of its breath—a breath that does not divide the living from the dead but instead joins them in the strike of the beat and its interval. The work song speaks of an accumulation without sedimentation or fossilization. It is an answer to the hierarchical organization of the orchestra—with which it is strictly contemporaneous—which moves in the direction of the consensual and the unanimous and must be directed from above with a baton. The cacophonous sophistication and textural saturation of the work song cannot be directed without becoming undone by this form of capture, without having its opacity stolen by culture. The becoming-bird of this chorus is another index of its gathering force, its ability to strike in the midst of the horrors of forced labor. Improvisation opens a space that did not exist before; it imagines deliverance even in the face of hopelessness, and *through* hopelessness. After all, an improvisation is a variation that has not yet been captured by musical notation, that remains fugitive because its movement has not been arrested.

Both the sorrow song and the work song are instances of the inscription of the slave into the shelter of community that the musical beat calls into being. Arendt's insights regarding natality become poignant in the context of what Orlando Patterson terms the "natal alienation" of slavery, the denial of social, cultural, and familial bonds, of anything that might constitute a heritage capable of anchoring a subject through belonging.[21] Slavery perverts the meaning of birth and belonging, reading them through the lens of property and disrupting the laws of generation and of social meaning. It expels the enslaved from the order of the human, which is always one of domination, and forces them into the living death of absolute alienation. The perpetuation of loss—experienced in the inability to claim natality either backward or forward because both parents and children are denied their generational bond—should be understood as a process of social delinking and enforced detachment. Such a process, however, is what allows Arendt to join the political and public sphere with a more private and existential space and to formulate the paradox by which the excluded and alienated become the stark reminder of the lack of control over the fact of one's birth—as the one "unproduced" element at the center of the human.

The context for Arendt's reflections is her analysis of the racialization of the modern political space and of the naked violence at its origins in slavery. It is the givenness of the slave's existence, the incalculability of a life with no acknowledged attachments, what Arendt calls an "unsurpassable affirmation" and "a disturbing miracle," that potentially reveals the limitation of the political scene as a product of human artifice: "The more highly developed a civilization, the more accomplished the world it has produced, the more at home men feel within the human artifice—the more they will resent everything they have not produced, everything that is merely and mysteriously given them."[22] Later in the same passage, Arendt matches the unqualified mystery of birth to the "unpredictable hazards of friendship and sympathy" in order to move on to the "incalculable grace of love," another event that emerges without any justification whatsoever:

> The human being who has lost his place in a community, his political status in the struggle of his time, and the legal personality which makes his actions

> and part of his destiny a consistent whole, is left with those qualities which usually can become articulate only in the sphere of private life and must remain unqualified, mere existence in all matters of public concern. This mere existence, that is, all that which is mysteriously given us by birth and which includes the shape of our bodies and the talents of our minds, can be adequately dealt with only by the unpredictable hazards of friendship and sympathy, or by the great and incalculable grace of love, which says with Augustine, "*Volo ut sis* (I want you to be)" without being able to give any particular reason for such supreme and unsurpassable affirmation.[23]

For Arendt, givenness refers to a singularity without identity, to an unprecedented birth that can never be prepared for and that constitutes a force of disruption. It is the disruptive nature of birth that Sala and Moondoc are intent on presenting in *Long Sorrow.* As Arendt counsels in her reading of Augustine, they will have to deploy grace, sympathy, and indeed love through an exploration of the nature of collaboration and of the transmission of sorrow through nongenerational bonds.

Once this birth is announced, visually and sonically, we are confronted with a series of disorienting camera moves in which Sala responds in kind to Moondoc's heightened experimentalism. The camera, moving outside the building, now shifts to the side to reveal the staging and the apparatus of the film: we see stage lights hanging and protruding out of a beam, and we get a first glimpse of Moondoc's head and the mouthpiece of his saxophone. The ground is now missing, and so is the reference to the horizon. Throughout the film, scale itself functions as a source of groundlessness. The change of scale is here matched by another, more aggressive cropping. In a disturbing visual echo of the beams of the tracking lights, Moondoc's head appears as hanging from the frame of the window in a suspension that further communicates the danger—the history of violence and death that has made the sorrow songs both possible and necessary—embedded in the music itself. The musician is in fact harnessed for safety and suspended on an eighteen-story-high small platform that we never see. Meanwhile, the visual apparatus of the film has been condensed into a lighting mechanism, light being, in turn, the immaterial scaffolding that sustains and holds any image.

The next three cuts are extreme and uncomfortable close-ups of fragments of Moondoc's face and head: his distorted cheek, his mouth, the top of his head, his furrowed brow, one of his eyes, his pores, his sweat, and hair follicles. Formally, the incompleteness and fragmentation of the visual scene before us becomes a delaying tactic akin to a musical tempo, a rhythm that appears in the form of delay. The effort and concentration of the production of music are made palpable by a zooming camera that echoes an almost invasive touch. The distortions of the face that make the music possible suggest that there can be no music without disfigurement, without fragmentation and breaks, an insight inscribed within the sorrow song. But here, the distinct fragments are held or rather suspended in a vertiginous midair flight by the music itself, just as the tracking lights in the previous shot were suspended by an architectural scaffolding. There is a conspicuous absence of hands in the film—a bit surprising, since there could be no music here without the movement of Moondoc's hands and fingers—in jarring and dissonant contrast with the excessive and violent close-up detail of the musician's face. The relationship between the intelligible and the tangible punctuates the faster tempo of this segment and points to music as a resistance to the void. In an interview with Hans Ulrich Obrist, Sala explains: "I wanted someone to improvise free jazz in the void, somebody for whom music is not only an ongoing conciliation with emptiness in life but is also what keeps him together, while being suspended outside the eighteenth floor. He is not only enduring emptiness as a lifetime experience, but also the void, physically speaking."[24]

Groundlessness is further emphasized in the more static shot that follows: a medium shot that crops Moondoc's hands.[25] It is not only that he is suspended but, more importantly, that the instrument that he holds onto and that symbolically supports him above the ground occupies the same compositional space as the literal platform that Sala will not let us see. The artist is adamant that we not see music or film as finished products but rather as the condition of possibility they both share—their conceptual leap into groundlessness and possibility. We are confronted not so much with music as with the promise of music as an intensification and refusal. Sala understands music as a state of permanent imminence, as becoming:

> One aspect that draws me to music is that it's highly communicative and can still resist meaning. I'm trying to film music in a way that feels closer to the pleasure of painting an apple than documenting a musical event. I look for simultaneous relationships between image, sound, and the viewer that avoid pre-existing sets of meanings, searching for a new sort of sense appeal and awareness. I'm interested in sounds as they become music. *Long Sorrow* shows the mouth and not the saxophone. Although what one hears makes one "see" the sax, what one really sees is a mouth and a face. Watching a mouth move and produce sax sounds fictionalizes the whole thing because a segment in the line of production is missing. It's never music as a final product, finished and available, that interests me, but music while it becomes, captured on the fly, before it reaches us for our pleasure.[26]

The role of fiction in Sala's work is often underestimated. Liminal spaces abound in Sala's work and often reflect on the imaginary and crepuscular location of his artworks and the role that fiction plays in them. These liminal spaces thrive in an intensification of risk and indistinction that, by adding variables to every stage of the production and execution of music, multiply uncertainty and leap into the fictional. Borrowing a felicitous phrase from Derrida's *The Politics of Friendship*, I would like to read *Long Sorrow* as a piece that remains "on the edge of fiction" and that seeks to understand improvisation as a modality of the fictional and the speculative.[27] The next shot in the film underscores this interpretation. The camera is now situated inside the room at a different angle, looking down on Moondoc's headpiece as it is surrounded by the lush spring greenery on the street below, his head marking the crossroads of four roads, two real and two reflected on the inclined glass pane and exactly divided in the middle by the edge of the window frame, so that even when one is a phantom image of the other, both remain structural equals. The trees below are now in focus, and Moondoc's head again becomes again a plant, but this time, the transformation speaks of life and communion. This regressive metamorphosis is now an elevation. The camera that in the first movement of the film was a source of revelation, an unveiling, is now a technology of fictionalization.

The next longish shot of Moondoc's blinking eyes is framed by two short captures of his headpiece that once more registers as soil and ground with increasing and mournful intensity. Again, working against his images, Sala shows eyes that do not see but that are completely in sync with the labor of sound as improvisation, as Moondoc's accelerated blinking recalls a camera's aperture, but a camera that no longer records the real but records instead the imagination, now a technology on the edge of a fiction. Indeed, the next shot is a wondrous leap: Moondoc takes flight, and the camera follows him outside the window as he glides over the trees and disappears to the right of the screen, the wind blowing as if to help support his movement. In a moment of synchronicity, wind, camera, and musician move in unison in the same direction. Moondoc's music has completely temporalized the space of the film, elongating architecture through time and detaching him from the harness that would hold him in place.

It is at this moment that Sala changes perspectives again, with two successive static shots. Moondoc has disappeared, but we still hear a few prolonged notes and their echo, a second instance of projection and doubling that reconfigures the music as a site of expanded resonance that views the world as a permeable architecture. Once the music and the sound of traffic that envelops it die away, we hear the wind and are shown a medium shot of the high-rise with track lights, now left as remainders of the film's setup, traces of the apparatus that made the fiction possible. In a way, we see the end of the film's logic before the actual end of the film. At this moment, as Moondoc stretches one final note, a plane emerges from the left, its movement in syntony with the music. It is as if the world now comes into being a second time in response to the music, which is extraordinary, considering the shot clearly conjures a visual echo of 9/11. However, the image in this case speaks of a fictional moment of harmony that does not fully erase catastrophe but reimagines it as contingent rather than necessary. History is still there, but it is no longer a dead weight. It has now acquired the lightness and possibilities of a fiction.

To emphasize this point even further, the film ends with the establishing shot that would have oriented the film earlier on but that now feels like yet another disorienting turn, a shift in scale, and a loop of sorts. The solidity of the Langer Jammer is now a reminder of the vertigo Moondoc must have felt while playing. Instead of being reassured by the clarity of the encompassing point of view, we are further displaced from any formal certainty. Moreover, this last shot is out of sync with the rest of the film and adds another layer of complexity to Sala's temporal experimentation, what we might call his *musicalization* of images.

Sala's work is an exploration of musicality as temporal plasticity, an effort to sustain a state of imminence: a relentless documentation of the fugitive moment when the present acquires the infinite plasticity of the imagined or the dreamt in order to tap into the reservoir of the possible. It presents a layering of the present in which the mobility of time is experienced as an endless transit and echo between modalities. Sala's musical understanding of the cinematic produces an image that is catching up to itself. Anachronism takes the place of syntax, so that temporalities are layered and juxtaposed, but hypotaxis and causality, as narrative elements, disappear altogether. We are left with temporal aftereffects that function like resonances and operate in a loop. Eliminating cause and effect, the experience of time turns into a transit between different modalities that reach into the hidden archive of the present through fictional protocols, the elusive subject of Sala's compositional practice.

In 2011, Sala restaged the performance *3-2-1* at the Serpentine Gallery in London, where saxophonists Andre Vida and Caroline Kraabel responded live to *Long Sorrow* in a series of daily duos with Moondoc's recorded music in the film. (More than four hundred performances had taken place by the end of the show.) At the Serpentine, the saxophonists continued to improvise a solo even after the film ended. This new configuration, typical of Sala's reengagement with his "finished" pieces, extends the logic of the film to delay its closure further. As I noted earlier, *Long Sorrow* is already a duet between the artist and the musician, if not many more. Yet it is quite clear that the sound of the film is not direct and has been carefully produced and that, in fact, it is already a reflection on the event of the film. Resonance in film goes backward and forward at the same time. Music can extend and accelerate time; it can temporalize sensation, but only film can reverse it. This is the key to Sala's complex intermedia exploration and explains his need to pit sound against image and vice versa. Only in this way can he move in all directions in space, as well as in time.

The poetic strength of the piece announces the creative potential of the dissolution of the sovereign subject, and not just the fictionalization of Sala's practice. Resisting both objectification and idealization means moving beyond the chronological logic of humanism to embrace sheer possibility instead. Moondoc and Sala's improvisation is a testimony to the contours of the lived experience, of the improvisation of the self as a fleeting experience that defies identification. Their combined practice is more about losing the self than about finding it. Sala's experimental abstraction announces the possibility of an encounter between fugitive subjects and objects, constantly metamorphosing into one another and bound by their very incompleteness to an ever-growing number of past and future others. As Fumi Okiji puts it, beautifully riffing off Benjamin's "Storyteller" with the "plural," "incomplete," and "iterative reworking" embedded in the storyteller's narrative:

> Could it be that jazz takes advantage of the inevitability of failure encoded in artistic pursuit? That it makes virtue of irresolution and incompletion? Similar to how a vignette, told well, can evoke the whole world of its protagonist but retain an indeterminacy that allows for others to retread and rework that world, does jazz work have future reworkings of its standards and (musical and social) themes encoded in it? Perhaps a creative form that encourages a teller's or a musician's peculiarities—their limitations, even—will inevitably allow space in the same story for many others.[28]

As a temporal situation that turns its own happening into its material, *Long Sorrow* underscores its musical conceptual organization as an "iterative reworking" of Moondoc's improvisation, visually occupying the void created by his music. However, in a twist that heightens the fictional complexity of Sala's images, Moondoc's music is itself a response to the void the artist has carefully constructed. Because of this, it is impossible to discern between the call and the response. While the fugitive subject has freely dematerialized into a musical fugue, it continues to oscillate between emergence and disappearance. Music is a fugitive form because it is anticipatory; it flees toward the future, into becoming, rather than being. The temporality of improvisation, literally "what cannot be foreseen," follows the structure of an indeterminate future as it carries the possibility of the yet unheard, the yet unseen, the new. Improvisation is the name of temporalized difference and the ultimate force of disidentification. Cecil Taylor spoke of the "unknown totality" of improvisation.[29] Musical totality, then, is structured like an open relation that cannot be fully captured or notated because it always takes flight.[30]

Phantom Limbs

> If you do know that here is one hand, we'll grant you all the rest.
> —Ludwig Wittgenstein, *On Certainty* (1969)

> The more we study this score the clearer the idea inspiring it, and the disparities of its episodes are erased: the thought of death, the nightmare of fear and of solitude. Whoever followed, as I did, the slow and cruel deterioration of our friend and saw the distant warning symptoms that assailed his lucidity, is bound to feel, with a pang of despair, that Ravel was carving his own destiny in his work. A work of this kind presupposes the perception of the beyond and requires, as Cocteau puts it, "receiving delegates from the Unknown."
> —Marguerite Long, *At the Piano with Maurice Ravel* (1973)

Sala's 2013 *Ravel Ravel* positions two screens on top of one another in a soundproofed anechoic chamber, each of them reproducing two different interpretations of Maurice Ravel's *Left Hand Concerto for Piano and Orchestra*. The temporal lag between the two performances by pianists Louis Lortie and Jean-Efflam Bavouzet, played at different tempos, is transformed into a resonance and phantom echo capable of moving in two directions, backward and forward, recomposing the melodic progression of Ravel's piece into a multiple and cinematic temporal entanglement. Once again, Sala's exploration of a spatial and acoustic expanse is also a reflection on the possibility and plasticity of an intermedial sculptural treatment of time and its historical inscriptions.[31] While he subtracts the echo from the room where the films are screening, he simultaneously layers and multiplies the internal echoes of Ravel's composition by doubling and redoubling them to ensure that the music is never identical to itself. In this way, the anechoic chamber allows us to hear the internal echoes and reverberations of the piece amplified so that the cinematic image becomes a loudspeaker by other means. In response to a pictorial and musical understanding of saturation in relation to color, Sala proposes the temporal and conceptual saturation that permeates his films and installations, mobilizing the secret archive of the present moment as a site of historical density through the interplay of visual and acoustic resonances.

Following the amputation of his right arm and his two-year captivity in a Russian camp, Viennese pianist Paul Wittgenstein commissioned Ravel to compose the concerto in 1929. Wittgenstein was intent on expanding the repertoire for the left hand and used his considerable family wealth to commission pieces from the foremost composers of the time. Benjamin Britten, Paul Hindemith, Alexandre Tansman, Erich Wolfgang Korngold, Sergei Prokofiev, Karl Weigl, Franz Schmidt, Sergei Bortkiewicz, and Richard Strauss all produced pieces for him. Ravel's concerto remains to date the most performed in this extensive repertoire. Wittgenstein, who was the brother of philosopher Ludwig Wittgenstein, was one of the many amputees of the First World War. However, the piano as a nineteenth-century instrument already carried within itself the memory of war. The 1844 innovation of the *sostenuto* pedal, which allows the sound of a note to linger after the pianist's hand has lifted from the key, was a technology developed as a result of war injuries and amputations. In this way, the musical instrument doubled as a prosthetic and was able to create the illusion of a sustained hand on the keyboard by means of a substitution and a fuller integration of the musician's whole body into the act of playing.

Furthermore, the entanglement of war and music is particularly audible in Ravel's composition. At the compositional and melodic level, Ravel's own description of the concerto's structure speaks of a rupture or a split. He describes how the two tempos that articulate the composition interrupt one another so that after a first part written in a more traditional way, a sudden change occurs and the jazz-like music begins.[32] In addition, the concerto concludes with

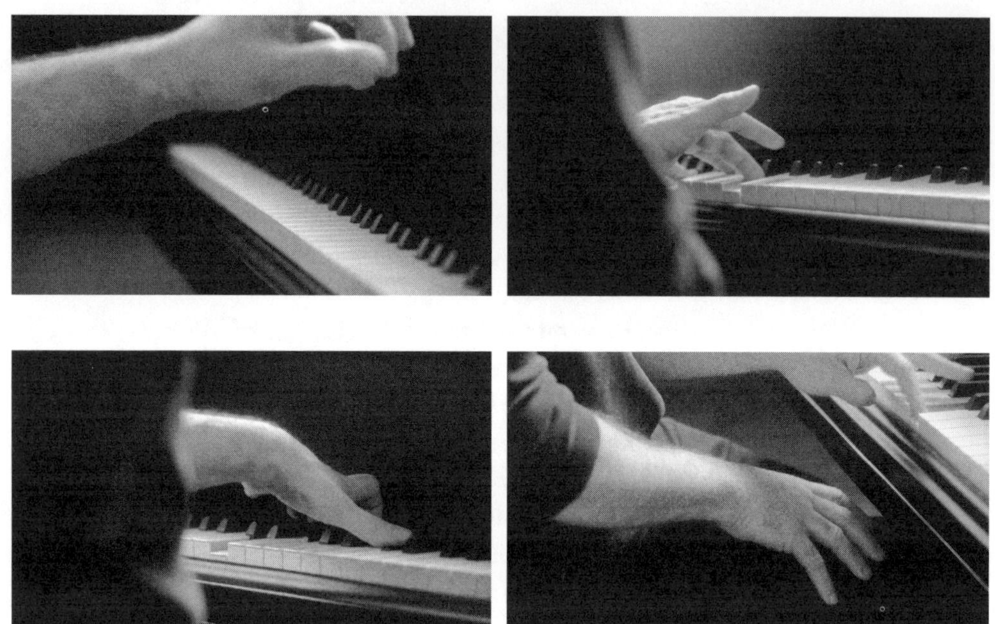

Anri Sala, *Ravel Ravel*, 2013.
Video stills. Courtesy of the artist.

a musical war of sorts, with the piano increasingly drowned by the percussive rhythms of the orchestra. Once again, Sala does not invent but intensifies, extends, and fictionalizes the musical logic of the piece into a spatial and cinematic exploration, very much as he did in *Long Sorrow*. Sala's practice is a conceptual and speculative portrayal of the ethico-political responsibility of musical artworks as an attentive and at times curiously violent form of listening, one that in turn dovetails with issues of historical legacy and cultural inheritance and the brutality they carry within them.[33] As Derrida puts it in *Specters of Marx*, "the *being* of what we are *is* first of all inheritance, whether we like it or know it or not."[34] Indeed, in *Ravel Ravel* the pianists' hands also pass down and transmit legacies and inheritances that are not just musical.[35]

The artist's intervention into the tempo of Ravel's piece relies on doubling and on delay to produce the fiction of an intermittent chase between the performances on the two screens. In Sala's work, legacy is the site of a temporal struggle that defies the break between the present and the past and that his artistic output often presents as the echo of an impossible and breathless chase, as a futile yet necessary exercise in catching up with one's cultural legacy. In the case of *Ravel Ravel*, the caesura separating what looks like the repetition of a proper name encapsulates not just the split that challenges the self-sameness of a name, a script, or a musical partition, but also the temporal lag between the legal status of the concerto within European copyright regulations. The temporal discrepancy in the legal status of the piece in the public domain in Germany and France at the time of Sala's installation in the Venice Biennale is yet another inscription of the violence of war.[36] Because the years of the Second World War are counted differently in Germany and France, by 2013, the concerto was in the public domain in Germany, but not yet in France. The fact that while representing France, Sala decided to show *Ravel Ravel* in the 1937 German pavilion, built during the Third Reich and bearing the inscription "Germania" on its entrance, further amplifies these resonances and differentials, so that temporal discontinuities echo inside each other, multiply, and become literally uncountable. The gesture is both extensive and intensive because it aggregates and deepens the reach of each partition in an effort to find a form that will match the historical and ethico-political entanglements of a Europe defined in relation to the inscription of violence.

To borrow from Theodor Reich's book title, *Ravel Ravel* should be understood as a quintessentially European "haunting melody," one that carries within it the memory of the war and holds and sustains it as an interval or spacing between inscriptions—a proper name, melody, performance, copyright law, or nationality—creating a conceptual *mise en abîme* that amplifies the losses and injuries of nationalist violence. In one single gesture within a proliferating syntax, Sala preserves, contains, and fictionalizes the violence of war and holds onto it as if were the pedal of a *sostenuto* until it becomes spectral, very much like a phantom limb. *Ravel Ravel*'s abstracted temporal figuration carries bellic violence within its movement, transforming it into a political undertone that colors the entirety of the composition in a musical version of chromatic saturation the artist has used before. With Sala, history becomes both the site of an absence and an insistent background noise. While sound takes precedence and organizes the movements of Sala's camera, Sala's camera, in turn, produces a perceptual abstraction that takes on impersonal and political undertones. While Ravel and Wittgenstein highlighted the role of personal and collective tragedy in their composition and performance, respectively, Sala depersonalizes that tragedy through an amplification that hinges on abstraction.

However, perhaps paradoxically, exposure, or even overexposure, is the condition of possibility of Sala's cinematic abstractions. His camera treatment of the human body provides the best example of this abstracting procedure. As was the case with Moondoc in *Long Sorrow*, the bodies of the two interpreters in *Ravel Ravel* are overexposed in a series of extreme close-ups that detail the micromovements of the hand and yet at the same time, are presented in a detached, impersonal, and abstracted manner. Sala emphasizes a point of view that cannot belong only to the camera, a mechanical contortion with which the audience cannot possibly identify and that remains impossible to humanize fully. The impersonality of Sala's camera abstracts the human body as a source of identity or as an anchor to orient the viewer and in doing so subtracts it.

Through a series of cinematic movements that emphasize plasticity and incompleteness, Sala approaches the human body as a distorted and tortured fragment that holds itself together through sound, the structural armature that prevents its collapse. The visual here is not tied to representation. It is instead a mechanism that further detaches the music from expression, pushing it into the realm of the conceptual as it strives to unify the visual caesuras that Sala's installation or, even better, the entirety of his perceptual composition, has meticulously devised and then multiplied. Abstraction in Sala's work is not a style or a static position but a practice, a mode of operation. It is a practice that consists in the oscillation and interplay between extreme closeness and a detached and mechanical cropping that produces a visual fragmentation that in turn finds its echo in the aural syncopation that characterizes *Ravel, Ravel*.

Like Wittgenstein's amputated hand, bodies in Sala are always in some sense phantom bodies, abstractions and ideas that carry forth the fictional armatures of his video pieces and installations.[37] The movements that the music triggers in the human body cannot be fully controlled by the pianists; indeed, their complex choreography is a spectral aftereffect of the music on the limbs, much as an amputated limb is a spectral aftereffect of the violence of war. Once again, Sala extends and intensifies this symbiotic relation when he shows us hands that continue to play even without the piano. As they absorb music as a muscle memory, these hands become silent instruments themselves. When they play a tune inscribed in the mind of the performer, they also hand down the trauma of war.

The human body is not the sole agent of the music but a plastic entity affected, transformed, and even shaped by the music. The illusion of autonomy cannot be sustained in the face of the responsive and composite being Sala carefully constructs and that in turn becomes the cinematic materialization of the relation between body and instrument. Like *Long Sorrow*, *Ravel Ravel* is a meticulous documentation of the body becoming an instrument, of a metamorphosis that travels from sound to image and then back again. Sala's exploration of musicality as plasticity can be understood as an effort to prolong the imminence of his work.

The speculative nature of Sala's approach in *Ravel Ravel* perfectly matches a reconfiguration of Europe as an uncertain community capable of acknowledging and surviving its constitutive violence. Such a political speculation hinges on the mobilization of two kinds of ontological inconsistencies: plasticity and incompleteness. Sala's use of the musical—like that of Santos, Portabella, or Allora & Calzadilla—highlights the medium's possibilities for the restaging of the relations between aesthetics and politics, making them manifest in all the plasticity and incompleteness of a performative event, stubbornly uncertain of its final configuration. In Sala's works, music is mobilized as an antidote to the inconsistencies of naming and the limitations of all identitarian formations, especially acute in the political realm, with Europe as one of its most poignant failures. In *Ravel Ravel*, both phantom limbs and phantom sounds provide an extraordinary aesthetic capture of the slippery "phantom Europe" Balibar has sought to outline in his extended, almost three-decades-long examination of Europe as a political concept, a concept that remains speculative because it repeatedly slips onto the terrain of the possible rather than of the real. Like Sala's practice of abstraction, Balibar's revised theoretical and conjectural approach is the result of the confrontation and maladjustment between the possible and the real, between history and ideas.

I would like to propose that this dissonance and friction present in Balibar's critique and in Sala's formal procedures—and in what I have called the wolf—should be understood as the mobilization of an idea in the direction of an intermittent and mutating practice of a community that takes the form of a transit among media, states, temporalities, and identities. Balibar's clearest articulation of this movement and its "community effects"—one that connects his reflection on Europe as the name for a formal and political problem with his return to Spinoza, a return inflected by the reading protocols of his Marxism, as well as by Freudian group psychology—could be the following:

> I will limit myself to the idea that *every identity as such is transindividual* (in psychoanalytic terms one would say "transferential"). . . . Individuals are always already implicated in a multiplicity of practices that put them in relation to "objects" in the Freudian sense, which is also the sense given to them in the classical age (Descartes, Spinoza, Hume), that is, other individuals who are sources of dependency, love and hate, fear and hope, and it is thus that they become subjects.[38]

We have already seen in the more detailed reading of *Long Sorrow* and even of *Intervista*—and with reference to Arendt's concepts of natality and givenness—how birth needs to happen twice: once as an illegible givenness that remains unpredictable, a "mere existence," and then again as a social birth, as the entry into the relations that constitute a community, bound by grace and fear, love and friendship. Balibar's Spinozan transindividual, a figure he borrows from Gilbert Simondon, thus becomes the underlying fabric of any community. This points to an act of transit between singular individuals that functions primarily as a linking mechanism that, mobilizing affects in a political way, aggregates and welcomes others as objects of love or expels and rejects them as objects of hate and fear. What connects Arendt and Balibar's reflections with Sala's artistic procedures is their shared insistence on interdependency as both a necessity and a practice. They all believe that community is an effect that can be achieved only through an open-ended and plastic understanding of a space that is caught midway between the realities of history, with its endurance encrypted in social memory, and the ideals that push the indeterminate future of the collective forward.[39] However, while for Balibar and Arendt the concept of the individual remains intact, despite their insistence on its dependency on others, Sala's acoustic and cinematic fictions present us with a model that pushes the concept even further.[40] In his work, the individual is in a constant state of transformation; it exists, as Catherine Malabou elaborates philosophically, as an "ontology of destructive plasticity," an ontology where nothing or anyone ever stays the same or is ever only one.[41] Like Moondoc's sorrow song, the phantom Europe Sala evokes in *Ravel Ravel* speaks of a performative approach to community formations, treating music and film as plastic media with no claims to stability of any kind. Sala's treatment of the medium echoes and transforms Balibar's description of the individual as a form that exists only in transit and in its entanglement with others. Indeed, the transmedia approach of his installations also is an instance of transport and gathering, yet its movements themselves modify the nature of his work so that it remains in a state of prolonged and endless metamorphosis, even at the risk of becoming undone.

Balibar returns to his notion of the transindividual in a more extended reading of Spinoza's ontology of relations as a political resource for the present. The volume, *Spinoza, the Transindividual*, does not mention Europe (that would be anachronistic), yet it clearly echoes and refines the previous passage in ways that philosophically describe the plasticity of the political as a social relation, as an activity of multiplication whereby "the liberation of the individual actually multiplies collective power, just as collective freedom multiplies the power of the individual."[42] Balibar here provides a new syntax for the thinking of political communities as sites of multiplicity and multiplication that resonates deeply with Sala's own desire for a syntax that takes its point of departure from the fugitivity of music.

While an understanding of community formation as an identitarian grouping can hinge only on an interplay between exclusion and inclusion—an interplay that does not question either the individual or the group and where the logic of inside and outside dominates — Sala and Balibar propose an alternative based on the abstraction of the multiple and the incomplete. Like Sala's practice of abstraction, Balibar's transindividuality is built on subtractions that need to be supplemented and must remain in transit, always becoming and ontologically in flux.[43] Rather than describing a scene of endangerment, this mobility and multiplicity describe a process of "preservation" by other means. Instead of exposing Europe as the political aporia and the reservoir of cultural capital that it is, we are presented with a performative fiction that gives us a glimpse of another kind of association. As Balibar puts it, in words that evoke Marx's penchant for the phantasmagoric, the nineteenth century's particular take on the fictional as spectral, the possibility of change depends entirely on coming to terms with the imaginary nature of any social and political formation: "social reality must take on a hallucinatory character, or be woven from fantasy, in order to exist as such, in history and in practice."[44]

If, as Sala reminds us, spectral sounds are central to musical transmission, the materialization of a community that is called into being through repeated performances must be equally complex temporally, involving both anticipation and afterlife, promise and memory. When Sala explores the intervals of becoming and their temporal disjunctions, he does so through the abstraction and fictionalization of historical situatedness. In *Ravel Ravel*, for instance, the trauma of history contained in bodies and sounds is both a memory of war, the afterlife of its violence, and an elaborate cinematic fiction of the unfolding of that memory in the present. Abstracting and fictionalizing Ravel's haunting melody, Sala binds the future to the past, creating a rhythmic continuum where the sound of history never stops and where the promise to listen carries an ethicopolitical weight that anchors the film in the present of its audience.

All the artists discussed in this book share formal procedures because they face, share, and respond to the political structures and conjunctures of the present and use music to make them manifest, even if in an unfixed, unnamed, and unfinished manner. They all present musical performance as a social form that cannot take place in isolation, that is anti-individual, that functions as an assemblage and a collaboration, as the collective labor of sound and its transmission. As we saw with Allora & Calzadilla, the complex temporality of the noncontractual promise contained in music as a model, and not just a medium, can acquire political resonances that mobilize the relationship between memory and promise so that the two become interdependent and activate the viewer's experience of the temporal into an expansive and intensive response to musical composition. Of the artists studied here, however, Sala may be the most attuned in his work to the temporal multidirectionality of historical existence and the most insistent on never presenting an unmediated musical performance, on highlighting the role not just of transmission, but of the medium of transmission.

Stravinsky's Snails

> The reign of birds seems to have been replaced by the age of insects, with its much more molecular vibrations, chirring, rustling, buzzing, clicking, scratching, and scraping. Birds are vocal, but insects are instrumental: drums and violins, guitars and cymbals.
>
> —Gilles Deleuze and Félix Guattari, *A Thousand Plateaus: Capitalism and Schizophrenia* (1987)

> Because she mourns, nature is mute.
>
> —Walter Benjamin, "On Language as Such and on the Language of Man" (1916)

Igor Stravinsky's 1944 *Elegy for Solo Viola*, his only composition for viola, was a commission from the violist Germain Prevost in honor of fellow musician and violinist Alphonse Onnou, who had died in 1940 while touring the United States. Onnou had performed some of Stravinsky's compositions as the first violinist and founder of the Belgian Pro Arte Quartet, a string ensemble. By 1940, Stravinsky, who knew Onnou, was already living in the United States, and it seems likely that he may have started working on the *Elegy* even before Prevost made his request.

Stravinsky's instructions for the piece, which do not contain a time signature, are worth noting. To begin with, the piece can be played either on a violin or a viola by going up or down a fifth accordingly. This indicates a first doubling or relay. In the Pro Arte Quartet, Prevost played the viola while Onnou played the violin. Once Onnou died, Prevost would become the first violin. Even at the level of his notes to the player, Stravinsky's solo already contains a duet. This viola solo was never *only* for a soloist but was a performance of internal relays, where one musician is traversed by the memory of another—as in the inscription of a relationship to the dead that an elegy is.

Stravinsky's instructions also indicate that the instrument should remain muted for the duration of the elegy, as if it was itself in mourning or short of breath, unable to be fully expansive in its vibrations through space.[45] The brief piece, about five minutes long, slowly unfolds like a chant with a three-part structure, broken into phrases at irregular and breathlike intervals. The *Elegy* is internally split as a composition, a polyphony for two voices that also suggests a loop through the coincidence of the beginning and the end of the composition. The two distinct voices come together in a fugue at the center of the composition before returning to the opening chant, which now feels like a delay.

Delay is the indeterminate procedure that opens the door to an entirely different temporal organization. Sala's 2018 *If and Only If (Ratio 1,89)* proposes a change in the ratios of the composition, a change, however, that he does not control. In the film, a garden snail travels the full length of a violin bow, gradually moving across it as violist Gérard Caussé plays Stravinsky's *Elegy*. Moving from the bottom to the top of the bow, enacting what Sala has described as a "road movie," the gastropod slows the composition, since the musician must adjust and adapt his playing to the cues of this batonless and deaf conductor.[46] Gastropods do not hear and hardly make any sound themselves.[47] While the camera follows the length of the bow, the bow is no longer a stable measure but the place of a highly constructed encounter.[48] The relational movement between the musician's hand and the snail is literally and conceptually supported by the bow, but it is entirely dependent on the musician and the snail's response to one another. At one point, Caussé delicately blows on the snail, as if to encourage its reluctant upward crawl. As he blows, his audible breath does not seem in the least out of place in the *Elegy*, a piece whose elongated musical lament often evokes the rhythms of human breathing. Paradoxically, and in more than one way, the snail does not interrupt Stravinsky's composition but intensifies its internal structure.

Sala's conceptual arrangement of the *Elegy*, his introduction of a third actor, manages simultaneously to delay Stravinsky's piece and to accelerate and multiply its compositional logic. The *Elegy* is shorter than the total duration of the film, which is nine minutes and forty-seven seconds. Paradoxically, by means of an unlikely and alien addition, Sala makes the *Elegy* coil further into itself. It becomes more internally divided and then cinematically multiplied by a looping that becomes potentially endless as it spirals into itself and unspirals. In order to maintain the two procedures, split and repetition, as somewhat distinct, Sala uses two screens in a cinemascope format that continuously circle through the video while remaining divided.[49] It is an infinitely fissured continuity, a game of ratios that recalls Zeno's paradox of Achilles and the tortoise and introduces a fictional or virtual element into the piece. Zeno's paradox is a reflection on the question of the continuum and of an interval or measure. Through a dichotomy, it aims to prove that Achilles will never outrun the tortoise because an infinite number of divisions cannot be overcome in finite time. The virtual comes into play because ratios and divisions are a labor of the imagination, while movement is actual. I mention this to call attention to Sala's sophisticated and meticulous approach to his visual and cinematic fictions and finally to his fictionalization of time.

In *If and Only If (Ratio 1,89)*, Sala employs several procedures to fictionalize further and call attention to the formal composition of the film—which appears as a single uninterrupted take only because of an extraordinary labor of montage that takes its cues from the music that results from a collaboration with a snail, and maybe more. Retakes, loops, multiplications, and repetitions are crucial to the fictional infrastructure of the film. As Caussé moves his bow up and down the strings, two snails, and not one, suddenly appear on the bow. Because of the careful editing, the doubling of the snail feels like a magic trick and colors the entire film with an atmosphere

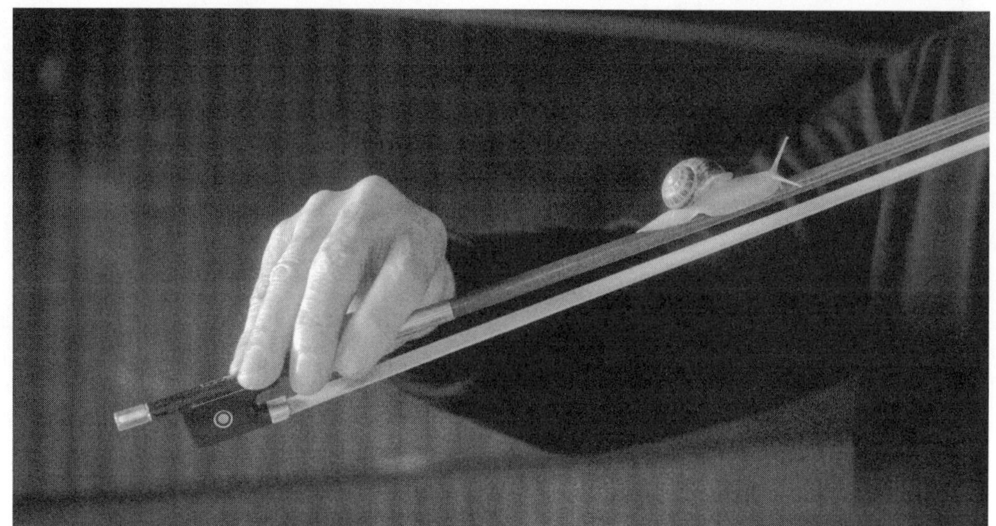

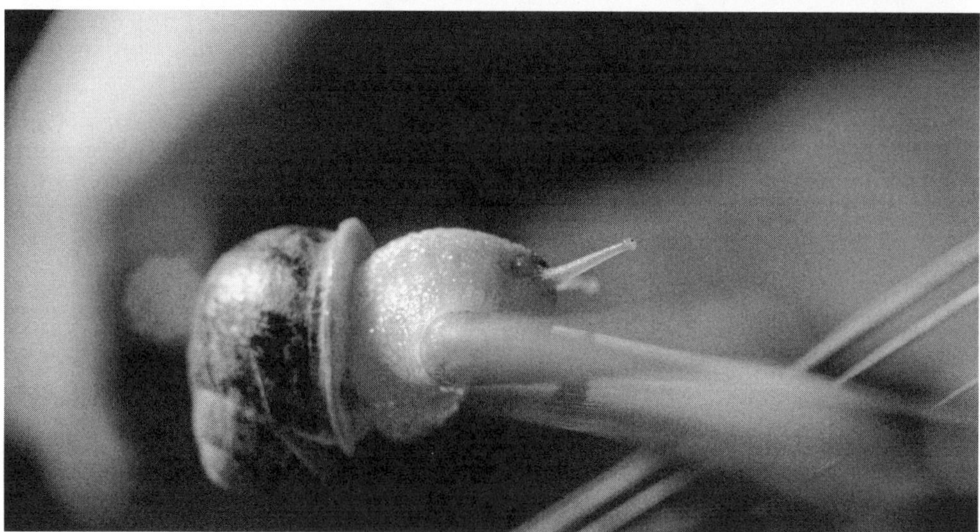

Anri Sala, *If and Only If (Ratio 1,89)*, 2018.
Film stills. Courtesy of the artist.

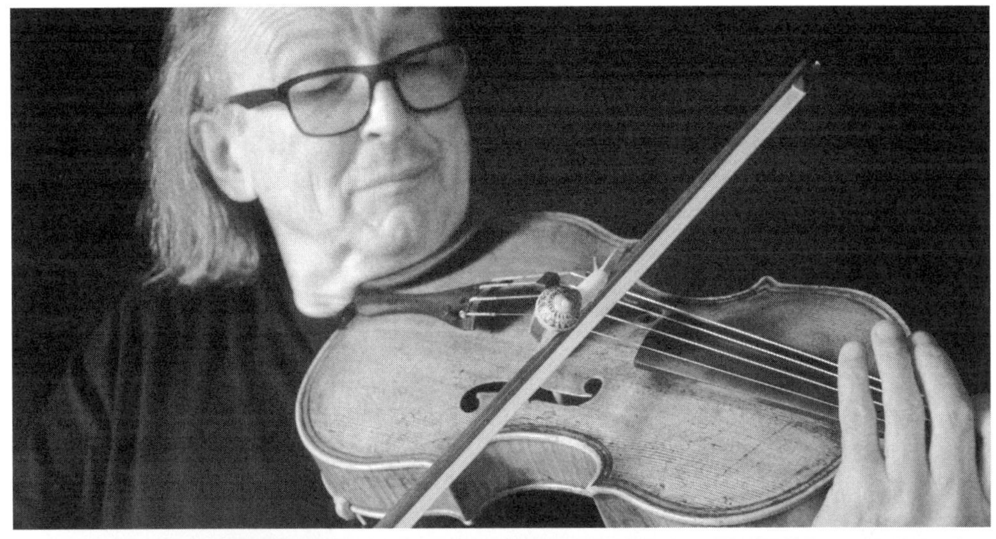
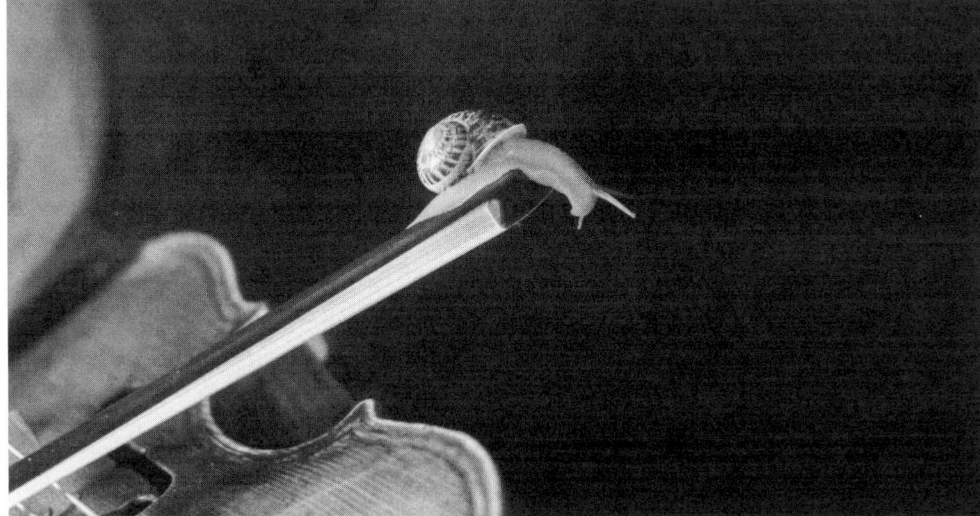

of make-believe. It also underscores the play on infinity suggested by the looping of the film and by the reference to Zeno's paradox. Interestingly, a detail unlikely to have escaped Sala, while playing the violin, a down-bow following a whole down-bow has a rather cinematic name, a "retake." Furthermore, the title of the piece, *If and Only If*, a reference to a biconditional logical connective between statements, functions like an anagrammatic inscription of the three-part compositional itinerary of Stravinsky's piece. Its looping is echoed by the clause's partial palindrome, with "only if" an encryption of the impossibility of the one being only one—an impossibility that Stravinsky's music and Sala's film perform and enact. The phrase is also quite literally the bracketing and the production of a logical measure, a division between the clauses that comply or do not comply with the biconditional. Sala exposes this restrictive logic to the vagaries of time and music as forces of becoming.

Nonetheless, time, here expressed through delay, does not precede music; instead, music produces time by borrowing it from movements in nature, at times imperceptible and mute. Sala reminds us here that music originates in the nonmusical, from what touches and surrounds music, as part of an organic and collaborative ensemble, as a shared labor of composition. This, in turn, allows him to detach music from the logic of humanism and its reductive relationship to the world. The snails in the compositions are not metaphors or props but actors that, knowingly or not, fully transform the music and its visual recording. What Sala's work documents is the becoming-snail of music, and the becoming-music of the snail, giving us an understanding of music as a transformation that consists in falling into another state of being, into another time.

Marxian Acousmatics

> Europe is for us, first of all, the name of an unresolved political problem.
> —Étienne Balibar, *We, the People of Europe?* (2003)

In his 2017 video installation *Take Over*, Sala explores the transits and ideological entanglements between "La Marseillaise" and "The Internationale." Unlike Moondoc's experimental sorrow song or Ravel's rendition of war trauma, both "La Marseillaise" and "The Internationale" are collective anthems composed under the influence of marching songs. They rely on regular and repetitive rhythmic patterns that are easy to memorize and devised to be repeated over a length of time. These rhythms are in fact measures of time that move in one single direction, forward, and aggregate into a steady crescendo that speaks of multiplication and of the force, and even violence, of a single-minded collectivity.

Composed by Claude Joseph Rouget de Lisle in 1792, "La Marseillaise" was originally titled "Chant de guerre pour l'Armée du Rhin" (War song for the Army of the Rhine) and alluded to the declaration of war by France against Austria (the song acquired its present name after being sung by volunteers from Marseille marching to Paris). It was a violent call to defend the "motherland" against a foreign military threat. Soon after, the song became the anthem of the French Revolution, as well as of other emancipatory causes beyond the French border, and was officially adopted—nationalized and domesticated—as the anthem of the French Republic in 1795 by the French National Convention.

In 1871, the lyrics of the "The Internationale," whose original French words were written by the Communard Eugène Pottier—and composed while in hiding to escape the "Semaine sanglante" of brutal repression against the Paris Commune—were initially sung to the tune of "La Marseillaise." In 1888, the Belgian Pierre De Geyter composed a new melody for it—a hardly modified version of the French tune "Chant du depart"—and the piece then became the shared hymn of socialism, communism, and anarchism. Additionally, being the most translated anthem in history, "The Internationale" has been interpreted and rewritten in hundreds of languages, and to this day, its text or meaning is far from fixed. Even the most cursory look at the history and reception of "The Internationale" reveals a permanent state of flux, a transit between languages, ideologies, and melodies, triggered by the repetition, reproducibility, and massification inherent to the composition. The musical figurations of the ideological and the political are intrinsically technological.

The borrowing of a national melody tied to the French Revolution and its subsequent transnational transit across borders and languages traces with uncanny precision the fate of universalism and its symbolic entanglement with a myriad of divergent ideologies—revolution, nationalism, state Communism, antifascism, anticolonialism, and so on. Like Sala, Balibar also traces a lineage between the ideals of the French Revolution, their appropriation by revolutionary communism, and their intimate connection to the idea of Europe as a political community after the demise of state Communism. The dream of the appropriation of the idea of Europe by the West

> began with the symbolic "transfer" of the Jacobin Revolution and the Paris Commune to Petrograd and Moscow and continued with each of the two "Europes" claiming to be the only authentic incarnation of the spirit of antifascist resistance, because the other was stigmatized by its impure collusion with Nazism (whether on account of Munich, or the German-Soviet Pact, or imperialism and monopoly capitalism, or totalitarianism, or the *Berufsverbot*, or else the gulag).[50]

The continued appropriation of the anthem is a testament to the liquidity and fugitivity of music in the face of ideological stagnation, but also to the weight of formal symbolism in group formations. Structurally, the piece collectivizes the role that the individual had in *Ravel Ravel*, where transindividuality became the effect of a multiplication and repetition that increased the resonance of the piece.[51] In *Take Over*, every new variation and translation of "The Internationale" is already present in the melody and the lyrics of the song, both of which are presented as variations and repetitions of a single verse and a rhythmic pattern, as musical accumulations.

Sala's *Take Over*, first conceived for and presented at the Esther Schipper Gallery in Berlin, takes its point of departure from the rhythmic kinship between these two political anthems. Sala's installation consists of three videos played in a loop, displayed on three different screens and divided by angled glass panels that reflect, amplify, and spectralize the screen's images. On one horizontally split screen, each section with a close-up of the keyboard of a Disklavier player, the two anthems are performed simultaneously by pianist Clemens Hund-Göschel and by a computer-generated algorithm. The embodied and mechanical performing and reproducing in overlapping and contrasting tempos is supplemented by two other individual projections of these same recordings, with "La Marseillaise" on one side and "The Internationale" on the other side. The architectural divisions created by the glass panel double as intimate acoustic chambers, so that the spectator's mobility and changing point of view figures as yet another element of transit and functions as a literal "cropping" of the projection's sound that further weaves body, sound, and image into a complex spatiotemporal arrangement. Sala's installation is presented as a choreography of different media, designed to multiply the possibility of encounters and crossovers between them. We are dealing again with a perceptual conceptualism that defies formal stasis in its commitment to imminence as a state of heightened attention.

However, instead of relying mostly on the doubling and internal echoes of the two pieces, as he did in *Ravel Ravel*, Sala disrupts the steadiness of the composition, its reliance on tempo as a measure,

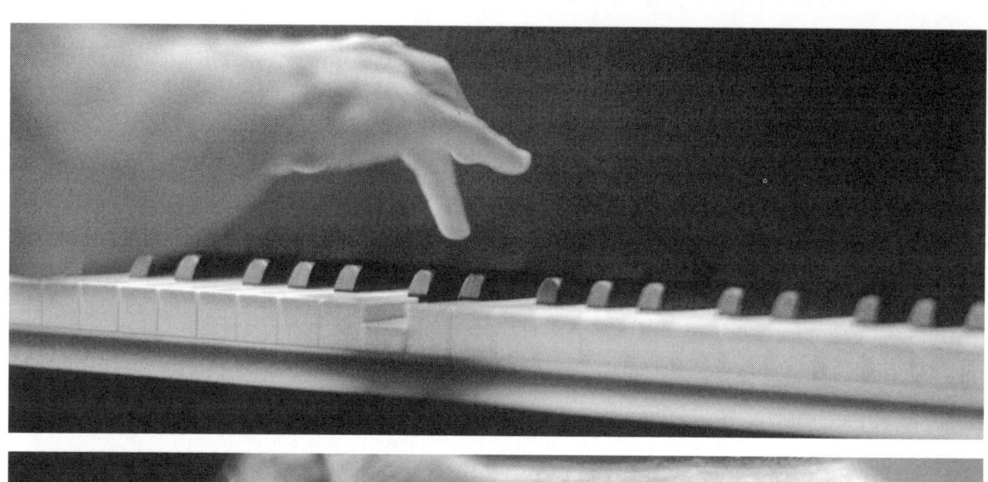

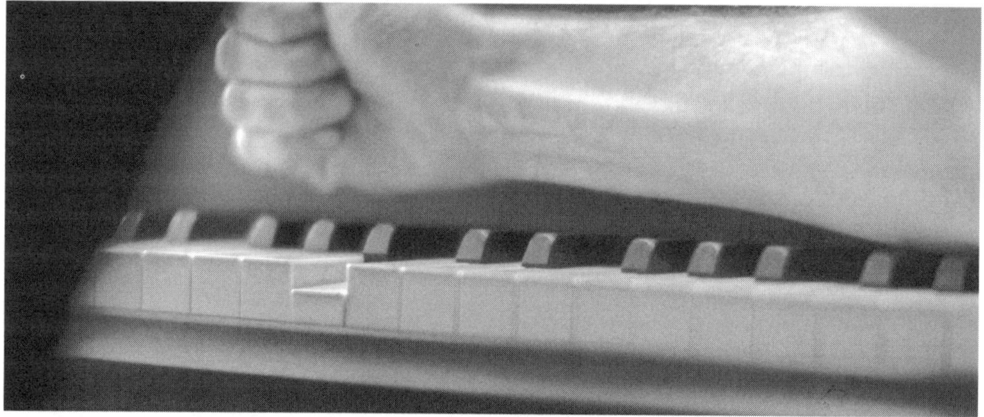

Anri Sala, *Take Over (La Marsellaise* [left] *and The Internationale* [right]), 2017. Video stills. Courtesy of the artist.

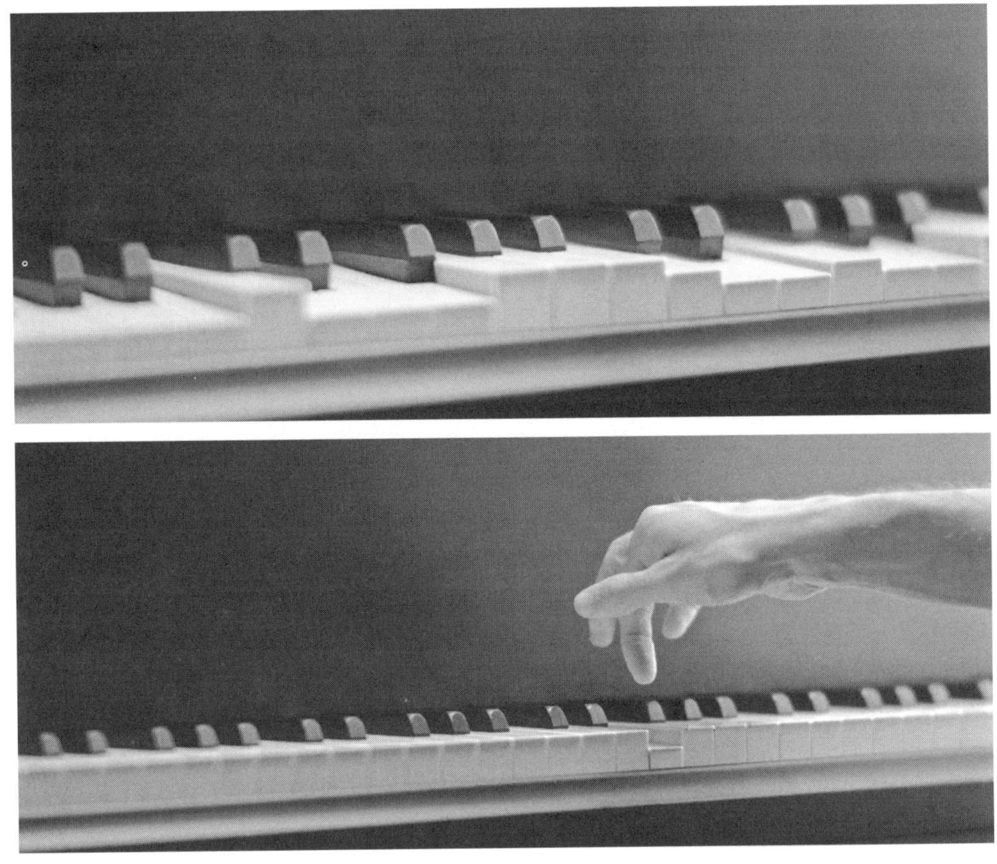

to force a change in the directionality and predictability of the musical theme, arguably the characteristic most readily appropriated by ideological narratives of progress. As is often the case with Sala, *Take Over* contains several self-referential echoes to previous films and installations, motifs and figures that circulate throughout and across his corpus. In this instance, Sala's sustained meditation on agency, mediation, and multiplicity, or more precisely, on the multiplicity contained in any mediation of agency, now reverses some of the elements of *Ravel Ravel*: one single pianist playing two different anthems is now substituted for the two pianists performing the piano concerto. This numerical interplay between different forms of multiplicity across human and technological media allows Sala's meditation to continue and to become increasingly complex by creating compositions and recombinations between different works. We are therefore able to experience his archive as unfolding and unfinished but also as thematically and affectively gathered. The beginning of *Take Over*, for instance, echoes the first images of *Ravel Ravel*, but this reference makes an absence of hands at the piano (an absence that now takes on an entirely different connotation) all the more conspicuous. In this self-referential echo, the addition of mechanical automation in the form of the player piano initiates one of the most important motifs of the piece: the blurring between technology and performance, the exploration of movements without agency, and more precisely, the disfigurations and reconfigurations of agency, political, ideological, and historical.

As was the case with *Long Sorrow* and *Ravel Ravel*, and despite Sala's early disavowal of a purely linguistic understanding of language in favor of a more extensive one, the title of the piece, *Take Over*, encapsulates and inscribes various forms of appropriation, replacement, and violent domination. It also brings back the figure of inheritance and the responsibility it entails, a constant undercurrent in Sala's various deployments of Europe's musical heritage. But this time, inheritance appears even more fully mediated by technology; indeed, it cannot exist outside technological reproduction and transmission. When the piano plays without the keyboard being touched, we are once more confronted with an (unchosen) inheritance that will only be altered with great effort. Through repeated performance, and musical technologies fully embedded in the pianist's body, inheritance can even become an unconscious muscle memory. Yet through the possibilities opened by endless reenactments, history itself becomes cinematic: it acquires the plasticity of fiction and becomes capable of containing endless possibilities. This cinematic history, carried across generations and across different cartographies, even if in disfigured, distorted, and fragmentary ways, can nevertheless help forge new compositions. However, even these new compositions and assemblages will continue to shift in their shape and in their relations and affiliations, which is exactly the way "La Marseillaise" and "The Internationale" are mobilized in *Take Over.*

In *Take Over*, Sala's transmedia labor of composition takes the form of defamiliarization, disintegration, and the multiplication of uncertainty and unpredictability. The fluctuation between closeness and detachment, anchoring and disorientation, punctuates the compositional variations of each of the two films and also between them. The regular and horizontal architecture of the keyboard is slanted so that, when shown on a split screen, the two diagonal keyboards appear more separated and distanced on one end and closer together on another. This contrast between distance and proximity is further accentuated by the intermittent focus of the camera, which follows the movements on the keyboard, so that the last resonance of a note is visual, rather than acoustic, and our expectations regarding the function of the visual and acoustic are reversed. The fact that there are three projections, one where the films are misaligned together in a split screen and then again fully detached from one another on separate projections, amplifies this contrast even further.

The compositional presentation of each film depends on the focus of the camera, which is shifting, offering a mirror effect without any clarity as if the body, or at least the visible, detached body parts, are at risk of vanishing. Meanwhile, the musical notes and mechanical sounds unfold very slowly and irregularly until the anthems suddenly become recognizable, but even then only in fragments. The anthems' melodies become as ghostly as the hands and forearms of the pianist, constantly in and out of focus, full of insurrectionary ghosts but also nationalist and conservative ones. Yet unlike the personalized tragedy of *Ravel Ravel*, these anthems, reproduced a million times and appropriated by multiple ideologies, reference not a single individual but anonymous masses, appearing and vanishing, inheriting and breaking with inheritance, unfolding in terms of rhythms and sounds that are at once predictable and unpredictable and that speak of both a shared historical memory and an indeterminate future.

It is possible to read the inscription of the masses in *Take Over* through the role of the numerical as a site of illegibility. The impersonal role of the computer-generated metronomic inscription that regulates the automated playing of the Disklavier remains enigmatic throughout the performance; its improvisations are entirely unpredictable and cannot be attributed to any particular or recognizable subject, in contrast to the tragic subjectivity that structures Ravel's *Left Hand Concerto for Piano and Orchestra*. In a somewhat counterintuitive manner, Sala locates the highest density of uncertainty in the machine and makes its animation a key component of the piece. The numerical as enigma hovers over the entire work, evoking the impossibility of political calculation and the failures of the utopianism inscribed in the two anthems, but most poignantly—after all, Sala is an Albanian citizen who witnessed the collapse of state Communism—in "The Internationale."

When the hands appear in *Take Over*, they do so visibly attached to their forearms, which are at times aligned with the keys, which move without being touched, rather than perpendicular to them, signaling and following a change of direction in the music. The forearm plays the keys as a violent percussive instrument, even as a hammer, emblematically recalling the association of "The Internationale" with communism and socialism but also miming and echoing the mechanical hammers of the piano itself—out of sight, but essential for the transmission and production of sound in the instrument. The visual echo and the reference to the working-class masses is clear; indeed, the working arms and hands of the anonymous masses were the bodily instruments appropriated by movements and political formations that sought to take over or mobilize their collective force.

The pianist's rhythmic gestures—the single gentle strokes, the violent bursts, and the touchless and eerie synchronization with the player piano—help transform the keyboard and the anthems it plays and stands for into an animated and unpredictable counterpart to the performer, whose increasingly forceful playing cannot entirely overcome the momentum of the player piano. Agency and autonomy become an effect no longer of the subject, the pianist, but of the transient gathering force of the music itself, which ends up taking over the entire acoustic, visual, and architectural assemblage of the piece, as was the case in *Long Sorrow.* Sala's work relentlessly emphasizes the difficulty and ephemerality of any convergence, so much so that when convergence happens, it is experienced as a highly elaborate fiction or as a disorienting and wondrous miracle—like the unreal and moving starry sky at the end of the film on "La Marseillaise," which recalls a planetarium, or the beautiful sequence of keys being played from a distance, with the hands and fingers delicately hovering over the keys.[52]

Sala's approach to different media (acoustic, cinematic, spatial) and discursive registers (aesthetic, political, historical) speaks of a series of relays, of insufficiency and relational dependence on one another. None of these elements ever functions in isolation. The term "acoustic immersive environment" seems insufficient to describe Sala's practice because his mobilization of resonance, although it departs from the acoustic, is much more extensive. It exhibits an all-encompassing network of relations that can never be fully extricated and that are held together by a fictional structure. The role of fiction in Sala's practice can hardly be overstated: it is the key to his artistic procedures as a whole and to his complex understanding of the historical as a site of political possibility, so that the function of "as if" may be transformed into a yet indeterminate but hopeful "what if." Fiction opens the door to speculation, and art becomes a possible entryway into a political imagination of increased plasticity.

The most original aspect of Sala's practice might be his fictionalization of music. Since 2003, the artist has continued to mine a variety of Western musical traditions (Beethoven, Arnold Schoenberg, Stravinsky, Olivier Messiaen, or The Clash) in his work as sites of potentiality, understood as a modality of fiction that refuses "to pass into actuality" and chooses instead to remain speculative.[53] Sala's sophisticated cinematic movement is sonically inflected, but the notion of "soundtrack" does not do justice to the passages and transports between sound, image, and space in his video installations.[54] His return to lens-based techniques associated with an earlier filmic avant-garde—such as focus, extreme close-up, or cropping—situates him at a high point of experimentation, but in an oddly anachronistic position.[55] Furthermore, his assimilation of the lens to musical tonality and saturation allows him to produce an intermedial perceptual abstraction that transforms our experience of the two media—Sala's fictions cannot be attributed to either of them alone. The complexity and intensity of attention his films demand and perform affects the audience's responsiveness to image and sound by engaging body, mind, and memory in a fictional and endless loop that establishes a new relation between the two media, an interval that plays in the mind.

In "From Recollections to Dreams: Third Commentary on Bergson," Deleuze reminds us that in postwar European cinema (with the proviso that all European cinema is postwar), "it is not the recollection-image or attentive recognition which gives us the proper equivalent of the optical-sound image, it is rather the disturbances of memory and the failures of recognition."[56] Sala's fictions, which Deleuze might have called "virtual" or "reflective," exist as "disturbances of memory" and "failures of recognition," insofar as cinema's dream-image "is not a metaphor but a series of anamorphoses which sketch out a very large circuit" that is potentially infinite—limitless, in fact, as it extends into "a movement of world." This movement, Deleuze adds, which must be impersonal and technologically mediated and is "marked by animals" and "peopled by inversions," belongs to the time-image as a musicalized temporality that only cinema can actualize by means of a transmedia anachronism. Blending Kant and Henri Bergson, the philosopher of cinema tells us that "we are internal to time" and its "unbridled depth," but time is already traversed by memory. Only cinema can begin to unfold this internal time, and it does so by borrowing its virtual intervals from music as the interiorization of time.[57] "What is opposed to fiction is not the real," he goes on to note, "it is not the truth which is always that of the masters or colonizers; it is the story-telling function of the poor, in so far as it gives the false the power which makes it into a memory, a legend, a monster."[58] This monster, I would add, is a monster in the ear, the limitlessness of a howl that survives us all.

CODA

Listening Beyond the Ear

> The act of listening is much broader and wider than just channeling sound through the ear. If we start to pay attention to other ways of listening, a whole horizon of building instruments, of working together, of occupying space, becomes possible.
>
> — Tarek Atoui (2023)

In 2006, composer, DJ, and artist Tarek Atoui returned to his hometown, Beirut, to record an album and to document the soundscapes of the city. Atoui was born just before the Lebanese Civil War, and the country was now at war with Israel for the second time.[1] Internally divided by quarters, an echo and legacy of Euro-American partitioning of the region at large after the Second World War, Beirut once had been dubbed the "Paris of the East" by French colonialists. During these intermittent and prolonged wars, propaganda and political songs were popular, and concert venues for more experimental and less politically legible music, often integrating sonic violence, continued to thrive. In this context, negotiating music's relationship to polyphonic discord, dissent, and displacement — reflecting, that is, on the centrality of the nonmusical in the musical — becomes a necessity. In a further entanglement of violence and the acoustic, because of his sound documentation in the streets of Beirut, Atoui was

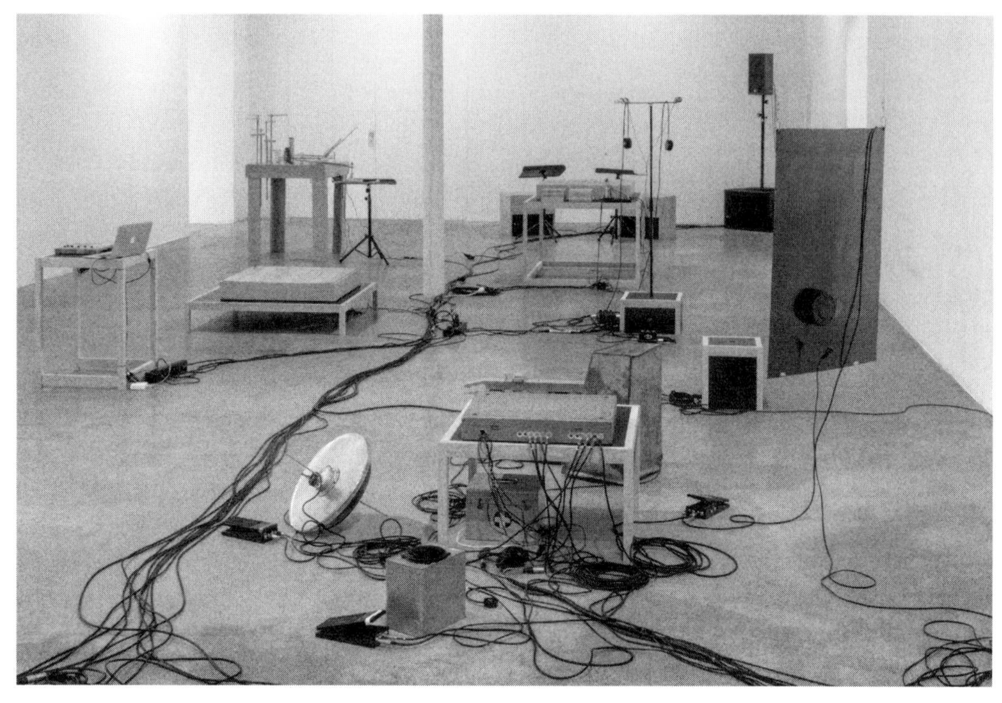

Tarek Atoui, *WITHIN*, 2017. Exhibition view, Galerie Chantal Crousel, Paris. Courtesy of the artist and Galerie Chantal Crousel. Photo by Florian Kleinefenn.

accused of espionage by Hezbollah. He was detained and hit in the head by his captors. Upon release, he was partially deaf in one ear.[2]

Since then, Atoui has been engaged in expanding what listening is through a series of experiments and with an ever-growing number of collaborators around the world. Among these collaborators, Deaf schools and different kinds of learning communities have played a key role. We already have seen several modified instruments — variations intent on accommodating the musician's nonnormative bodies, including Beethoven's pianos — and artworks that question what listening may mean to an elephant, a vulture, a bat, a snail, or a human ear. Atoui expands and intensifies these speculations by asking what hearing is.

His response, one borne of continued experimentation, improvisation, and fabrication, begins in a perceived reduction that opens onto a world of possibilities — learning to hear, that is, more deeply and otherwise. Learning from how Deaf listeners hear, through lower frequencies of vibration and resonances felt in the body, Atoui returns sound to the sense of touch and music to the percussive rhythms of the oldest of instruments — moving from the eardrum to the drum, externalizing a bodily organ into a sculptural organism. Additionally, further blurring the lines among composition, performance, and installation, he extends acoustic resonance into an instrument of attention that far exceeds the event that each exhibition makes possible as it continues to resonate into the everyday life of the listener as a kind of attunement.

His first collaboration with Deaf collectives, during his work on the 2009 *Un-drum / strategies for surviving noise* for the Sharjah Biennial 15, involved the Al Amal School for the Deaf, with students ranging from eight to twenty years old. Together with the students in the school, he designed instruments that amplify sound by using coils and metal bars that when struck, transmit their sounds though wooden boxes with deep grooves in them. In 2012, he began the multiyear project *WITHIN* in collaboration with the duo Council—Sandra Terdjman and Gregory Castera—as a direct exploration of the Deaf understanding of sound, instrumentation, and performance.[3] Tapping into the knowledge of the Deaf, Atoui moves beyond orality, the ear, and the tympan toward an Epicurean swerve, a frequency that animates everything and everyone equally. The acoustic is a source of endless distortion and plasticity, mobilizing perceptual experience away from identification and toward a process of becoming.

Establishing *instrumentarium* workshops and residencies with hundreds of participants, Atoui develops—together with sound engineers, Deaf and hearing listeners, composers, and software designers—new instruments that double as sound sculptures and portable laboratories. The project requires a great deal of institutional support, a combination of different kinds of knowledge or practice, and involves an entire collective well before it reaches a gallery or museum audience.[4] It is an accumulation that proceeds through improvisation and that none of its participants can fully own. When the instruments are tested for the first time—in Bergen, for instance, they were installed in a resonant abandoned pool—an inclusive and expansive group of players is invited: musicians and nonmusicians, the Deaf and the hearing, ensembles and soloists. This relational network is literally materialized through the web of cables across the floor, an entanglement of conductors out of which sound circulates and remixes.

At one point, Atoui and his collaborators realized that the Deaf participants, when talking to the hearing, described the physicality of sound using concepts borrowed from hearing culture, a vocabulary sensorially less expressive, and decided to integrate sign language into the piece. Heavily inflected by mood and sensation, sign language easily allowed for an expansion of the vocabulary used to describe sound during these workshops, which is where the artworks were conceived and produced, once again turning an insufficiency, the limits of the verbal, into an anchor for transformation and expansion by inscribing sensation into the sign itself.

Following the same logic, Atoui adapts the concept of DeafSpace, devised by architect Hansel Baumal in 2005,[5] to the collective manufacture of modified and new instruments, ranging from complex software interfaces to simple alterations: a drum covered in glass marbles, with the player's hands striking the drum with marbles, visualizing music in the clash of the marbles; Sub-Ink, a modular instrument that can synchronize a set of four units with a single subwoofer each so that the listener can sit and touch an ink drawing prepared beforehand while the musician plays;[6] or 33 Soft Cells, a sampler made of thirty-three touch-sensitive textile panels that, when connected to a computer with an acoustic output, allows music to be perceived through touch alone. As the project continues to evolve and transform as the sessions are recorded, a repertoire for both Deaf and hearing listeners begins to form that can be used in music schools, becoming publicly available.[7] In more recent installations—incorporating vibration, rotation, and sound transmission through water—the difference between hearing through the tympan or through muscles and bones becomes increasingly less significant.

While the project may have started with Deaf communities, it is simultaneously an entryway into a more layered, complex, and heterogeneous understanding of sound and its endless configurations. As Atoui puts it, "it gradually became an exploration of what hearing is, aside from the aural: hearing in our dreams, hearing voices of the dead, listening to birds or recording unexpected and imperceptible sounds. Beyond the hearing and non-hearing binary, it brought together expertise and knowledge which one does not generally encounter, therefore challenging a set of preconceived ideas."[8] A limitless listening that exceeds the bounds of hearing allows us to feel the complexity of time as a living organism—a composite organism that can inhabit the body and connect us to the world around us, a world composed of an accumulation of interconnected layers of sound, at once perceptible and imperceptible. The projects that followed *WITHIN* experiment with, among other things, wildlife sounds, birds singing, amoebae breathing, and even photosynthesis; water sounds and their underwater amplification: splashing, dripping, bubbling; recordings of harbors around the world: Dubai, Athens, and Singapore; and sounds transmitted through stones, each sound affected by the stone's porosity and levels of sedimentation. If, in Atoui's world, artworks become instruments in the full sense of the word — in the way Socrates becomes an instrument to be a philosopher — it is because they equip us to listen more profoundly. They are a reminder that we are all hard of hearing; we are all children of deaf adults — CODA.

During the COVID lockdown, Atoui brought his acoustic workshops to the kindergarten school in Paris his son was attending, to one of the "hearts of Europe," that is. As the children became more daring in their interaction with the project's water instruments and turntables, less afraid of breaking them, and more comfortable with the breakdown of the border between listening and playing, a little girl, Greta, began to howl like a wolf.[9]

Acknowledgments

Writing and reading are conversations where the living and the dead partake in equal measure to become partners on the page. This book is the result of a constellation of conversations that continue to expand and deepen, and this brief acknowledgment an attempt to gather onto one single page some of the friends and interlocutors who made it possible—so that they too know they belong to the shared network that sustains this project and sustains me as well.

This necessarily incomplete list includes my family and particularly my nephews, Tomàs, Gerard, Liam, and Marc, who have become my relationship to the future (it is often to them that I imagine I talk when I write); Agnieska Kurant, because thinking with her is thinking better; Jorge Coronado, whose friendship has remained an anchor even when everything else becomes uncertain; Manuel Cirauqui, who sent me the image that opens this book (because he understood that much); Jo Labanyi, whose version of the university should be everyone's model; Barbara Held, who shared her love and understanding of Carles Santos with me; Anthony Graves, whose acuity can spot hidden hesitations and remind me to think them through; Douglas Ross, who read the entire manuscript with his finely tuned musical ear; Jennifer Allora and Guillermo Calzadilla, who trusted me with their survey show at Barcelona's Fundació Tàpies and forever changed my thinking with artworks, and not just theirs; Mónica de la Torre, whose writing and conversation make me want to be better at both; Glenn Ligon, whose work is a miraculous reminder, among many other things, of the force of words, and even letters; Gregg Bordowitz, who welcomed me into the Whitney ISP, a study community that quickly felt like an intellectual refuge; and Eduardo Cadava, who insisted that finishing our *Politically Red* first would make returning to *Europe and the Wolf* both easier and more enjoyable. I resisted but he was right, so very right. Gracias, Eduardo! And finally, Patrick Killoran, whose comedic timing lovingly interrupts my worst inertias and makes our everyday sing a happier tune—with some major help from our beloved and floppy-eared Lula.

I thank Films 59, Actar, Fons Carles Santos at Caixa de Vinarós, Jennifer Allora and Guillermo Calzadilla, Anri Sala, and Galerie Chantal Crousel for kindly granting me permission to reproduce images of artworks, performances, and films—none of which can capture the wonder and complexity of the pieces they document. I also thank the Slought Foundation/Public Trust in Philadelphia, where I was a Writer-in-Residence while I finished this book, and the Vartan Gregorian Center for Research in the Humanities at the New York Public Library for providing a much needed study room.

Everyone at Zone has been simply wonderful and I cannot imagine this strange book being at home anywhere else. Bud Bynack made my prose clearer and more direct with every suggestion. Elizabeth Benninger kindly checked all my references. Meighan Gale steered the whole production process with the most efficient grace. Jonathan Crary gave the space and trust I needed to write the book I wanted and very much needed to write. Julie Fry's creative labor is the envelope that introduces this book to you. An early fragment of Part 1 appeared in *Catalan Cinema: (In)Visible Traditions and the New Avant-Garde* (2023). Small bits and pieces of Part 2 were included in *Allora & Calzadilla* (2018).

This book is dedicated to Carla Herrera-Prats, whose commitment to the work of thinking and making with others endures as an affectionate encouragement to just keep going, because somehow it matters, and because we are in it together.

Notes

INTRODUCTION: THE WOLF AND EUROPE

1. For the most erudite study of Pythagoras's understanding of harmony, see Daniel Heller-Roazen, *The Fifth Hammer: Pythagoras and the Disharmony of the World* (New York: Zone Books, 2011). I heard a preliminary fragment of this text for the first time at a talk Heller-Roazen gave at *Après-Coup* in New York City, and it remained with me. It made me think of wolf tones but also about the symbolic and political weight they carry.

2. The original reads, "Lupus est homo homini, non homo, quam quails sit non novit." Titus Maccius Plautus, *Asinaria, or the One about the Asses*, trans. John Henderson (Madison: University of Wisconsin Press, 2006), p. 53 (translation modified).

3. Thomas Hobbes, *De Cive, or The Citizen*, ed. Sterling P. Lamprecht (New York: Appleton-Century-Crofts, 1949), p. 1. In Hobbes, the paradox and the tension between nonhuman animals and the positing of the sovereign-animal-law suggests that nonhuman animals have no rights, since the law will always need an outside, an outlaw. The bond between the sovereign and the wolf must be retroactively broken once the law has been posited.

4. Jacques Derrida, *The Beast and the Sovereign*, ed. Michel Lisse, Marie-Louise Mallet, and Ginette Michaud, trans. Geoffrey Bennington, 2 vols. (Chicago: Chicago University Press, 2009), vol. 1, p. 17.

5. Ibid., p. 26.

6. Sigmund Freud, *Civilization and Its Discontents*, trans. James Strachey, in *The Standard Edition of the Complete Psychological Works of Sigmund Freud*, ed. James Strachey, 24 vols. (London: Hogarth Press, 1961), vol. 21, p. 111.

7. Derrida, *The Beast and the Sovereign*, vol. 1, pp. 4–5.

8. I of course refer here to Schmitt's 1932 *The Concept of the Political*. See, Schmitt, *The Concept of the Political*, trans. George Schwab (Chicago: University of Chicago Press, 2007).

9. The National Center on Disability and Journalism's style guide advises that the word "deaf" be lowercased when referring to a hearing-loss condition but capitalized when referring to the Deaf community.

10. Jacques Derrida, *Athens, Still Remains: The Photographs of Jean-François Bonhomme*, trans. Pascale-Anne Brault and Michael Naas (New York: Fordham University Press, 2010), p. 55.

11. Jean-Luc Nancy, *Listening*, trans. Charlotte Mandell (New York: Fordham University Press, 2007), p. 12.

12. Étienne Balibar, *Politics and the Other Scene*, trans. Christine Jones, James Swenson, and Chris Turner (London: Verso, 2002), p. xi.

FIRST INTERLUDE: EUROPA 2005, OCTOBER 27

1. In the wake of the uprisings, Balibar writes that "*the 'banlieue' as such is a frontier, a border-area and a frontline*." He adds that this logic "culminates in the construction of a juridically and humanly monstrous social category: the *hereditary status of immigrant*—'once an immigrant, always an immigrant,' generation after generation, whatever nationality is acquired. And hence 'foreigners in their own country,' since they do not (or no longer) have any other." See Étienne Balibar, "Uprisings in the *Banlieues*," trans. James Ingram, *Constellations* 14.1 (2007), pp. 48 and 58 (emphasis in the original).

2. Jean-Jacques Rousseau, *Discourse on the Origins and Foundation of Equality (Second Discourse)*, in *The First and Second Discourses*, ed. Roger D. Masters, trans. Roger D. and Judith R. Masters (New York: St. Martin's Press, 1964), p. 132, translation extensively modified. See KINO SLANG, "Joachim Gatti (2009)," April 4, 2001, https://kinoslang.blogspot.com/2010/04/joachim-gatti-2009-video-by-jean-marie_04.html.

3. Balibar, "Uprisings in the *Banlieues*," p. 66.

PART ONE: THE LABOR OF SOUND

1. Portabella has told this anecdote many times in interviews and in conversations and has also written about it in his text for Santos's retrospective, "Flashback," where he recounts their experience in the Modelo prison. See *Carles Santos: ¡Visca el piano!*, exhibition catalogue (Barcelona: Actar and Fundació Joan Miró, 2006), pp. 73–86.

2. Later in Santos's career, pianos become as mobile as motorcycles, carrying and containing bodies in a similar manner. Throughout his more than three decades of work, pianos will function as metaphors and sculptures, as ideas and objects. They will be constantly tampered with, manipulated, and deconstructed, with all these forms of displacement culminating in his 2006 series *Pianos intervinguts*, Santos's own version of John Cage's "prepared pianos."

3. Not be confused with the Assemblea Nacional de Catalunya or ANC, founded in 2011 with the exclusive aim of promoting Catalan independence and calling for a referendum.

4. Before the term "fugue" became widely accepted, the earlier Italian "ricercar" ("to seek"), which Bach himself uses, was used to describe the speculative characteristics of this archaic and complex musical form.

5. Theodor W. Adorno, *Introduction to the Sociology of Music*, trans. E. B. Ashton (New York: Continuum, 1988), pp. 221 and 224.

6. Trinh T. Minh-Ha, *The Cinema Interval* (New York: Routledge, 1999), p. xiii.

7. This attack recalls Adorno's intuitive term *Einschlag*, which could be translated as an "impact," "hit," or, even better in the context of our discussion, as a "woof." As Lydia Goehr notes, "Adorno used the noun usually with a modifier: the *virtuosic impact*, the *suave*, *exotic*, *catatonic*, *nationalistic*, but also the *tonal* or *compositional*." She adds that his use of the term contains an "element of protest that is possible given only the ongoing mediation between *technique* and *technology*, *spirit* and *mechanism*." See Goehr, "Did Bach Compose Musical Works?," *New German Critique* 48.1 (2021), pp. 16 and 17 (emphasis in the original).

8. Their first official collaboration was the 1966 performance of Josep Mestres Quadreny's *Suite Bufa*, with Brossa's theatricalization, followed in 1968 by Santos's *Concert irregular* at the Fundació Maeght of Josep Mestres Quadreny to celebrate Joan Miró's seventy-fifth birthday—an action that Portabella directs. It is there that for the first time, Santos declares the piano a "useless piece of furniture" and uses this declaration as an invitation to play and tamper with the instrument in novel ways and eventually to transform it into a sculptural object that links and articulates his musical and artistic output. It is also the last segment of the performance, "Homenatge al Vietcong," where the pianist uses an American flag as a towel after shaving, an act that outraged the US delegation present at the event. See Fèlix Fanés, "Portabella, Brossa, Santos: Un triangle irregular," *Hispanic Review* 78.4 (Autumn 2010), p. 477.

9. I first heard the story of Santos meeting Brossa from art historian Fèlix Fanés, but while their encounter and Brossa's response is well documented, whether Santos did or did not play Bach remains unverified. Most of the musician's friends agree that Bach being his musical center, it would be unlikely for him to play anything else. As Fanés put it in a recent email exchange, "se non è vero, è ben trovato"—"if it is not true, it is well founded." Although Santos's New York period has not been extensively researched, we do know that in addition to Cage, he was in contact with and carefully studied Steve Reich, La Monte Young, Terry Riley, and Philip Glass.

10. The subtitle is a reference to Bach's biographer Johan Nikolaus Forkel, author of *Johann Sebastian Bach: His Life, Art, and Work* and considered one of the founders of modern musicology. Forkel corresponded with two of Bach's sons, Carl Phillip Emmanuel and Wilhem Friederman, for his research.

11. It is not an accident that the panther is not native to Europe. That Santos chooses to name his piano and the composer he so often performs—and deforms—after this foreign animal is consonant with his effort to displace and ruin any European sovereignty that would take its force from a cultural patrimony. Put differently, Santos's panther is another name for the wolf at the heart of Europe, fissuring its harmony and self-sameness from within.

12. As Adorno notes in an aside in a series of radio lectures, collected in his *Introduction to the Sociology of Music*, during Bach's time and beyond, composers, who often came from impoverished backgrounds, "belonged to the so-called 'third persons.'" The term was used to describe those who work in the service of others, such as servants. See Theodor W. Adorno, "Classes and Strata," in *Introduction to the Sociology of Music* (New York: Continuum, 1988), p. 58.

13. Arthur Cravan, born Fabian Avenarius Lloyd (1887–1918), was a Swiss Dadaist poet, artist, performer, and boxer. Cravan was also the director and sole contributor to the journal *Maintenant*. One of his most famous boxing matches, against world champion Jack Johnson, galvanized the city of Barcelona in 1916. The match, in which he was quickly knocked out, was in fact a means to raise money for his trip to the United States in an attempt to avoid conscription during the First World War. On board the ship, he befriended Leon Trotsky, then en route to Mexico.

14. Theodor W. Adorno, "Bach Defended against his Devotees," in *Prisms*, trans. Samuel and Shierry Weber (Cambridge, MA: MIT Press, 1967), p. 142.

15. Ibid., p. 145.

16. Theodor W. Adorno, *Aesthetic Theory*, trans. Robert Hullot-Kentor (Minneapolis: University of Minnesota Press, 1997), p. 301 (translation modified).

17. Gilles Deleuze and Félix Guattari, *A Thousand Plateaus: Capitalism and Schizophrenia*, trans. Brian Massumi (Minneapolis: University of Minnesota Press, 1987), p. 8.

18. Gould's humming does not always follow Bach's score; rather, it offers a counterpoint that escapes notation. It literally breathes new life into the score of the *Variations* by adding new elements—elements having to do with the breath and rhythm of the pieces themselves.

19. Adorno, "Bach Defended against his Devotees," p. 146.

20. Theodor W. Adorno. "On the Contemporary Relationship of Philosophy and Music," in *Essays on Music*, trans. Susan H. Gillespie (Berkeley: University of California Press, 2002), p. 148 (translation modified).

21. Here is a complete list of Grup de Treball's members: Francesc Abad, Jordi Benito, Jaume Carbó, María Costa, Alicia Fingerhut, Xavier Franquesa, Carles Hac Mor, Imma Julián, Antoni Mercader, Antoni Munné, Antoni Muntadas, Josep Parera, Santi Pau, Pere Portabella, Àngels Ribé, Manuel Rovira, Enric Sales, Carles Santos, Dorothée Selz, and Francesc Torres. For the only publication dedicated to the group to date, see Antoni Mercader, Pilar Parcerisas, and Valentín Roma, *Grup de Treball*, exhibition catalogue (Barcelona: MACBA, 1999).

22. Ibid., inside front cover.

23. Most of these performances were linked to his role as director and performer in the Grup Instrumental Català (GIC), active from 1976 to 1979 at the Fundació Joan Miró, a location that archives manifold dissidences, dating back to the Spanish II Republic Pavilion at the World's Fair, and that plays a densely symbolic role in Santos's artistic production. It is the location for his Miró films in collaboration with Clovis Prévost, as well as for *¡Visca el piano!* (Long live the piano!) and *Die Stille vor Bach* (The silence before Bach).

24. His 1970 recorded performance *Playback* and his 1973 *Acció Santos* (Action Santos) were already meditations on transmedia recording technologies that intensified the delays and repetitions already inherent in musical experience.

25. I will use the original German title of the film throughout because it underscores the role of translation and the transport between languages in the film. Portabella uses a modified German translation of a Lars Gustafsson poem from 1983, whose original Swedish title, "Välderns tystnad före Bach," is more accurately "The Stillness of the World before Bach."

26. Alain Badiou, "Cinema as Philosophical Experimentation," in *Cinema*, trans. Susan Spitzer (Cambridge: Polity, 2013), p. 202.

27. Gilles Deleuze, *Cinema 2: The Time-Image*, trans. Hugh Tomlison and Robert Galeta (Minneapolis: University of Minnesota Press, 2001), p. 217.

28. Portabella repeats the gesture in his film 2008 *Mudanza* (Removal), which documents workers removing furniture from Federico García Lorca's Casa Museo in Huerta de San Vicente and the camera's itinerary through the bare walls and rooms of his home—in this way, making the poignant absence of the poet and playwright, murdered by Spanish Fascists in 1936, all the more present. The film was screened during ten days in a wooden cinema built in the garden while the house/museum stayed empty. The request for an intervention in the museum space came from curator Hans Ulrich Obrist, under the title *everstill/siempretodavía* (in Catalan and Spanish, everstill/always still), which took over the space and commissioned site-specific works from a variety of artists from 2007 to 2008.

29. Nowhere is this clearer than in his Miró trilogy—*Miró l'altre* (Miró the other) in 1969, *Miró forja* (Miró forge) in 1973, and *Miró tapis* (Miró tapestry) in 1973, where, rather than focusing on Miró's creative process, he examines the labor of production of foundry workers and textile weavers. He makes an exception in the first film in the series, where Miró (who remains silent for the entire duration of the film) draws a mural on the windows of Barcelona's School of Architecture to have it then erased by a crew of female cleaners, who effectively complete the performance, or rather, in the parlance of the time, the "happening." Miró's own "assassination" of painting remains a reference throughout, his legacy never more clearly transmitted than here.

30. Adorno uses the phrase "thinking with one's ears" (*mit den Ohren zu Denken*) in "Cultural Criticism and Society," in *Prisms*, p. 19 (translation modified).

31. There is indeed a syntactical relationship between all of Portabella's extraordinary experimental films of the 1960s and 1970s. However, I will not address any of them here because the stated goal of my project is to think *with* a select and reduced number of artworks that specifically experiment with Europe's musical legacy, and not to give an art historical or critical account of any of the artists with whom I engage. In regard to the financial aspect of Portabella's clandestine film production and its anachronic relation to the Francoist milieu, it is striking that the filmmaker often used expired film stock. It is hard not to read into this minor detail an inscription of the layered and contradictory temporal spaces his films inhabit.

32. This choice is a bit surprising since Straub, who had started work on the film by 1954, always emphasizes his collaboration with Huillet: "I would probably never have made a film if I had remained alone. Because I wouldn't have found the courage and I was too lazy and still am. And I would probably have failed or given up." Quoted in Peter Nesler, "For Danièle and Jean-Marie," in *Tell It to the Stones: Encounters with the Films of Danièle Huillet and Jean Marie Straub*, eds. Annett Busch and Tobias Hering (Berlin: Sternberg Press, 2021), pp. 44–45.

33. On a biographical note regarding violence and borders, Straub was born in the town of Mets, which was part of Germany until the end of the end of the First World War, then became French, only to be annexed to Germany during the Second World War then returned to France at the end of the war.

34. Jean Marie Straub, "The Bach Film," in Danièle Huillet and Jean Marie Straub, *Writings* (New York: Sequence Press, 2016), p. 74.

35. Ibid., p. 70.

36. Immanuel Kant, *The Critique of Judgement*, trans. Werner S. Pluhar (Indianapolis: Hackett Publishing, 1987), p. 45.

37. Hannah Arendt, *Lectures on Kant's Political Philosophy*, ed. Ronald Beiner (Chicago: University of Chicago Press, 1992), pp. 64–65.

38. Kant, *The Critique of Judgement*, p. 161 (translation modified).

39. Michel Chaouli, *Thinking with Kant's Critique of Judgment* (Cambridge, MA: Harvard University Press, 2017), p. 90.

40. Michael Wayne, *Red Kant: Aesthetics, Marxism, and the Third Critique* (London: Bloomsbury, 2014), p. 7.

41. Gilles Deleuze, *Kant's Critical Philosophy*, trans. Hugh Tomlinson and Barbara Habberjam (London: Athlone Press, 1984), pp. 60 and 63.

42. See Kojin Karatani, *Transcritique: On Kant and Marx*, trans. Sabu Kohso (Cambridge, MA: MIT Press, 2005), and Georg Lukács, *History and Class Consciousness*, trans. Rodney Livingstone (Cambridge, MA: MIT Press, 1972), p. 134.

43. Kant, *The Critique of Judgement*, p. 154 (italics in the original).

44. Chaouli, *Thinking with Kant's Critique of Judgment*, p. 85.

45. Kant, *The Critique of Judgement*, p. 151.

46. Éric Alliez, *Capital Times: Tales from the Conquest of Time*, trans. Georges Van Den Abbeele (Minneapolis: University of Minnesota Press, 1996), pp. xii-xiii.

47. To this, Kant adds a "secret article" at the end of his "philosophical sketch" that

retroactively demands that his counsel as a philosopher be heard and be freely given, with the proviso that the request be carried out "silently" and not be given any priority. "Simply listen," he seems to say.

48. Immanuel Kant, *Perpetual Peace, and Other Essays on Politics, History, and Morals*, trans. Ted Humphrey (Indianapolis: Hackett Publishing, 1983), p. 115.

49. Ibid., pp. 117, 115, and 116–17.

50. Ibid., p. 117.

51. Ibid., p. 118.

52. Ibid., p. 119.

53. Ibid., p. 120.

54. Kojin Karatani, *The Structure of World History: From Modes of Production to Modes of Exchange*, trans. Michael K. Bourdaghs (Durham: Duke University Press, 2014), p. xx.

55. Like Kant, Adorno also sees the "nationalization of music paralleled [in] its bourgeoisization" and points out that with Bach, "the national element is truly voided into universality." By contrast, Wagner's musical nationalism "exerted a power over other countries that harmonizes exactly with the newcomer-country's success in world markets." See Adorno, *Introduction to the Sociology of Music*, pp. 158, 159, 167.

56. Kant, *Perpetual Peace*, p. 64.

57. Adorno, *Aesthetic Theory*, p. 158.

58. These included taxidermy animals, automated slaughterhouses, and vampires — all figurations of a suspended state between life and death and of the abstraction and industrialization of the latter.

59. Deleuze, *Cinema 2: The Time-Image*, p. 86.

60. Sergei Eisenstein, "A Dialectical Approach to Film Form," trans. Jay Leyda, in *Film Form: Essays in Film Theory* (London: Dennis Dobson, 1963), p. 49.

61. Although Santos recorded many video pieces during and after the 1980s to document his work, the vast majority of these recordings remained unarchived and unedited.

62. Gilles Deleuze, *The Fold: Leibniz and the Baroque*, trans. Tom Conley (Minneapolis: University of Minnesota Press, 1993), p. 77.

63. Lars Gustafsson, *The Stillness of the World Before Bach: New Selected Poems*, ed. Christopher Middleton, trans. Philip Martin (New York: New Directions, 1988), p. 95.

64. John Cage, *Silence: Lectures and Other Writings* (Middletown: Wesleyan University Press, 1973), p. 8.

65. Kant, *The Critique of Judgement*, p. 68.

66. Deleuze, *Cinema 2: The Time-Image*, p. 170.

67. It becomes clear in the next scene that his interlocutor, who remains silent during the conversation and who turns out to be a musician, as well, is also guilty of this misconception. When he asks after the whereabouts of a hidden gun, which was previously given as an example of the generalized assumptions about the perceived violence and road rage of truck drivers, linguistic miscommunication becomes sadly comic.

68. The choice of Györgi Ligeti opens several resonances. The composer's ability to move between and beyond the avant-garde and the music of the past, understood as rigid ideologies, would be a good case in point. In 1993, he states: "I am in a prison: one wall is the avant-garde, the other wall is the past, and I want to escape." However, the film's choice of Ligeti is as much a matter of compositional agility and aesthetic freedom as an inscription of the extreme violence that punctuated his life. Alex Ross gives a succinct summary that encapsulates the kind of barbarism to which Portabella alludes throughout his film:

> *He was born in 1923, in Transylvania, to a family of Hungarian Jews. Three years before he was born, Transylvania became part of Romania, and Ligeti went to study at the conservatory in Cluj, which had been called Kolozsvár. In 1940, the fascist government in Hungary regained control of Transylvania, and Cluj became Kolozsvár again. Ligeti was mobilized into a forced labor gang in 1944, wearing the yellow armband required by anti-Semitic regulations, and carried heavy explosives on the eastern front. The Nazis took over the country later that year, and deportations to the death camps began. Calculating the likelihood of his being either killed in action, shot by the SS, or sent to the camps, Ligeti deserted from the front line. He immediately fell into the hands of Soviet troops, but once again managed to slip away. After a long walk home, he found that the Russians were now in control and that strangers were living in his parents' house. When the war ended, he learned of his family's fate: his father had been killed in Bergen-Belsen, his brother in Mauthausen, and his aunt and uncle in Auschwitz. His mother somehow survived.*

For the next decade, Ligeti lived under Soviet Stalinist control until he escaped in 1956, hiding in a postal train. In Alex Ross, *The Rest Is Noise: Listening to the Twentieth Century* (New York: Farrar, Straus, and Giroux, 2007), pp. 465–66.

69. Lauren Berlant and Lee Edelman, *Sex, or the Unbearable* (Durham: Duke University Press, 2014), p. 125.

70. Jean-Luc Nancy, *Listening*, trans. Charlotte Mandell (New York: Fordham University Press, 2002), p. 66.

71. Attali develops his argument on composition and new technologies with claims that echo Santos's experiments with recording technologies: "The new instrument thus emerging will find its real usage only in the production, by the consumer himself, of the final object, the movie made from virgin film. The consumer, completing the mutation that began with the tape recorder and photography, will thus become a producer and will derive at least as much of his satisfaction from the manufacturing process itself as from the object he produces. He will institute the spectacle of himself as the supreme usage." See Jacques Attali, *Noise: The Political Economy of Music*, trans. Brian Massumi (Minneapolis: University of Minnesota Press, 1985), p. 144. The argument of Attali's entire text—which, as Fredric Jameson notes in his preface, is heavily influenced by Adorno—hinges on the anticipatory nature of the acoustic. Attali's text, in turn, is clearly a reference for Nancy's *Listening*. The theoretical texts I refer to throughout in Part 1 are themselves an exercise in historical composition, because they resonate and accumulate together and are mostly contemporaneous with the artworks I discuss here.

72. Portabella further emphasizes this point by presenting us with one of Bach's female descendants, played by an actress, posing on a couch as if for a portrait and in diegetic silence. By adding this fictional parenthesis, a reminder that female lineages are the first to be lost, the filmmaker questions the entire logic of the patronymic, which is itself the ancestry of national formations. Regarding the inheritance of permanent, inherited patronymics, see James Scott, *Seeing Like a State: How Certain Schemes to Improve the Human Condition Have Failed* (New Haven: Yale University Press, 1998).

73. Incidentally, "composition" is the same term Marx uses to describe the activity of "actual free labor" in the *Grundrisse*, a text Attali, Santos, and Portabella surely know well. See also Karl Marx, *Capital: A Critique of Political Economy, Vol. 3*, trans. David Fernbach (New York: Penguin Books, 1991), p. 959.

74. And this despite the fact that a number of Portabella films were screened in international festivals. His most successful film in the US, *Vampir-Cuadecuc*, which attained cult status, was famously screened by MoMA in 1972 and eventually was purchased by the museum. However, Portabella could not travel to the presentation because his passport had been confiscated by the regime. In Spain, the film did not even legally exist and could not be screened publicly.

75. Notably through his participation in Documenta 11 at Kassel in 2002 and having

entered the MACBA permanent collection a year earlier.

76. Quoted in Lynne Walker, "Bach to the Here and Now," *Herald*, August 12, 1998, p. 16. The piano was the point of origin for Santos's retrospective, *¡Visca el piano!*, at the Fundació Joan Miró between June 30 and November 5, 2006, featuring dismembered, battered, and reconfigured pianos collected under the title "Pianos intervinguts," and celluloid prints and images of Santos practicing, his Imperial Bösendofer grand piano transported from his Vinarós home, and the errant, wandering pianola from *La pantera imperial*. For further details, see *¡Visca el Piano!*, pp. 45–72.

77. Earlier in the same film and under the direction of Santos, Miró's name and address in Mallorca becomes the script for a polyphonic performance in five languages that transforms the iconography of Miró's Balearic retreat into a cacophony of splintered voices, with serialization and parataxis as forms of endless multiplication. Santos had used a similar approach in his 1970 *Playback*, directed by Portabella. There, the choir of the Liceu opera house sings by reading each from the notes on the fragments of *Tannhäuser*, *Lohengrin*, and *Die Walküre* while ignoring the melody and finally walking around the stage in confusion as they increase the speed of their delivery. This search for chaos within perceived order and identity is a constant in Santos's treatment of musical and artistic national legacies. The rehearsal with the choir that Portabella documents here is part of Santos's recording of the soundtrack for Clovis Prévost's 1970 film on Gaudí.

78. Aden Evens, *Sound Ideas: Music, Machines, Experience* (Minneapolis: University of Minnesota Press, 2005), p. 84.

79. It is hardly a coincidence that Portabella's 2016 *Informe General II: El nuevo rapto de Europa*, which was commissioned by the Museo Nacional Centro de Arte Reina Sofía to document a conference on European austerity measures, signals Europe as a problem from the very beginning. The film, once it had already been finished, was presented as a continuation of his 1976 *Informe General: Sobre algunas cuestiones de interés para una proyección pública*, a polyphonic fictional documentary on the changing political landscape during Spain's troubled transition to democracy after forty years of Francoism. *Informe General II* follows the country's political reactivation after the 15-M movement, which mounted protests, demonstrations, and occupations against austerity policies in Spain, and proposes an understanding of this movement as the inauguration of a second transition, one perhaps capable of fulfilling the promises of the first one. Nevertheless, the title of the film clearly indicates that the austerity policies and the social failures of contemporary Spain need to be understood within the frame of the European Union's neoliberal loyalties.

80. Gerhard Richter, *This Great Allegory: On World-Decay and World-Opening in the Work of Art* (Cambridge, MA: MIT Press, 2022), p. 124.

81. Nancy, *Listening*, p. 8.

82. Badiou, "Cinema as Philosophical Experimentation," p. 228.

SECOND INTERLUDE: A MONSTER IN THE EAR

1. Quoted by Javier Rivero Ramos in his introduction to *Raphael Montañez Ortiz*, ed. Javier Rivero Ramos (New York: El Museo del Barrio, 2021), p. 9.

2. The clearest confirmation of this is Raphael Montañez Ortiz's theatrical reenactment of the Kent State massacre by the National Guard. His Blood and Flesh Guerrilla Theater stages the action within days of the event, both at Kent State and in New York City.

3. James Baldwin, "Of the Sorrow Songs: The Cross of Redemption," in *The Cross of Redemption: Uncollected Writings*, ed. Randall Kenan (New York: Pantheon Books, 2010), p. 124.

4. Maya Kronfeld complicates and vindicates Adorno's understanding of the relationship of jazz to the military marching band in her essay "The Philosopher's Bass Drum: Adorno's Jazz and the Politics of Rhythm," *Radical Philosophy* 205 (Autumn 2019), pp. 34–47.

5. The phrase is from Puerto Rican philosopher Nelson Maldonado-Torres's "Outline of Ten Theses on Coloniality and Decoloniality," Foundation Frantz Fanon (2016), https://fondation-frantzfanon.com/wp-content/uploads/2018/10/maldonado-torres_outline_of_ten_theses-10.23.16.pdf, p. 11. I will return to this notion in the context of Allora & Calzadilla's artistic practice in the next section.

6. That this found 8-mm and 16-mm film footage is chopped, scratched, and cut out can also be read as a materialization of the original violence of decoupage and montage intrinsic to cinema as a medium—as the visible inscription of a structural violence we rarely perceive.

7. "In the case of Puerto Rico, coloniality posits the colony anew. As a form of coloniality, debt posits the colony anew—within and through the strictures of financialized neoliberal capitalism. The present is the past. Second, and for this reason, decoloniality is a matter of turning the present into the past." Rocío Zambrana, *Colonial Debts: The Case of Puerto Rico* (Durham: Duke University Press, 2021), p. 14.

8. Pedro Reyes, in Pedro Reyes, ed., *Laser/Disc/Scratch/Destruction: Raphael Montañez*

Ortiz and Pedro Reyes in Conversation, exhibition catalogue (Mexico City: Labor, 2011), pp. 2 and 3.

PART TWO: ACOUSTIC RELATIONS

1. Édouard Glissant, *Poetics of Relation*, trans. Betsy Wing (Ann Arbor: University of Michigan Press, 1997), pp. 37–42.

2. María Zambrano, "Isla de Puerto Rico: Nostalgia y esperanza de un mundo mejor," in *Islas*, ed. Jorge Luis Arcos (1940; Madrid: Editorial Verbum, 2007), p. 19. All translations from Zambrano's Spanish texts are my own.

3. The fact that the Spaniards of her generation, through the influences of the philosophers of 1898 (notably Miguel de Unamuno and José Ortega y Gasset), associated the Caribbean and the Philippines with the ruins of an old empire at the hands of a modern empire (the United States), together with their understanding of Spain as an island within the European continent, resonates deeply in Zambrano's thought.

4. In 1955, Zambrano uses "desmoronamiento"—at once a confusion, a shattering, and a degrounding—to describe the undoing of the European subject and its philosophico-political certainties in *El hombre y lo divino* (Madrid: Siruela, 1992), p. 169.

5. See María Zambrano, "Una metáfora de la esperanza: Las ruinas," in *Islas*, ed. Jorge Luis Arcos (1951; Madrid: Editorial Verbum, 2007), pp. 123–28. Lena Burgos-Lafuente has addressed the relationship between islands and ruins in Zambrano's Caribbean essays without, however, connecting it to her critique of sacrificial history in "¿Qué es entonces una isla?: Ruinas, islas y escritura en el Caribe de María Zambrano," *Journal of Spanish Cultural Studies* 16.4 (2015), pp. 375–96.

6. Zambrano, *El hombre y lo divino*, p. 169.

7. The Spanish Empire did reverse its stance, even though the legal change failed to prevent an industrial-scale Indigenous genocide when it understood that Indigenous populations were a source of wealth through indentured labor and Christianization.

8. Gilles Deleuze, *Desert Islands and Other Texts 1953–1974*, ed. David Lapoujade, trans. Michael Taormina (New York: Semiotext(e), 2004), p. 10. Later in the same text he goes on to say, in an exact echo of Zambrano, "The deserted island is the origin, but a second origin" and a "second birth" (p. 13).

9. Zambrano, "Isla de Puerto Rico," p. 11.

10. Ibid., p. 8.

11. Zambrano, *El hombre y lo divino*, p. 8.

12. María Zambrano, *Agonía de Europa* (1945; Madrid: Trotta, 2000), p. 25.

13. Ibid., p. 46.

14. María Zambrano, *Filosofía y poesía* (1936; Mexico City: Fondo de Cultura Económica, 2006), p. 22.

15. María Zambrano, "La Cuba secreta," in *Orígenes*, no. 20 (1948), p. 4.

16. Zambrano, "Isla de Puerto Rico," p. 5.

17. María Zambrano, "Las catacumbas," in *Islas*, pp. 56–58.

18. The characteristic polysemy of Zambrano's frequent use of "nostalgia" as a mediatory and secret affect, caught between hope for the future and longing for the past, belongs to her intensification of and investment in the temporal and experiential. That her unfinished dissertation, while she was a student of Ortega y Gasset in Madrid, focused on Baruch Spinoza's "affectus" and his figure of the "person in the world" is hardly a surprise, because one can find traces of this earlier work throughout her general emphasis on sensation.

19. Zambrano, *Agonía de Europa*, p. 75.

20. María Zambrano, *Los bienaventurados* (1979; Madrid: Siruela, 1990), pp. 14 and 16.

21. Zambrano, "Isla de Puerto Rico," p. 10.

22. Puerto Rico was part of the collective Insular Cases, fourteen rulings between 1901 and 1904 that debated the application of the US Constitution and the Bill of Rights to overseas territories. For a full account of the cases, see Christina Burnett and Burke Marshall, eds., *Foreign in a Domestic Sense: American Expansion and the Constitution* (Durham: Duke University Press, 2000).

23. Zambrano, *El hombre y lo divino*, p. 77.

24. Michel Serres, *Geometry: The Third Book of Foundations*, trans. Randolph Burks (London; New York: Bloomsbury, 2017), p. 64.

25. Jacques Derrida, *The Animal That Therefore I Am*, trans. David Wills (New York: Fordham University Press, 2008), p. 12.

26. For the most up-to-date survey of Archipelagic studies, see Michelle Stephens and Yolanda Martínez-San Miguel, eds., *Contemporary Archipelagic Thinking: Toward New Comparative Methodologies and Disciplinary Formations* (London: Rowman & Littlefield, 2020).

27. This is the phrase Humboldt uses to describe his Caribbean and American voyages in his multilingual and fractal *Personal Narrative of Travels to the Equinoctial Regions of the New Continent during the Years 1799–1804*. For five years, Humboldt traveled to the Canary Islands, Colombia, Perú, Mexico, and Cuba. For a detailed engagement

with Humboldt's transatlantic context and his relationship to a vexed ecological and epistemological colonialism, slave economy, and emergent globalization, see Susanne Schlünder and Rolando M. Carrasco, eds., *Asymmetric Ecologies in Europe and South America around 1800* (Berlin: De Gruyter, 2022).

28. See William H. Babcock, "Antillia and the Antilles," *Geographical Review* 9.2 (1920), pp. 109–24.

29. Glissant, *Poetics of Relation*, p. 34.

30. A meta-archipelago is a complex island formation with indistinct boundaries and without a center. The difficulty in delineating the precise contours of the Caribbean speaks to this indistinction but also to overlapping colonial regimes and their cartographic efforts.

31. As Megan Raby shows, the notion of "biodiversity" is itself the result of American tropical biology's encounter with the Caribbean rainforest in the mid-1980s. As she argues, "the ideas, attitudes, and institutions forged at field sites in the colonies and neocolonies of the circum-Caribbean are crucial for understanding the emergence of this new paradigm in biology and conservation at the end of the century." See Megan Raby, *American Tropics: The Caribbean Roots of Biodiversity Science* (Chapel Hill: University of North Carolina Press, 2017), p. 4.

32. Antonio Benítez-Rojo, *The Repeating Island: The Caribbean and the Postmodern Perspective*, trans. James Maraniss (Durham: Duke University Press, 1992), p. 2.

33. Ibid, p. 4.

34. Stanley Cavell, *The Senses of Walden* (Chicago: University of Chicago Press, 1972), p. 106n.

35. Herman Melville, *Moby-Dick, or, The Whale*, ed. Harrison Hayford, Heschel Parker, and G. Thomas Tanselle (Evanston: Northwestern University Press, 1988), p. 308.

36. Ibid., p. 143.

37. Jane Bennett, "The Force of Things: Steps toward an Ecology of Matter," *Political Theory* 32.3 (June 2004), p. 365.

38. Stanley Cavell, *Must We Mean What We Say?* (Cambridge: Cambridge University Press, 2002), p. 257.

39. Ibid., p. 263.

40. Thomas Nagel, "What Is It Like to Be a Bat?," *Philosophical Review* 83.4 (October 1974), pp. 440–41.

41. More recent findings indicate the existence of this kind of flute dating back

forty-two thousand years, significantly earlier than previous estimates.

42. Similarly, Allora & Calzadilla's 2014 performance *Lifespan* pairs the irreconcilable geological temporal scale of a Hadean rock — Hadean rocks are the oldest rocks known — with the lung capacity of three vocalists through an encounter that literally puts them in contact. The reduced size of the stone ironically belies the enormity of the temporal scale it carries within it. The piece is a musical event that sustains the gap between multiple temporalities, indifferent to each other, by turning the possibility of their touch into the structure of the composition. The rock's movements, as well as those of the singers, sway and oscillate between the marking of incompatible times and the choreography of the body. The four-billion-year-old rock, displayed hanging from a string, moves like the pendulum for an impossible clock that would measure the immeasurable. The singularity of the human voice, reduced here to whistling and breathing, carries with it a reminder of bodily transience and fragility, while the geological endurance of the stone speaks of the extended temporality of mineral life. The multiple temporalities at play in this acoustic event disturb the autonomy of a presumed subject and of language by pointing to an exteriority that precedes them both. By restricting singers to breaths and whistles, David Lang's composition harks back to an original scene that precedes the linguistic, but also the musical, understood as a harmonically organized expression. The acoustic intimacy of the piece is also reminiscent of a whispered confession, a mental reverberation where one breath echoes another and brings us closer to contact. Like the Hadean rock, we are in fact touched by sound, exposed to it and approached by it. The intimacy of the sonic and the aural produces a shared, multiple, and tactile temporality, a reminder of the primary emotion of sound in its movement through space and time.

43. Stanley Cavell, *The Claim of Reason: Wittgenstein, Skepticism, Morality, and Tragedy* (Oxford, UK: Oxford University Press, 1999), p. 178.

44. This piece has relays with Allora & Calzadilla's 2013 film, *3*, a highly speculative project on the Upper Paleolithic Venus de Lespuge, a small prehistoric mammoth-ivory statuette discovered in 1922 in the Rideaux cave. During their research, an important stage in their practice, they encountered the work of Ralph H. Abraham, a mathematician and chaos theorist, and of William Irwin Thompson, a social philosopher, critic, and poet. Abraham and Thompson speculated that the measurements of the figure coincided precisely with the diatonic scale of the Vedic Aryans — what ancient Greeks referred to as the Dorian mode. The artists then asked composer David Lang, a frequent

collaborator, to compose a solo for cello based on this diatonic scale. In the film, the visual and the acoustic work in tandem to animate the statue through an auratic and filmic inscription of ancient intervals.

45. Georges Bataille, *Prehistoric Painting: Lascaux or the Birth of Art*, trans. Austryn Wainhouse (London: Macmillan, 1980), p. 25.

46. Bataille, *Prehistoric Painting*, p. 120.

47. Ibid., p. 12.

48. Albert Skira, foreword to the 1955 edition of *Prehistoric Painting*, originally published as the first volume in a series called The Great Centuries of Painting published by Skira in Switzerland, unpaginated.

49. Cavell, *The Claim of Reason* p. 421.

50. Bataille, *Prehistoric Painting*, p. 130.

51. Stanley Cavell, "Declining Decline: Wittgenstein as a Philosopher of Culture," in *This New Yet Unapproachable America: Lectures after Emerson after Wittgenstein* (Chicago: University of Chicago Press, 1989), p. 42.

52. Jakob Johann von Uexküll (1864–1944) argued that living beings experience their environment in species-specific spatiotemporal frameworks, in different environment worlds. He called this perceived surrounding an *Umwelt*. Such a stance, distinct from how humans perceive these organisms, transforms every single organism into a subject within a specific biosemiotic system. Uexküll was an important referent for Martin Heidegger, Michel Foucault, Maurice Merleau-Ponty, Deleuze and Guattari, and, more recently, Giorgio Agamben.

53. As Gerhard Richter points out, "Both the English word 'world' and the German *Welt* are akin to the Gothic *wer-alt*, which means 'human age' or 'human seed or sowing,' which in turn translates the Greek *aeon* (αιών) as well as the Latin *mundus*." Gerhard Richter, *This Great Allegory: Of World-Decay and World-Opening in the Work of Art* (Cambridge, MA: MIT Press, 2022), p. 6.

54. One of the mysteries of prehistoric cave art is that the very few human figures depicted are completely abstract, faceless, and schematic.

55. Richter, *This Great Allegory*, p. 88.

56. Although it may seem like a cliché, I find it hard not to recall Seth Bernardette's stunning reading of the Platonic allegory of the cave here, part of a fascinating conversation in his miniscule office at New York University's Department of Classics when I was a graduate student. Probably because of Smithson, I thought of Plato's cave as

proto-cinema in my intent to prove that cinema has been with us from the beginning, that it is the medium of our every thought. Bernadette, who remains without peer in his readings of Plato, reflected that in Plato *both* the cave and the world outside the cave are projections of reflected light, one of the burning fire inside, the other of the sun. The brief blindness of the freed prisoner marks his transition between different scales of projection, of modes of mediation. In this version, there is only the oscillation between blindness and projection, nothing else. The world cannot be grasped, because it is made of reflections, and the direct sources of light burn and blind us. This seems very close to what Giuliana Bruno suggests in her book or to the painters of Chauvet and Lascaux. In Bruno's reading, Pliny's Dibutades also inhabits the Platonic cave, although her focus is on the technological dispositif that undergirds her world, projection and desire, rather than on its phenomenological limits. For Bruno's discussion of Dibutades, see Giuliana Bruno, *Atmospheres of Projection: Environmentality in Art and Screen Media* (Chicago: University of Chicago Press, 2022), pp. 1–10. The other significant reading of Dibutades/ Butades and the origin of drawing is Derrida's *Memoirs of the Blind: The Self-Portrait and Other Ruins*, trans. Pascale-Anne Brault and Michael Naas (Chicago: University of Chicago Press,1993), pp. 49–57.

57. Bruno, *Atmospheres of Projection,* p. 8.

58. Ibid., 11.

59. Ibid., p. 51.

60. The irony of the location and founding for *Puerto Rican Light*, the Americas Society, adds another layer to Allora & Calzadilla's critical occupation. Founded in 1965—the same year as Flavin's piece—by Nelson Rockefeller, the Americas Society was conceived as the New York headquarters for an expansionist policy to increase US influence in Latin America, the Caribbean, and Canada. In 1985, it absorbed the Center for Inter-American Relations.

61. The trajectories of Dan Flavin's piece are fascinating on their own right. For a detailed account, see Molly Nesbit, "All Together Now," in *Puerto Rican Light (Cueva Vientos)* (New York: Dia Art Foundation, 2016), pp. 47–64.

62. Yates McKee, "Cave Art and Climate Debt," in *Puerto Rican Light (Cueva Vientos)*, p. 32. Electricity and the recurrent blackouts of the Puerto Rican grid have been key for a number of Allora & Calzadilla's sculptures and performances. The 2017 *Blackout*, for instance, activates a relic from a power transformer explosion that, like *Puerto Rican Light*, emits an almost imperceptible vertical hum, while a choir of singers, scattered

among the audience in the gallery, respond to the vibrations of this sculptural amorphous mass as if it were a tuning device, the acoustic orientation to their own humming. David Lang's original composition, *mains hum*, uses a quotation by Benjamin Franklin: "In going on with these Experiments, how many pretty systems do we build, which we soon find ourselves oblig'd to destroy! If there is no other Use discover'd of Electricity, this, however, is something considerable, that it may help to make a vain Man humble." "Blackout, 2017," TBA21 Thyssen-Bornemisza Art Contemporary, https://tba21.org/allora_calzadilla_blackout. However, the singers exhale and hiss rhythmically, shaping the words of the text with their mouths without ever fully uttering them. The gestural traces of speech function as structuring patterns to their signing. The verticality of the generator's humming, produced by the vibrations of electrically charged copper, contrasts with the horizontal organization of the singers gathering voices and materializes political contestation, a call for accountability in Puerto Rico's ongoing state of emergency amid a transnational circuitry that relies on a manufactured colonial energy dependence on fossil fuels.

63. The artists spent a fair amount of time settling on this cave and considered different sites in the Caribbean. It is in this search that their artmaking can be said to begin. It is not unlike the activity of assembling an orchestra or the process of finding collaborators.

64. Dan Flavin, "'. . . in daylight or cool white': an Autobiographical Sketch," *Artforum* 4.4 (December 1966), p. 24n. That same year, Robert Smithson published his "Entropy and the New Monuments," with echoes of George Kubler's hugely influential *The Shape of Time: Remarks on the History of Things* (New Haven: Yale University Press, 1962). In it, Smithson describes Flavin's sculptures as monuments where "a million years is contained in a second." See Robert Smithson, "Entropy and the New Monuments," *Artforum* 4.10 (June 1966), p. 27.

65. Robert Smithson, "A Cinematic Atopia" (1971), in *Robert Smithson: The Collected Writings*, ed. Jack Flam (Berkeley: University of California Press, 1996), p. 142.

66. Magic Architecture: Its Origins and Future is the title of Kiesler's manuscript, written immediately after the Second World War and never published. A critical edition by Spyros Papapetros and Gerd Zillner is forthcoming from MIT under the title *Frederick Kiesler's Magic Architecture: The Story of Human Housing.*

67. Interestingly, very much like Robert Smithson and his cinema cavern, Kiesler was profoundly disappointed with contemporary movie theaters and in particular their

predisposition to flatness, which had merely updated the theatrical stage. He believed they did not do justice to the temporal and spatial complexity of the cinematic experience, to its endlessness and circularity as an environment of sound and light. See Frederick Kiesler, "The Universe as Architecture," in *Magic Architecture*, quoted in Spyros Papapetros, "The Portable Cave," in *Puerto Rican Light (Cueva Vientos)*, pp. 74–75.

68. After repeated government failures to protect this ecosystem, several grassroots organizations initiated a public campaign to preserve the area and stop real-estate projects nearby. In 2004, The Conservation Trust of Puerto Rico gave protected status to 630 acres of this southern subtropical dry forest. When Allora & Calzadilla began to project *Puerto Rican Light (Cueva Vientos)*, they partnered with the activist land trust of Para la Naturaleza, an organization intent on buying back a third of Puerto Rico's land for ecological conservation to ensure that the access to the cave did not damage this delicate ecosystem.

69. To further complicate matters, the Flavin Estate did not allow direct documentation of the light sculpture, protected through copyright.

70. I visited the cave with Allora & Calzadilla in February 2016. We got caught in a big storm and had to be picked up by the Para la Naturaleza park rangers because the trails had flooded. The description in this section transcribes the notes I took then.

71. Quoted in Walter Putnam, "Captive Audiences: A Concert for the Elephants in the Jardin Des Plantes," *TDR* 51.1 (2007), p. 155 (his translation).

72. Before the Revolution, the private royal ménagerie had already housed elephants. Derrida recounts the French king, Louis le Grand and Roi Soleil, attending the 1681 autopsy of one of the pachyderms as the encounter "between two very great bodies, the beast and the sovereign, of course. Between two immense living beings first of all: the kings of kings, the greatest of kings, Louis le Grand, and the greatest animal," and "this hand-to-hand is a duel, or rather the end, the aftermath, of a duel (a warlike duel, perhaps, or unconsciously amorous, therefore narcissistic, after a scene of seduction, hunt, or capture, captation or predation)." The philosopher, oddly, does not mention it, but after the king died from gangrene, he would undergo a public autopsy, as well, his remains paraded and his body dissected—a repetition of the elephant's postmortem that binds them even further. See Derrida, *The Beast and the Sovereign,* eds. Michel Lisse, Marie-Louise Mallet, and Ginette Michaud, trans. Geoffrey Bennington, 2 vols. (Chicago: University of Chicago Press, 2009), vol. 1, p. 281.

73. Quoted in Hector Chomet, *The Influence of Music on Health and Life* (New York:

G. P. Putnam's Sons, 1875), p. 186.

74. In 2012, Tim Storms had won the Guinness World Record for the Lowest Note Produced by a Human, 0.189 Hz (G-7).

75. Consider the productive use of silence in the sculptural installation *Intervals* (2014), where fragments of dinosaur bones are displayed on top of acrylic lecterns, as if to acknowledge the unknown sounds these remains still contain: where there was once a sound, there is now the trace of a sound. Absence is not the same as disappearance.

76. Georges Cuvier (1769–1832), considered the founder of paleontology, also formulated and demonstrated the existence of global extinction phenomena through an analysis of fossils. He also provided the theoretical basis for the development of "scientific racism."

77. These lines appeared in an anonymous Paris paper and were reprinted in the *Kentish Weekly Post or Canterbury Journal* (March 28, 1817), p. 3.

78. Tracks and "land marks" feature prominently in Allora & Calzadilla's interventions in the island of Vieques, Puerto Rico, in the mid-2000s as the civil disobedience campaign for the demilitarization of this weapon-testing site was gaining momentum. Under the title *Land Mark*, the artists produced a series of sculptures, videos, and photographs that documented Vieques as a marked, damaged, and occupied landscape, using the trace as their preferred medium and performative concept. The series coincides with Allora & Calzadilla's decision to leave New York and move to Puerto Rico, embracing the precarity and ambiguity of the island's colonial realities. For a brilliant analysis of this series of works, see Yates McKee, "Wake, Vestige, Survival: Sustainability and the Politics of the Trace in Allora & Calzadilla's *Land Mark*," *October* 133 (2010), pp. 20–48.

79. To this day, this breed is the most popular for police, prison, and military crowd control. German Shepherd Dogs (GSD) were bred for the first time in 1910, and the German army started using them in the First World War. The practice was soon extended to other national and colonial armies throughout the world. It is ironic that this breed, the closest in appearance to a wolf and with an equally powerful bite, functions as the symbolic counterpoint to the figure of the wolf—the former stands for the law, the latter for the unlawful. Famously, Hitler was very attached to his GSD Blondi, who was often used by the National Socialist propaganda machine to present him as an animal lover. The breed became a Nazi icon, because it was made to represent German purity of blood. Blondi died in the Führerbunker in a test for the cyanide capsules his owner would take a day later.

80. This landscape of rubble also echoes Rossellini's *Germany Year Zero*, shot on location in a Berlin that had been razed to the ground by Allied bombing.

81. This logo remains a well-known advertising icon, along with the motto "his master's voice," and was used by a number of recording labels. The painter Francis Barraud recalls how the idea of depicting his dog Nipper with a gramophone occurred to him: "It is difficult to say how the idea came to me beyond the fact that it suddenly occurred to me that to have my dog listening to the Phonograph, with an intelligent and rather puzzled expression, and call it 'His Master's Voice' would make an excellent subject. We had a phonograph and I often noticed how puzzled he was to make out where the voice came from. It certainly was the happiest thought I ever had." Mournfulness, absence, and inheritance, however, are also deeply embedded in Barraud's painting. Nipper was already dead when the painting was made, and so was Mark Barraud, who was Francis's brother and the dog's original owner. Both the dog and the voice are inscriptions of loss. Quoted in Joan and Robin Rolfs, *Nipper Collectibles: The RCA Victor Trademark Dog*, 2 vols. (Hortonville, WI: Audio Antique, 2007), pp. 1–7. Deutsche Gramophone is the world's oldest acoustic recording company and still the most renowned classical music label. Despite being a global company, it is fully identified with a national project connected to high culture.

82. This modified bell digger belongs to a long list of mechanisms retrofitted with acoustic components in the artists' work—including motorcycles, boats, tables, pianos, and bicycles.

83. After pleading guilty to charges relating to the manufacture and distribution of adulterated drugs, GlaxoSmithKline closed the Cidra manufacturing facility. Pharmaceutical companies, by far the island's most important industry, originally settled in Puerto Rico to take advantage of federal tax incentives. Once these incentives expired, many companies moved their production to China, Brazil, India, and South Korea.

84. Sound reshapes the gallery space in invisible ways. It is an architect of resonances whereby walls are traversed, expanded, and contracted. The acoustic functions as a transient sculptural medium that transforms sites into events as a multiple and spatio-temporal phenomenon that contaminates them with its reverberations. The survey show at the Fundació Tàpies was conceived as an intermittent score, as an exercise in musical composition. Following this compositional approach, the visitor was acoustically guided from one piece to another. The compositional unfolding of the show enacted the anticipatory structure of the acoustic: the sound of one piece announced the sound of

another, and so on. The same logic allows Allora & Calzadilla's compositions to spill over into other spaces such as the library, the screening room, staff offices, the pavement in the parking lot, or even an unused attic room.

While the appearance of the quasi-empty gallery space may bring to mind Minimalism and the stark formalism of its site-specific structures, together with its universalist assumptions regarding aesthetic priorities, Allora & Calzadilla mobilize their art historical precedents only to upset these same priorities. Rather than reduce the formal to the aesthetic as a universal principle, their nonautonomous formalism engages art as a practice whereby form functions as a singular by-product or support. The visual is subordinated to the aural, so that both behave sculpturally to modify the space they inhabit. Yet the places these artworks occupy are called into being by the acoustic, creating a loop or a transfer by which the visual and the aural activate one another in an expressive continuum of call and response. By shifting back and forth between the material and the immaterial, Allora & Calzadilla recover the idea of music as movement. Acoustic temporality is finally socialized through space, so that its duration is traced onto the gleaming gallery floor as an itinerary, as the menacing dance of a piano, for instance. The score of the exhibition functions as a temporal organization of acoustic intensities and attentions by treating the gallery space as an echo chamber of resonances. The temporal spacing between a sound and its resonance, the movement of its vibration through space, always brings something other with it. Sound always returns transformed, having folded the outside into the inside. The acoustic cannot be concerned with representation or appearance, but with the relations established by sonority and its durational expansion through space. The acoustic is an uninterrupted expanse. If there was once a sound, there will always be the trace of a sound. The visitors, as viewers and listeners, must let these traces find each other midair in their unreconciled difference. Adapted from Sara Nadal-Melsió, "To Be All Ears, To Be in the World: Acoustic Relation in Allora & Calzadilla," in *Allora & Calzadilla* (Barcelona: Fundació Antoni Tàpies, 2018), pp. 9–10.

85. The artists have also accumulated an archive on the uses of music as a weapon of war and "no-touch" torture. The US military started using acoustic torture consistently beginning in 1989 during the invasion of Panama, escalating these activities during the two Iraq wars and in prisoner camps in Afghanistan, Iraq, and Guantánamo.

86. Sara Binzer Hobolt and Sylvain Brouard, "Contesting the European Union? Why the Dutch and the French Rejected the European Constitution," *Political Research Quarterly* 64.2 (2011), pp. 309–22.

87. It should be noted that one of the targets of Slavoj Žižek's essay is Ernesto Laclau's theorization of populism, understood by Žižek as an empty floating signifier and universal equivalent that effectively deactivates actual class struggle. See Slavoj Žižek, "Against the Populist Temptation," *Critical Inquiry* 32.3 (2006), p. 568.

88. Ibid., pp. 569 and 571.

89. Ibid., pp. 569–70.

90. In another turn in this long history, Gail K. Hart notes that during the celebrations of the fall of the Berlin Wall in 1989, "Leonard Bernstein conducted the Ninth in the Berliner Schauspielhaus and the concert was televised internationally. Before Bernstein began, he announced that he had instructed the singers that instead of 'Freude' they were to sing, 'Freiheit,' thus transforming the 'Ode to Joy' into an 'Ode to Freedom.'" Gail K. Hart, "Schiller's 'An die freude' and the Question of Freedom," *German Studies Review* 32.3 (October 2009), p. 488.

91. While the police violence against peaceful voters was alarming and shocking, it did show the face of Spanish nationalism and the resilience of sociological Francoism. The referendum itself was a mere symbolic gesture, a performative democracy that failed to represent the heterogeneity or complexity of Catalan citizens.

92. Hurricanes and capitalist—as well as colonial—exploitation function like catastrophic convergences in Puerto Rico and can never be disengaged fully from one another. In 1867, Hurricane San Narciso devastated Puerto Rico and set the stage for the first pro-independence uprising against Spanish rule in the island. By then, Catalan and Mallorcan colonialists had settled in the interior, western, and southern regions of the island. Very much like the Catalan Diada (which commemorates the fall of Barcelona in 1714 during the War of the Spanish Succession), the commemoration of the Lares revolt on September 23, 1868, known as the Grito de Lares (the Lares Shout), ostensibly celebrates a defeat, yet much more importantly, it stands as a reminder that history carries within itself the seeds of political possibility. An element of Puerto Rico's exceptionality vis-à-vis the United States is a heightened awareness of the complicities that prepare the ground for catastrophes that superimpose the cycles of nature onto manufactured political and economic crises. While slavery and colonialism were in the eye of Hurricane San Narciso, debt as a new form of capitalist coloniality and as an erosion of sovereignty was in the eye of Hurricanes Irma and María. Hurricanes have the ability of capturing the Puerto Rican political imagination because they visualize a seemingly unstoppable motion that structures the prolongation of a state of emergency.

If hurricanes are the high point of a slow war of attrition, the final blow in the slow death of a people's sovereignty, they also offer the potential for interrupting the spiraling motions of capitalism. They are expressions of a *kairos*, a Greek word that describes both "the times" and "the weather" and that as such signals, like the Lares Shout, a complicity between capitalism and coloniality as ways of relating to time. Benjamin engaged in a rethinking of the temporality of politics and history through *kairos* as a nonchronological understanding of time. In *kairoi*, the past becomes visible as present, and temporal limits are traversed and crossed. Historical experience becomes a form of immediacy felt in both the body and the mind as the spiraling of time. From the beginning, the temporality of natural disasters appears as an abrupt interruption and culmination of the standstill enforced onto colonial subjectivities, the calm before the storm. Workers in Puerto Rico's US sugar corporations were employed only during the harvesting season and as temporary workers. The rest of their time was labeled as "dead time" and was an expression of the slow death neoliberalism imposed on the island, as well as of the waiting time for an ecological catastrophe in the making. Global capitalism and disaster capitalism as its most lethal by-product collapse economic precarity into existential precariousness by putting Puerto Rico's entire population at risk. Crises are never solely economic, but in the world of capitalism, they are always expressed in economic terms.

93. Lydia Goeher, "After 1800: The Beethoven Paradigm," in *The Imaginary Museum of Musical Works* (Oxford, UK: Oxford University Press, 1992). As she puts it, "To describe musicians as having composed so many individual works is misleading, of course. Many of their compositions would have involved significant overlap and repetition of musical material. And such overlap would not have existed within a single composer's output, but among compositions by any number of composers" (p. 183).

94. Romanticism brings the notion of artistic freedom to musicians; they are no longer viewed as servants or employees who do not own their work or even attempt to preserve it, as was Bach's case. Musicians moved from subservience to the need to construct and perform the role of the artistic genius and instead were seen to embody the emergent ideas of aesthetic autonomy and of full authorship and ownership of works through the imprimatur of copyright. These changes deeply affected notational systems, which became more precise and standardized. Music became more textual.

95. This occasional piece was originally composed for the Panharmonicon, a musical instrument invented in 1805 by Johann Nepomuk Maelzel (a friend of Beethoven). The Panharmonicon could imitate the sound of cannons and gunfire, as well as several

orchestral instruments. Maelzel also manufactured metronomes and musical automata.

96. Quoted in Nicholas Cook, "The Other Beethoven: Heroism, the Canon, and the Works of 1813–14," *19th-Century Music* 27.1 (2003), p. 14.

97. Jacques Attali, *Noise: The Political Economy of Music*, trans. Brian Massumi (Minneapolis: University of Minnesota Press, 1985), p. 65.

98. See Daniel Chua, *Absolute Music and the Construction of Meaning* (Cambridge: Cambridge University Press, 1999).

99. A year later, Allora & Calzadilla's 2008 *A Man Screaming Is Not a Dancing Bear*, shot in New Orleans in the aftermath of Hurricane Katrina, presents us with an even more poignant assemblage of body and instrument. The images of the film move between three different locations in Louisiana and between the human, the inorganic, and a natural ecosystem. In one of them, Isaiah McCormick uses a set of window blinds in his damaged house to play music. McCormick's predominately African American neighborhood, the Lower Ninth Ward, was flooded by a failure of the levees on the Mississippi River. Other scenes of the film document the traces left by water damage in the house's interior and a slow and eerily peaceful boat ride along the stunning wetlands of the lower Mississippi River Delta, scenes that seal within them the unimaginable violence of the Middle Passage. The flickering of the image on the screen functions as a counterpoint to the play of sound and light produced by the musical movement of the blinds. The piece encourages a musical reading of all of its elements: McCormick's own body, which has also become an instrument, and the empty house, which amplifies the sound by acting as a resonating chamber, together with the soundscapes of the bayou. The play of light and darkness, of revelation and concealment, a texture that flickers and reverberates like sound itself, insists on the instability and precariousness inscribed in the scene. The intervals of light in the film, the glimmering produced by the blinds in McCormick's house, speak of movement and, bitterly, of displacement. The threat of displacement, eviction, and loss underlines the percussive rhythms of the film. Presenting vision as the touch of light, the artists remind us of the relational qualities of the visual, bringing it closer to its analogue in the intimate caress of sound and music. In this process, however, the precariousness and fragility of the tactile also comes to the surface. The music in the film depends on McCormick's contact with the blinds of his condemned dwelling. Where there is intimacy, there is the possibility of loss. The film puts into play questions of cultural inheritance and its evisceration. Legacy is at risk, beginning with the quote from the Caribbean poet Aimé Césaire in the title of the piece, the references to both early and low-budget cinema through the use of 16-mm

film stock and to different recording technologies, and especially to the African American musical traditions of the South through the use of domestic percussion instruments. Connecting and extending these cultural legacies to the natural soundscapes of the bayou, Allora & Calzadilla highlight their ties to ecological and social justice. The film socializes sonic environments without directly resorting to acoustic ecology, which in the end must always decide which sounds deserve protection and preservation. It proposes instead the intermittence and fragility of an invisible and impossible belonging.

THIRD INTERLUDE: THE TALKING KNEE

1. The name of Kluge's production company is Kairos, a clear allusion to an unexpected eruption of time not bound by chronological order.

2. As Anton Kaes has noted in regard to *Die Patriotin*, Kluge transforms historical information into a materialist sensorium. Its protagonist, Gabi Teichert, he writes, "'bores her way into history'; she 'makes history a part of herself'; she 'digests' it, and so on—all figures of speech which, translated from their Heideggerian literal meaning, generate surrealistic dream images. As an amateur archaeologist, she participates in illegal excavations at the city wall in the hopes of finding prehistoric everyday objects in order to 'grasp' (*be-greifen*) the past; only when she can touch it does she understand it sensually." See Kaes, "In Search of Germany: Alexander Kluge's *The Patriot*," in Tara Forrest, ed., *Alexander Kluge: Raw Materials for the Imagination* (Amsterdam: Amsterdam University Press, 2012), p. 98.

3. The film is an urgent political intervention in the aftermath of the alleged suicides of Red Army Faction members Ulrike Marie Meinhof, Jan-Carl Raspe, and Andreas Baader in a German high-security prison, the Lufthansa plane kidnapping, a resurgence of state-sanctioned police violence, and a collective rethinking of German identity. See Miriam Hansen, "Alexander Kluge, Cinema and the Public Sphere: The Construction Site of Counter-History," *Discourse* 6 (1983), pp. 53–74.

4. The Mayerling incident refers to the suicide of Rudolf, Crown Prince of Austria, and his teenage mistress in January 1889 in an imperial hunting lodge in Mayerling. The Royal Prussian Military Railway was built after the Franco-Prussian War to train troops in the wartime use of railways. It was one of the things proscribed by the Treaty of Versailles after the First World War. The Sparticist uprisng refers to the brief 1919 revolt that sought to transform Germany into a Soviet-style republic. It resulted in the execution of Sparticist League leaders Rosa Luxemburg and Karl Liebknecht.

5. Walter Benjamin, "Theses on the Concept of History," trans. Harry Zohn, in *Walter Benjamin: Selected Writings, Volume 4, 1938–1940*, eds. Howard Eiland and Michael W. Jennings (Cambridge, MA: The Belknap Press of Harvard University Press, 2006), p. 391.

6. Christian Morgenstern, "The Knee," trans. W. D. Snodgrass and Lore Segal, in Ted Hughes and Seamus Heaney, eds., *The Rattle Bag: An Anthology of Poetry* (London: Faber & Faber, 1985), p. 228.

7. The fraught reception of Beethoven's Ninth has been addressed and complicated by numerous filmmakers intent on a critical rearticulation of Europe's musical heritage, among them, Jean-Luc Godard, Andrei Tarkovsky, Dušan Makavejev, Hans-Jürgen Syberberg, and Stanley Kubrick. In particular, in the context of the New German Cinema to which Kluge belongs, Helke Sander's feminist 1977 *The All-Round Reduced Personality—Redupers*, a documentary essay about the Berlin Wall, stands out. In the film, a collective of feminist photographers intervenes in Berlin's ruined cityscape by pointing out the connections and similarities between East and West Berlin. Sander uses "The Ode to Joy" to cacophonous effect, combining it with images of urban blight, rubble, and demolition. At one point in the film, the photographers mount a curtain to separate two buildings facing one another on opposite sites on the wall; in another, we meet one of the "Grey Panthers," as the film calls them, a group of East Berlin senior citizens who are eligible for day passes to West Berlin and become conduits of information between the two sides, as well as smugglers of goods.

8. Similarly, in *Deutschland im Herbst*, the "Deutschlandlied" (a fragment of Haydn's *Emperor* Quartet that became a national anthem) appears in various parts of the film, but in Kluge's section, the text is critically analyzed.

9. Repetition with a difference is key to Kluge's unsystematic method. Again, in the 1988 *Changing Time, Quickly*, the same image of the New Year's Eve celebration contains simultaneously 1988, 1923, 1908, and 1812. As the celebration takes place, a group of women again struggle to remember the words of the third stanza of Friedrich Schiller's "Ode to Joy."

PART THREE: *INTER CANEM ET LUPUM*

1. Zubin Mehta conducted the concert and guest artists included José Carreras, Ruggero Raimondi, Cecilia Gasdia, and Ildikó Komlósi. Interestingly, images of the concert are now hard to find. They have been replaced by the image that illustrates Steven Galloway's novel *The Cellist from Sarajevo* (2009) and that also inspired it. The picture, staged and taken by Mikhail Evstafief in 1992, shows musician Vedran Smailović playing in the

ruins of the National Library. That the more international collaborative performance is marginalized and almost forgotten in favor of the representation of a single artist and musician performing a cultural resistance to death and tragedy suggests the privilege granted to the idea of the individual artist. Much of what follows is meant to demonstrate that every artistic act is always in advance collaborative, and indeed, to think about how such collective activism can be generated and enacted. Such collaboration asks that we rethink our conception of the artist, and even of the subject in general, in relational terms.

2. I refer to Sala's video pieces as "films" throughout these pages, as I did with Allora & Calzadilla. As I will explain at length later, the artist's return to lens-based cinematic procedures cannot be separated from his mobilization of a musical understanding of the image, one that transforms and integrates these two media infrastructures through technological means that remain belated and anachronistic.

3. The Catalan conceptual artist Joan Fontcuberta translates Pandora's infamous box into what he calls *Pandora's Camera*, a figure that seems appropriate to Sala's explorations in this early film. This camera-box functions as an archive of all the greed, hatred, poverty, and war that overwhelmed Albania after the fall of the Berlin Wall, but also as an archive of the technological interplay between the visual and the linguistic, sound and meaning, subjectivity and its displacement, the past and the present, that Sala will inscribe within all his work.

4. Translation is the structuring procedure of other pieces by Sala, such as *Answer Me* (2008) or *Làk-kat* (2015).

5. It is tempting to read Sala's elaborate staging of this "primal scene" for the origin of his film as an allegory of his birth as a filmmaker and artist. Especially since "his" camera is already in the box, and in a structural sense, it precedes his discovery of the reel, or at least its registration in film.

6. I will return to Sala's images in my epilogue, where I address Lebanese artist and composer Tarek Atoui, who mobilizes Deaf culture to compose and perform with new instruments that demand a different modality of listening in his collaborative project *WITHIN*.

7. Anri Sala, quoted in Robert Barry, "Venice Preview: Anri Sala Unveils His Project for the French Pavillion," *Frieze*, May 27, 2013, https://www.frieze.com/article/venice-preview-anri-sala-unravels-his-project-french-pavilion.

8. The first time we hear this fragment of the symphony's first movement, it registers as a quotation from a film soundtrack. This is hardly surprising, since, after all,

arrangements of Tchaikovsky are ubiquitous in classic Hollywood film.

9. I use the term "film" rather than "video" because Sala shot the original footage in 16-mm film, making the whole process logistically much more difficult, and then transferred it to video. As I will discuss later in this chapter, Sala's use of earlier and even anachronistic lens-based technologies is key to his reconfiguration of the art video as an art historical "genre." I will analyze this film almost frame by frame and then move more quickly with the next two interrelated ones, *Ravel Ravel* and *Take Over*, because *Long Sorrow*'s slow unraveling allows us to witness, almost in real time, the movements of Sala's thinking with a camera, as a way to relate to the unfolding, and even birth, of the world as a complex acoustic environment. The film's commitment to attention, in particular in connection to the art historical "absorptive tradition," is also discussed in detail by Michael Fried, but in relation to his 1967 "Art and Objecthood" essay in *Artforum*. However, Fried fails to read the intensity of attention the film displays historically and thus to make its "sorrow" concrete. See Michael Fried, *Four Honest Outlaws: Sala, Ray, Marioni, Gordon* (New Haven: Yale University Press, 2011).

10. I am fully aware of the racist connotations of the word "dreadlocks." However, when I tried using "locs" or "dredlocks," most readers assumed it was a spelling mistake. It was then that I realized that "sanitizing" the word was not the way to proceed. Racism indeed has a place in Sala's piece because it walks a very fine line between acknowledgement (a concept I discuss at length in relation to Allora & Calzadilla) and cultural appropriation. The risk is never quite erased from *Long Sorrow*, and quite simply, it should not be. It is also hard not to recall the young Sala sporting locks of braided hair as he talks to the sound engineer Todi Lubonja in *Intervista*.

11. Moondoc's name, echoing "moon dog," carries uncanny resonances to the figure of the wolf in both literal and allegorical ways. In addition, and biographically, the name is an abbreviation of "moondoctor" and a reference to his enslaved great-great-grandmother, Katie, who had participated in moonshine medicine shows. Musically, it also inscribes the name of the blind American composer, theoretician, as well as inventor of musical instruments, Louis Thomas Hardin, who performed as Moondog. Influenced by jazz and by street and ambient sounds, the highly experimental Moondog lived as a street musician in New York until he finally moved to Germany.

12. With the demise of manufacturing in downtown and midtown New York after the Second World War, old industrial lofts had been vacated and were either left empty or were taken over by squatters as their surrounding neighborhoods became depopulated

and decayed. By the mid-1950s, artists, and especially jazz musicians, realized these large open spaces could be used as studios and performance spaces and because of their neglect could be surreptitiously inhabited, usually with a small rental fee. By the early 1970s, close to twenty such lofts were established and provided jazz musicians—especially those engaged in newer, less commercially viable musical styles—with a much-needed place to live cheaply, meet, rehearse, and perform. As Michael Heller notes: "the lofts were not an organization, nor a movement, nor an ideology, nor a genre, nor a neighborhood, nor a lineage of individuals. They were, instead, a meeting point, a locus for interaction" that exhibited "various forms of political consciousness, often connected to racial identity and economic inequality." Michael Heller, *Loft Jazz: Improvising New York in the 1970s* (Berkeley: University of California Press, 2016), pp. 125 and 60.

13. James Baldwin, "The Uses of the Blues," in *The Cross of Redemption: Uncollected Writings*, ed. Randall Kenan (New York: Pantheon, 2010), pp. 57 and 59.

14. W. E. B. Du Bois, *The Souls of Black Folk: Essays and Sketches* (Amherst: University of Massachusetts Press, 2018), pp. 247–48.

15. Later in the same text, Du Bois writes about the place of restlessness and silence in the sorrow song:

> *Yet the soul-hunger is there, the restlessness of the savage,*
> *the wail of the wanderer, and the plaint is put in one little phrase:*
>
> My soul wants something that's new, that's new
>
> *Over the inner thoughts of the slaves and their relations one with another*
> *the shadow of fear ever hung, so that we get but glimpses here and there,*
> *and also with them, eloquent omissions and silences.* (Ibid., pp. 249–50.)

16. Germany was already an important referent for Du Bois, who completed part of his graduate education in Berlin. As he described his experience, "I found myself on the outside of the American world, looking in. With me were white folk—students, acquaintances, teachers—who viewed the scene with me. They did not always pause to regard me as a curiosity, or something sub-human; I was just a man of the somewhat privileged student rank, with whom they were glad to meet and talk over the world; particularly, the part of the world whence I came." Quoted in Aldon D. Morris, *The Scholar Denied: W. E. B. Du Bois and the Birth of Modern Sociology* (Berkeley: University of California Press, 2015), p. 17. As Tina Campt notes, Du Bois's experience underscores how

"Germany depended as much as any other European nation on the distinction from non-European populations in the constitution of national identity." See Tina Campt, *Other Germans: Black Germans and the Politics of Race, Gender, and Memory in the Third Reich* (Ann Arbor: University of Michigan Press, 2004), p. 6.

17. Hannah Arendt, *The Origins of Totalitarianism* (New York: Houghton Mifflin, 1973), p. 466.

18. Hannah Arendt, "The Concept of History: Ancient and Modern," in *Between Past and Future: Eight Exercises in Political Thought* (New York: Penguin Books, 2006), p. 61.

19. Baldwin, "Of the Sorrow Songs: The Cross of Redemption," in *The Cross of Redemption*, p. 124.

20. Quoted in Fumi Okiji, *Jazz as Critique: Adorno and Black Expression Revisited* (Stanford: Stanford University Press, 2018), p. 69.

21. See Orlando Patterson, *Slavery and Social Death: A Comparative Study* (Cambridge, MA: Harvard University Press, 1982).

22. Arendt, *The Origins of Totalitarianism*, pp. 300–301.

23. Ibid., p. 301.

24. "Interview: Hans Ulrich Obrist in Conversation with Anri Sala," in Mark Godfrey ed., *Anri Sala* (New York: Phaidon, 2006), pp. 17–19.

25. There might be also a practical explanation for the absence of Moondoc's hands. Because the sound of the film is not direct but recorded in the studio after the image editing was completed, seeing the musician's hands may have given away the artificiality of the film perhaps a bit too soon.

26. "Interview: Hans Ulrich Obrist in Conversation with Anri Sala," p. 21.

27. As Derrida puts it, "We would, however, hesitate on the edge of a fiction." See Jacques Derrida, *The Politics of Friendship*, trans. George Collins (London: Verso, 2005), p. 75.

28. Okiji, *Jazz as Critique*, p. 68.

29. Cecil Taylor, "Sound Structure of Subculture Becoming Major Breath / Naked Fire Gesture," liner notes, *Unit Structures*, LP 84237, Blue Note, 1966.

30. As Okiji points out, Adorno's utter deafness to the compositional and polyphonic complexity of jazz and its sociohistorical conditions, its capacity to resist culture and its barbarism, does not prevent the philosopher from theorizing the negative and dialectic movement of the Black musical tradition with virtuoso accuracy—particularly when he bemoans the rigidity with which Bach or Beethoven have been met in their full disclosure and appropriation, in the consensus, that is, of their reception. It is never

a question of understanding, however, but of listening, listening beyond structure or meaning—not a "thinking ear" but an ear traversed by unintelligibility. Adorno's limits are the limits of understanding composition as a process closer to writing than a continuation of listening, performing, playing, singing, and breathing.

31. In the context of Sala's anachronistic return to cinema (to which I will turn later in this chapter), the role of memory in the work of Andrei Tarkovsky, what the Russian director calls "imprinted time," immediately comes to mind: "What is the essence of the director's work? We could define it as sculpting in time. Just as a sculptor takes a lump of marble, and, inwardly conscious of the features of his finished piece, removes everything that is not part of it—so the film-maker, from a 'lump of time' made up of an enormous, solid cluster of living facts, cuts off and discards whatever he does not need, leaving only what is to be an element of the finished film, what will prove to be integral to the cinematic image." See Andrei Tarkovsky, *Sculpting in Time: Reflections on the Cinema*, trans. Kitty Hunter-Blair (London: Bodley Head, 1986), pp. 63–64.

32. Maurice Ravel, *Lettres, écrits, entretiens* (Paris: Flammarion, 1989), p. 329.

33. It is a listening that resists by paradoxically intensifying the logic of "structural listening." Rose Subotnik argues that Adorno developed this kind of listening as a response, or even an endorsement, of Schoenberg's compositions. In her words: "This concept of structural listening, as Schoenberg and Adorno presented it, was intended to describe a process wherein the listener follows and comprehends the unfolding realization, with all of its detailed inner relationship, of a generating musical conception or what Schoenberg calls an 'idea.' Based on an assumption that valid structural logic is accessible to any reasoning person, such structural listening discourages kinds of understanding that require culturally specific knowledge of things external to the compositional structure." Subotnik then notes that because of its abstract nature, structural listening takes place by reading a score because music and its notation are virtually identical. Rose Subotnik, *Deconstructive Variations: Music and Reason in Western Society* (Minneapolis: University of Minnesota Press, 1996), p. 150. For his part, Sala insists—as he does in many of his musicalized films—that the unfolding of the internal logic of a composition can be better achieved through another medium capable of returning music to a place of utter differentiation and estrangement.

34. Jacques Derrida, *Specters of Marx: The State of the Debt, The Work of Mourning and the New International*, trans. Peggy Kamuf (New York: Routledge, 1994), p. 54.

35. Peter Szendy bases his extensive analysis of Sala's work on the notion of

"manutension," the holding together of music and time through the allegorical and narrative role of hands in the artist's work. See *Bendings: Four Variations on Anri Sala* (Luxemburg: Mousse Publishing, 2019).

36. Laurent Pfister writes about the legal status of Ravel's concerto in "Private versus Public: The Legal Status of Ravel's Work Creates Franco-German Discord," in *Anri Sala: Ravel Ravel Unravel* (Paris: Manuella Éditions, 2013), pp. 149–53.

37. It is hard not to speculate whether the "mirror" therapy currently used to treat phantom limb pain plays a role in the conception of Sala's piece. The therapy helps reorganize the proprioception of the body through visual feedback, so that when the patient sees the projection of her limb on the mirror, she is able to integrate that image mentally as the substitute for the missing limb. The "trick" image thus acts as another fiction superimposed on the "original" phantom one. It is therefore a modality of healing through semblance.

38. Étienne Balibar, *We, the People of Europe?: Reflections on Transnational Citizenship*, trans. James Swenson (Princeton: Princeton University Press, 2004), p. 26.

39. In all these instances, the difficulty is how to move from birth and its radical givenness to political rights, which are a normative construction. I believe Sala's work may provide a model for imagining a community as pure means, where givenness instead of sovereignty becomes the basis for an abstract yet ethico-political structure that, rather than ever being fully constituted, is always in the process of constituting itself through performance. For a detailed reading of the political possibilities of Arendt's natality, see Miguel Vatter, *The Republic of the Living: Biopolitics and the Critique of Civil Society* (New York: Fordham University Press, 2014).

40. Simondon's revision of "identity," which takes inspiration from Ionic philosophers, Merleau-Ponty, and thermodynamics, is much further reaching than Balibar's. It could be summarized in this way: in a relational system, difference is always differentiation and cannot be reduced to a monadic and autonomous state; there are no individual identities, but only relations that, for a brief moment, as they continue in their transit toward a new relation and a new form, appear to take on individual identities.

41. Catherine Malabou, *Ontology of the Accident: An Essay on Destructive Plasticity*, trans. Carolyn Shread (Cambridge: Polity, 2009).

42. Étienne Balibar, *Spinoza, the Transindividual*, trans. Mark G. E. Kelly (Edinburgh: Edinburgh University Press, 2020), p. 74.

43. In "A New Querelle of Universals," Balibar distinguishes between three modalities of the universal: the real, the fictive, and the ideal. Sala's artistic practice

demonstrates their interdependence; in his work, fiction and composition are deployed in unison as the bond between the real and the ideal. See *Philosophy Today: An International Journal of Contemporary Philosophy* 61.4 (Fall 2017), pp. 929–45.

44. Balibar, *Spinoza, the Transindividual*, p. 154.

45. This simple technical modification attaches a small device, often a rubber tourte mute, to the bridge of the instrument to limit vibrations. The overall effect is a shallower and leaner sound, but it can also affect the timbre of the violin.

46. Sala used this rather wonderful description during a conversation with Peter Szendy on March 3, 2018, at the Marian Goodman Gallery in New York City.

47. Snails make sounds only when they eat, but even then, our ears cannot hear them unless one uses specialized sensitive sound equipment. Because the snail produces its own trail by secreting slime, there is little friction with the surface they slide on, making them extremely quiet. Sala's snails may not make audible sounds, and we may not even hear them, but they nonetheless radically alter the tempo of the music, directing it with the slowness of their slithering movements.

48. The logic of the bow, which has remained unchanged since the nineteenth century, is also one of mediated and organically composite touch. An undetermined number of horse tail hairs treated with tree rosin erode with every touch of the violin's bow on the strings.

49. This is another manipulation of ratios on Sala's part. The use of cinemascope, with a 2.35:1 screen ratio, can be seen as expansion that echoes the slower musical ratio that Sala introduces into Stravinsky's *Elegy*. It is yet another interval between Sala's technique and the technologies he uses.

50. Balibar, *We, the People of Europe?*, p. 89.

51. Interestingly, Ravel used exactly this aggregating structure in what remains his most popular composition, his 1928 orchestral piece *Boléro*.

52. Artist and theorist Brandon LaBelle has devoted a series of texts to the acoustic as the site for a new economy of attention that might herald what he calls "acoustic justice," a balancing act whereby a collective performance of "sonic agency" can become a "generous infrastructure" onto which to build a more equal distribution of social power. LaBelle deploys Balibar's "strategies of civility," in turn a set of critical reconfigurations of Hegelian "civility," as a means to sustain collectively the possibility of the political through restrained social behavior. See Brandon LaBelle, *Acoustic Justice: Listening, Performativity, and the Work of Reorientation* (London: Bloomsbury, 2021), pp. 5–6.

However, in the contexts of the slippages, caesuras, disappearances, ellipses, and even violence that punctuate Sala's work, I believe a somewhat less conciliatory structure emerges, one where the acoustic is a force of both dispersion and gathering, of memory and forgetting, of love and violence. The asymmetries between hearing and being heard, or between demand and response, are never resolved and cannot easily accommodate predictable behaviors, since they exist only in the performance of their becoming. In Sala's work, the notion of justice as a sort of social equilibrium or agency, as an expression of freedom or autonomy, is put into question. What we are left with, instead, is an acoustic and cinematic fiction that continues to unfold in its present and remains incomplete that forces us to wonder at the strange and resonant plasticity of possible futures. From this fiction a politics or a justice may perhaps emerge, but if it does, it will take a form that we may not immediately recognize: it may look like an unexpected leap of a body into space, the intuitive and fragile choreography of body and machine, or a concert hall metamorphosed into a planetarium—emerging as a givenness that can never be fully anticipated by already existing infrastructures.

53. The phrase is used by Catherine Fowler in her essay, "Obscurity and Stillness: Potentiality in the Moving Image." Fowler, however, then argues that the cinematic practices of someone such as Sala, David Claerbout, or Tacita Dean blurs the opposition between actuality and potentiality, whereas I find it more productive to emphasize the role of fiction as a way to sustain potentiality artificially, so that it amounts to a reconceptualization of cinematic time as an expansive and suspensive structure. See Fowler, "Obscurity and Stillness: Potentiality in the Moving Image," *Art Journal* 72.1 (2003), pp. 64–79.

54. The other artist that comes to mind in his early mastery of the possibilities of a new medium is Charlie Chaplin, and in particular, the interplay in his work between the gesture and the camera as a new hybrid form that expanded the poetic and perceptual possibilities of cinema, even as he incorporated earlier forms and remained out of sync with the times for a large part of his career. (He resisted the talkies longer than anyone thought possible.) Chaplin conceived his films by experimenting directly on camera, so that technology was not a recording device but an inanimate and central agent that allowed that actor/director's body to become animated as a response. Both Sala and Chaplin thematize anachronism and deploy it as a structural armature in their work. A century separates their practices, but they both occur in a politically fraught context when their chosen medium has been too often appropriated for propaganda of one sort or another. The 1983 documentary series *Unknown Chaplin* offers a rather extraordinary view into the director's mode of production by giving us access to his private film archive.

The film was written and directed by film historians Kevin Brownlow and David Gill.

55. While video art emerged with conceptualism in the 1970s, it was often a medium for the documentation of performance and because of this was fully invested in the notion of presence. It has developed a truly complex and nuanced cinematic vocabulary only in the last twenty years, with Tacita Dean, Steve McQueen, Christian Marclay, and Douglas Gordon, to name only a few of the artists whose work has expanded this lexicon.

56. Gilles Deleuze, *Cinema 2: The Time-Image*, trans. Hugh Tomlinson and Robert Galeta (Minneapolis: University of Minnesota Press, 1989), p. 55.

57. Ibid., pp. 56, 59, 60, 82, 108.

58. Ibid., p. 150.

CODA: LISTENING BEYOND THE EAR

1. Allora & Calzadilla's 2007 *Wake Up* also originated with the war in Lebanon, when the artists heard the trumpet player Mazen Kerbaj's 2006 "Starry Night," with Kerbaj responding to the sounds of Israeli bombs, improvising on his balcony. Their sound and light installation builds on that cue and invites several trumpet players across the world—the number and the order of the recorded interpretations is not set—to improvise on the military "Reveille." *Wake Up*'s interpellation of the trumpet's military origins takes the form of a series of riffs on the American sunrise reveille song for the troops. The gesture is already implicit in the appropriation of the reveille in early jazz, such as "The Bugle Call Blues," and is connected to the participation of Black musicians in military bands during the First World War. These variations on the tune render it inoperative as an order while expanding its expressive potential as a meditation on music and war. The light display that accompanies and responds to each rendition evokes the violence of bombings, very much like the ones that populated TV screens worldwide during the wars in Iraq or the sonic and toxic warfare to which inhabitants of the island of Vieques were subjected for decades by American military training exercises.

2. While the detention is undisputed, according to ethnomusicologist Thomas Burkhalter, in what he calls "strategic self-positioning," Atoui's account has a different emphasis depending on the interlocutor: "Tarek Atoui, an electro-acoustic musician, said in a Lebanese book that during the 2006 war between Israel and Hizbullah, he hit the streets to collect sound recordings. 'He was arrested and detained for three days, during which time he was whacked on the head and lost partial hearing in his left ear, permanently' (Wilson-Goldie 55). To me Tarek Atoui told a different story, just after

the war: He did not do much more than watch TV." See Burkhalter, "Between Art for Art's Sake and Musical Protest: How Musicians from Beirut React to War and Violence," *Popular Music and Society* 34.1 (2011), p. 56.

To me, though, the instability of Atoui's accounts is an index to the complexity of memory and war and to the inscription of borders in the mind. Later in this same essay, Burkhalter relates the accusations against Kerbaj for recording the bombings while living in a wealthy quarter of Beirut unlikely to get hit. It would seem, and this is hardly surprising, that there are no perfect war victims.

3. *WITHIN* has been performed in several venues, including the Sharjah Biennial (2013), Berkeley Art Museum, USA (2015), Experimental Music and Performing Art Center, EMPAC, USA (2015), Zentrum für Kunst und Medien, Germany (2016), and the Bergen Assembly, Norway (2016). It has evolved and been modified with each new iteration.

4. The Paris performance, for instance, had the support of INJS (Institut National de Jeunes Sourds de Paris), Centre Pompidou, and IRCAM (Institute for Research and Coordination in Acoustics/Music).

5. Commissioned by Gallaudet University, a higher-education center for the Deaf founded in the nineteenth century, the DeafSpace Program established by Bauman outlines five ways Deaf people relate to space: sensory reach, space and proximity, mobility and proximity, light and color, and acoustics.

6. These instruments continue to transform, like the complex organisms that they are. In *Whisperers*, the Sub-Ink is connected to a small stone trough that transforms the electricity of water dripping on it into bass kicks and heartbeatlike sounds.

7. This pedagogical impulse, this continuity in transmission, has remained consistent in later projects. It is evident in his work with Parisian kindergarten schools, using instruments that would be part of *Whisperers Playground*; in his 2021 *Cycles in 11* for the Sharjah Art Foundation, which created a residency and education hub; and in the *Whispering Manual*, which gives instructions that allow Atoui's workshops to be activated elsewhere by other collectives.

8. Tarek Atoui, *WITHIN* (Paris: Les Cahiers ASSN and Galerie Chantal Crousel, 2017), p. 9.

9. See Tarek Atoui, *The Whisperers* (Santa Fe: Radius Books, The Contemporary Austin, and the Flag Art Foundation, 2024), p. 9.

Index

Images are indicated by italic page number

Zone Books series design by Bruce Mau
Image placement and production by Julie Fry
Typesetting by Meighan Gale
Printed and bound by Maple Press